Locality in Vowel Harmony

Linguistic Inquiry Monographs
Samuel Jay Keyser, general editor

A complete list of books published in the Linguistic Inquiry Monographs series appears at the back of this book.

Locality in Vowel Harmony

Andrew Nevins

The MIT Press
Cambridge, Massachusetts
London, England

© 2010 Massachusetts Institute of Technology

All rights reserved. No part of this book may be reproduced in any form by any electronic or mechanical means (including photocopying, recording, or information storage and retrieval) without permission in writing from the publisher.

For information about special quantity discounts, please e-mail special_sales@mitpress.mit.edu

This book was set in Times New Roman and Syntax on 3B2 by Asco Typesetters, Hong Kong. Printed and bound in the United States of America.

Library of Congress Cataloging-in-Publication Data

Nevins, Andrew.
Locality in vowel harmony / Andrew Nevins.
  p. cm. — (Linguistic inquiry monographs)
Includes bibliographical references and index.
ISBN 978-0-262-14097-3 (hardcover : alk. paper) — ISBN 978-0-262-51368-5 (pbk. : alk. paper)
1. Grammar, Comparative and general—Vowel harmony. I. Title.
P234.N48   2010
415—dc22
                                        2009040462

10 9 8 7 6 5 4 3 2 1

Contents

Series Foreword   vii
Acknowledgments   ix
Abbreviations   xi

1 What Is Vowel Harmony, How Does It Vary, and Why Study It?   1
   1.1   The Computation of Locality   3
   1.2   Vowel Harmony Is Distinct from Coarticulation   8
   1.3   Locality Is Not Measured by Pure Distance in Syntax Either   10
   1.4   Overview of the Major Claims   11
   1.5   The Need for a New Model of Vowel Harmony   17

2 The Search Principle   23
   2.1   Harmony and Agree Are Both a Process of Finding a Value   23
   2.2   Back Harmony and Round Harmony in Turkish Suffixes   27
   2.3   Harmony Can Iterate from Morpheme to Morpheme   28
   2.4   Turkish Vowel Harmony Reflects a Phonological Computation   30
   2.5   Nonundergoing Morphemes Can Still Be Donors   32
   2.6   "Exceptionally" Nonseeking Vowels in Turkish   34
   2.7   Nonharmonizing Root Vowels in Turkish and Finnish and Their Nonfate in Language Games   35
   2.8   Bidirectional Harmony in Woleaian   39
   2.9   Directionality in Kalenjin "Dominant/Recessive" Harmony   45
   2.10 Split-Source Harmony: When a Consonant and a Vowel Are Each Copied From in Turkish   53
   2.11 Lack of Lookahead in Barra Gaelic Epenthesis Harmony   57
   2.12 General Conclusion: Search Must Be Recipient-Initiated   61
   Appendix: Harmony Necessitated by Deletion   62

3 Contrastiveness, Markedness, and Feature-Based Locality   69
   3.1   Contrastiveness Cuts Potential Donors in Finnish Harmony   69
   3.2   Finnish Transparent Vowels Are Excluded from Harmony   72
   3.3   What If No Contrastive Source Exists?   76

3.4 Why Contrastiveness? 79
3.5 Contrastiveness Determines Karaim (Consonant) Harmony 83
3.6 Markedness in Binary Feature Systems 88
3.7 Sibe Harmony and the Context-Free Markedness Value [+low] 90
3.8 Context-Sensitive Markedness and Sources of [+round] 99
3.9 Microvariation in Yoruba Dialects 103
3.10 Variation in Obstruent Transparency in [±nasal] Harmony 105
3.11 Microvariation in Finnish Loanwords 109
3.12 Set Union of Marked and Contrastive Values in Oroch 111
3.13 Conclusion: Transparent Items Are Pruned Away Because of Irrelevancy 115

4 Defective Intervention: When Search Comes Back Empty-Handed 121
4.1 The Grammatical Elements of Minimality 121
4.2 No Second Chances after Search Fails 123
4.3 "Opaque" Blockers of Harmony: Consonants in Nawuri 126
4.4 Parasitic Harmony: Conditional Requirements for [±high], [±round], and [±ATR] Copying 130
4.5 Intervention and Skipping Coexist in Khalkha Mongolian [±round] Harmony 136
4.6 Defective Intervention Due to All-Value Relativization in Oroch 140
4.7 Derived-Environment Effects in Harmony 141
4.8 Conclusions 146

5 Domain Limitations on Search 149
5.1 Distance Parameters Limit the Extent of Search 150
5.2 Sonority Peaks Are Barriers 168
5.3 Implicational Sonority Thresholds 184
5.4 General Conclusion: Extrinsic Bounds on Search 189

6 Minimalist Computation of Vowel Harmony: Implications 191
6.1 Expanding the Terrain of Minimalist Inquiry 192
6.2 Are Assimilation and Dissimilation Subroutines of Harmony? 196
6.3 Vowel Harmony and Impossible Languages 204

Notes 209
References 223
Index of Terms 239
Index of Languages 243

Series Foreword

We are pleased to present the fifty-fifth in the series *Linguistic Inquiry Monographs*. These monographs present new and original research beyond the scope of the article. We hope they will benefit our field by bringing to it perspectives that will stimulate further research and insight.

Originally published in limited edition, the *Linguistic Inquiry Monographs* are now more widely available. This change is due to the great interest engendered by the series and by the needs of a growing readership. The editors thank the readers for their support and welcome suggestions about future directions for the series.

Samuel Jay Keyser
for the Editorial Board

Acknowledgments

There is a kind of poetry and elegance in the rules governing the way words are formed. It is a thrill to see how languages around the globe conform to these rules of how the vowels in a word fall into place. In my discovery of the principles and parameters of vowel harmony, I greatly appreciate the guidance and support of my mentors in graduate school, Morris Halle, Michael Kenstowicz, Donca Steriade, and Bert Vaux, for their intellectual guidance in developing a wholly new model of vowel harmony and helping me to find the right case studies to make the arguments. I would like to thank many students and colleagues at Harvard, in particular Marc Hauser, Jay Jasanoff, Peter Jenks, Beste Kamali, John Lechner, Patrick Liu, Tim O'Donnell, Gabriel Poliquin, Bridget Samuels, Kobey Shwayder, and Daniel Wallach, for the opportunity to discuss this model extensively in courses and individually. David Braun, Brian Gainor, Max Guimarães, John McCarthy, Raphael Nevins, and Cilene Rodrigues read through a number of chapters of the manuscript and provided invaluable feedback. The reports of three anonymous *LI Monographs* reviewers were extremely insightful and enabled me to clarify and rethink many details of the proposals advanced here. I would also like to extend my gratitude to Ada Brunstein, Jay Keyser, and Anne Mark for their extensive editorial support. And finally, I would like to thank *you*, dear reader, without whom this book would be but a tree falling in a forest.

Abbreviations

1,2,3	1st, 2nd, 3rd person
ABIL	ability
ABL	ablative
ACC	accusative
AGENT	agentive
ALLTV	allative
AOR	aorist
CAUS	causative
COMIT	comitative
COP	copula
DEF	definite
DIM	diminutive
DIR	directional
DIST	distant
ESS	essive
FEM	feminine
FOC	focus
FUT	future
FV	final vowel
GEN	genitive
GER	gerundial
IMPF	imperfective
INCL	inclusive
INF	infinitive
INTR	intransitive
LOC	locative
MASC	masculine
NEG	negation
NEUT	neuter

NMLZ	nominalizer
NONCOMPL	noncompletive
NONDIR	nondirective
OBJ	object
OBJCTV	objective
PARTIT	partitive
PERF	perfect
PFCTV	perfective
PL	plural
POSS	possessive
PROG	progressive
Q	question
REC	recent
RECIP	reciprocal
REFL	reflexive
REP	repetitive
REVERS	reversative
SBJNCT	subjunctive
SG	singular
SR	surface representation
SUBJ	subject
UR	underlying representation
VEG	vegetable gender

1 What Is Vowel Harmony, How Does It Vary, and Why Study It?

It's common when typing an e-mail that our fingers hit the wrong key, and a savvy spell-checker underlines the misspelled word in red. Suppose I'm writing about the rodent protagonist of an animated film and make a mistake in typing *rat*. The resulting typo might create a real word that's different from the one I intended (e.g., *ray* instead of *rat*), or it might create an "impossible word" such as *rta*. The three-letter sequence *rta* could never be a word of English because of a constraint prohibiting the consonant sequence *rt* at the beginning of a syllable. The study of syntax begins with the observation that the words of a sentence cannot go in any order they like, and the study of phonology begins with the same observation for the consonants and vowels (the *segments*) of a word. Thus, *tra* is a possible segmental sequence in an English syllable, while *rta* is not. Vowel harmony, in languages that have it, is a set of restrictions that determine the possible and impossible sequences of vowels within a word.

These cooccurrence restrictions are largely based on the principle of dividing the vowels of the language into two sets—let's call them "even vowels" and "odd vowels" for now—and ensuring that no mixing and matching of vowels from the even set and the odd set can occur in the same word. Thus, in the idealized vowel harmony language, the only permissible words would be those containing only even vowels (e.g., *2426*) or only odd vowels (e.g., *1153*).

The example with "even" and "odd," while formally very close to how vowel harmony works, is analogical. In reality, a vowel harmony language divides its inventory of vowels into two sets along some phonetic/phonological dimension. For example, one articulatory parameter that divides vowels up neatly is whether they are pronounced with the body of the tongue aimed toward the front or the back of the mouth. In Turkish, the front vowels /i,ü,e,ö/ cannot mix with the back vowels /ı,u,a,o/

within the same word if it is to be considered "harmonic." Even when suffixes pile up, they keep to this restriction. Consider the word formed by adding the following thirteen suffixes to the root *Avrupa* 'Europe':

(1) Avrupa- lı-   laş-   tır-   a-   ma- yacak- lar- ımız- dan- mı-
    Europe- from- become- CAUS- ABIL- NEG- FUT-   PL- 1PL- ABL- Q-
    y-   dı-   nız
    COP- PAST- 2PL
    'Were you one of those whom we are not going to be able to turn into Europeans?'

Avrupa has vowels in which the tongue is pulled back, and owing to harmonization, all thirteen suffixes have the tongue body pulled back as well. By contrast, if the last vowel in the root is a front vowel, like the /i/ in *Akdeniz* 'Mediterranean', all thirteen suffixes have front vowels.

(2) Akdeniz-   li-   leş-   tir-   e-   me- yecek- ler- imiz- den-
    Mediterranean from- become- CAUS- ABIL- NEG- FUT-   PL- 1PL- ABL-
    mi- y-   di-   niz
    Q-   COP- PAST- 2PL
    'Were you one of those whom we are not going to be able to turn into Mediterraneans?'

Like the phonotactic restrictions banning certain sequences of consonants in some languages but not others (e.g., *rta* is disallowed in English but allowed in Russian), the restrictions banning certain sequences of vowels are subject to language-specific variation. But the restrictions governing possible orders and combinations of vowels within a word rest on completely different sets of principles than those related to consonants. This is because, for one, the articulatory dimensions along which these "harmonic sets" can be divided require a certain degree of symmetry among the vowels in a language (witness Turkish, with four back and four front vowels); the instantiation of harmony from one language to the next may differ because not every language has a perfectly balanced vowel inventory. Furthermore, the description of the syntax of vowel sequences is more complicated than that of consonant sequences in large part because vowels are rarely strictly adjacent to one another; the resulting cooccurrence restrictions become a type of "action at a distance," unlike the strictly local rules dictating that *t* cannot immediately follow *r* at the beginning of a word. Vowel harmony is one of the only phonotactic processes across human languages that consistently instantiates a long-distance relationship.

1.1 The Computation of Locality

Though we will examine the variety of long-distance dependency relationships in vowel harmony languages, this book is about much more than vowel harmony. Instead, it is about a rather nonintuitive discovery of a much more general aspect of cognition—the way humans measure distance—and illustrates this principle with the patterns of vowel harmony found in many languages around the world. The nonintuitive discovery about distance measurement (or the computation of "locality," more technically put) is easily introduced by considering the subway map of Boston and Cambridge.

Boston and Cambridge are two cities in eastern Massachusetts that are separated by a river, the Charles. The Boston area subway system, the oldest in the country, is organized into a network of color-coded lines (the Red Line, the Orange Line, etc.). The subway system was incremented over time as the city and important sites within it (often organized into "squares," such as Harvard Square, Central Square, Porter Square, and Kenmore Square) grew in various ways. Now, suppose we are sitting in the Harvard Square subway station (which is on the Cambridge side of the river, and on the Red Line) and you turn to me and ask, "I want to take the subway into Boston. What's the closest Boston stop we can get to from here?"

The answer that any Boston-area subway commuter would give without thinking twice would be "Charles Street," which is near Beacon Hill. But of course, strictly speaking, this answer is completely false. As the crow flies, the closest stop from Harvard Square (our "source") is not Charles Street at all. As measured by absolute distance, BU Central (one of the Boston University stops) is much closer to Harvard Square than Beacon Hill. From Harvard Square, it is 1.7 miles to BU Central, but 2.9 miles to Charles Street; these three stations form a textbook example of the Pythagorean theorem, as shown in figure 1.1. However, when you asked "What's the closest Boston stop we can get to from here?," if I had actually answered "BU Central," this would have been an irrelevant and smart-alecky response that took your question far too literally (much like when pedants respond to "Can I have a glass of water?" with "I don't know, *can* you?"). The reason is, when you said *closest*, you meant "closest as measured by stops on the subway"—not closest in an absolute, as-the-crow-flies measurement of pure linear distance. And on the subway from Harvard Square, it is in fact only three stops to Charles Street, but twelve stops to BU Central, as figure 1.2 shows (and if I had a nickel for

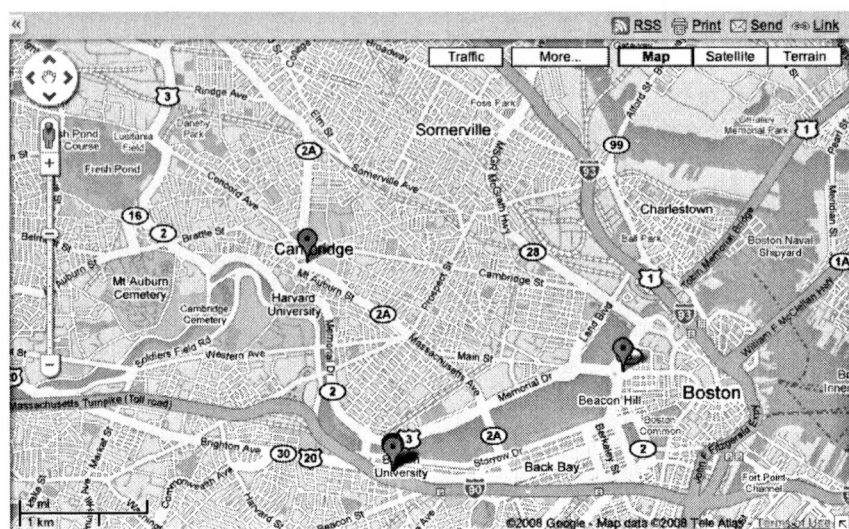

Figure 1.1
Actual locations and relative distances of Boston subway station locations. Left to right, the flags mark the Harvard Square, BU Central, and Charles Street subway stops.

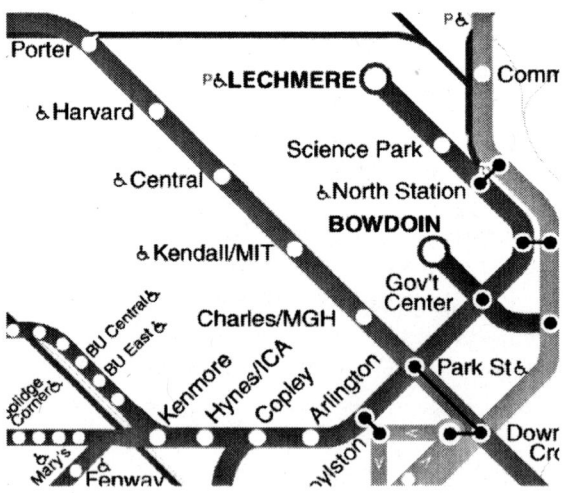

Figure 1.2
Boston subway connection map (not drawn to scale)

every time I heard a complaint about this, I could buy the subway system). While Harvard Square and Charles Street are both on the Red Line, getting from Harvard Square to BU Central requires transferring to the Green Line, a different subway line altogether. Therefore, when you asked, "What is the closest Boston stop?," I provided the answer that was most relevant given the structure we were traveling within, namely, the subway system. The Boston stop closest to Harvard Square *that is on the Red Line* is definitely Charles Street. Identical scenarios can no doubt be constructed for subway systems in other cities, and perhaps for flight routes and highway layouts as well.

This short subway dialogue illustrates the surprising centrality of *relativized locality* within human cognition. When we are measuring from point A (the "source") to the closest "goal" (a stop in Boston being the goal above), and when there are two possible targets, B and C, it can turn out that we decide on C as being closer to A than B, *even when further away in terms of linear distance*, if C is closer as measured by some other system of measurement based on the properties it has, such as *being a stop on the Red Line*. Thus, Charles Street is not the closest Boston stop to Harvard Square, but it *is* the closest Boston stop relativized to the property of being on the Red Line, and the closest Boston stop as measured by the logic of subway lines, rather than absolute distance.

One of the key arguments in this book will be that in languages with vowel harmony, the relationships between vowels are governed by this relativized rather than absolute form of locality. Thus, when a vowel A has to decide whether vowel B or vowel C is closer, in certain cases it will choose C, even when C is further away in terms of linear distance, because C turns out to be the closest *relevant* vowel. In a certain sense, this is a surprising result, because one might expect that in order to figure out the closest goal from a given source, you just get out your measuring tape, so to speak. But human cognition, particularly in the domain of language, does not seem to work that way; rather, we employ a metric of minimality that says that when we search for the closest Boston stop on the subway, or the closest harmony-valuer among vowels, locality must be defined with respect to the *properties* borne by the elements in question. Not all subway systems are laid out identically, and similarly, not all vowel harmony systems look at the same types of properties in order to determine closest-relevant-goal. A central objective of this book will be to delimit a system of parametric options that vowel harmony languages may choose from. Given the overarching and invariant principle of relativized minimality that holds across all such systems, these limited parameters determine how the variation in "what is relevant" is computed.

As a simple demonstration that vowel harmony may flout simple metrics of absolute distance, we may consider the ways that vowels compute distance in Yoruba (a Niger-Congo language spoken by around eighteen million people in Nigeria and Benin). In Yoruba, vowel harmony is a pattern that determines where the *advanced* mid-height vowels [e,o] will show up as opposed to the *retracted* mid-height vowels [ɛ,ɔ]. The latter two are lax vowels, produced with a retracted tongue root, much like the short vowels in English *bet* and *cot*. While Yoruba and English share these four vowels, there is an important difference: a pattern like English *robot* [ro.bɔt] (or *apex* [e.pɛks]) would be against the rules of vowel harmony in Yoruba's native vocabulary, because the first vowel, [o], is tense and the second, [ɔ], is lax. The rules of vowel harmony for Yoruba words ensure that lax [ɛ,ɔ] can only occur when another lax vowel follows. Thus, the following words are all well formed according to the rule that "[ɛ,ɔ] are allowed when the next vowel is lax." (The diacritics ´ and ` indicate high and low tone, respectively.)

(3) *Yoruba vowel harmony in disyllabic words*
    a. èwé   'lip'
    b. olè   'thief'
    c. èrò   'crowd'
    d. òdʒò   'rain'
    e. ègɛ́   'cassava'
    f. ɔsɛ   'soap'
    g. èfɔ́   'vegetable'
    h. ɔwɔ́   'hand'

However, the concept that is used to measure "next vowel" in Yoruba is not, as one might think looking solely at the above examples, strictly based on absolute distance. Since what is relevant to vowel harmony is the rule that forces all mid-height vowels in a word to share the same feature along the tense/lax dimension, other vowels that are not relevant to this distinction (i.e., vowels other than /e,o,ɛ,ɔ/) could presumably intervene without interfering in the dependency relation between [e] and [o] and between [ɛ] and [ɔ].

Examining the variety of Yoruba spoken in Ifẹ, and comparing it with Standard Yoruba, we find that these two closely related dialects differ only in how they measure locality. The two dialects have the same inventory of vowel sounds, and in large part they share the same lexical vocabulary. However, vowel harmony operates rather differently in these two dialects. In Ifẹ Yoruba, the tense/lax harmony-value of the first vowel in a word is determined with respect to the next *relevant* vowel. In other words, if the second vowel in the word is a high vowel like /i/ or /u/ (which are tense vowels), it is not counted as "next" in Ifẹ Yoruba. This is because the tense/lax distinction *is not important* in the high vowels /i,u/ in Ifẹ Yoruba, and so these vowels are not counted in the computation of "adjacent" vowel. (In chapter 5, we return to the pattern of the low vowel /a/ in Yoruba harmony.) This relativization of the measurement of "next-to" in such a way that it computes distance as determined by the relevance of a particular property (in this case, the tense/lax contrast), rather than absolute distance, exemplifies the core of our study of the locality of vowel harmony.

(4) *Ifẹ Yoruba vowel harmony skips the irrelevant second vowel (Ola Orie 2001)*
    a. ɔrúkɔ   'name'
    b. èlùbɔ́   'yam flour'
    c. ɛúrɛ́   'goat'
    d. ɔdídɛ   'parrot'
    e. ɔ̀títɔ́   'truth'

What is most interesting about the pattern of Ifẹ Yoruba is that this dialect counts locality differently from Standard Yoruba, which does measure locality in absolute, as-the-crow-flies terms (i.e., counts the "closest vowel" as indeed the closest vowel), as can be seen by comparing the pronunciation of these same words:

(5) *Standard Yoruba counts the second vowel as the next vowel*
    a. orúkɔ
    b. èlùbɔ́
    c. ewúrɛ́
    d. odídɛ
    e. òtítɔ́

In Standard Yoruba, the tense/lax value of *any* vowel matters for counting what's next and therefore /ɔ/ cannot precede /u/. In Ifẹ Yoruba, harmony only looks at the tense/lax value among the vowels /e,o,ɛ,ɔ/, and so the intervening /u/ in (4a) is not even counted in the computation.

This brief comparison highlights the fact that two languages with the same vowel inventory—indeed, two dialects of the same language—

may conduct their search for vowel harmony features entirely differently, depending on what counts as closest. The locality of vowel harmony in Ifẹ Yoruba is determined by the closest vowel contrastive for the tense/lax distinction, while the locality of vowel harmony in Standard Yoruba is determined by the closest vowel, period. In essence, each language may relativize its concept of closest vowel based on properties of the vowel inventory as a whole.

1.2 Vowel Harmony Is Distinct from Coarticulation

A slight twist arises in the harmony patterns of Central Ede dialects of Yoruba, which include Ijẹsa Yoruba. In Standard Yoruba, the high vowels /i,u/ have no lax counterparts /ɪ,ʊ/. However, in the Central Ede dialects, there *is* a contrast between tense /i,u/ and lax /ɪ,ʊ/, as seen in Ijẹsa [rín] 'laugh' versus [rɪ́n] 'walk' and [mún] 'be sharp' versus [mʊn] 'drink' (Bamgboṣe 1967; Akinlabi, in preparation). Since the high vowels /i,u,ɪ,ʊ/ can vary along the tense/lax dimension, they too participate in vowel harmony.

(6) *Ijẹsa Yoruba vowel harmony affects the high vowels*
    a. ɔ́úkɔ   'he-goat'
    b. eúrɛ́   'she-goat'
    c. ɛrʊ̀pɛ̀   'sand'
    d. orúkɔ   'name'
    e. èlùbɔ́   'yam flour'

What makes Ijẹsa high vowels undergo harmony, while Standard Yoruba high vowels don't? Some scholars of dialect variation might consider the participation of high vowels in harmony an innovation; then, as with all instances of phonological distinctions, they might investigate the seeds for these types of change. In a broader sense, why Ijẹsa high vowels undergo harmony and Standard Yoruba high vowels don't undergo it can be seen as the question of why some languages develop vowel harmony and others don't, writ small.

One proposed answer is that vowel harmony rules in a language are the result of elevating certain phonetic tendencies of the articulators to the status of hard-and-fast grammatical rules. For example, it is well-known from experimental phonetics that in a great deal of languages, the movement of the tongue body involved in articulating vowels, like many muscular articulations, displays anticipation (approaching its target before it actually needs to) and carryover (staying at its target longer than it actually should). This type of "bleedthrough" of an articulation from one sound to the preceding or following sound happens in all languages and is known as *coarticulation*. Coarticulation does not happen all the time for every vowel, and it happens to varying degrees, depending on many factors such as how fast and how carefully one is speaking.

According to the foremost proponent of this view, John Ohala, "Vowel harmony, *phonological* co-occurrence constraints between the features of vowels in polysyllabic words, is a *fossilized* remnant of an *earlier* phonetic process involving vowel-to-vowel assimilation" (1994, 491; italics mine). Provided that we interpret *fossilized* to mean phonologized (i.e., part of the phonological computation) and *earlier* to include the possibility of a no longer extant phonetic process, this statement is orthogonal to an analysis of harmony in a synchronic description. Indeed, Ohala emphasizes that this fossilization involves a transformative difference between what was once a gradient, variable, coarticulatory, phonetic process and what has become a categorical and symbolic phonological process, stating that "whereas the magnitude of the phonetic variation may vary continuously as a function of the strength or proximity of the contextual environment, the phonological variation is typically of an 'all-or-none' sort" (1994, 491).

The proposal that vowel harmony is the phonologized all-or-none version of a once-variable phonetic process of coarticulation, though speculative, has sparked much interest and research. In fact, pursuant to the question of whether the harmony affecting the high vowels in Central Ede dialects of Yoruba has developed from coarticulatory trends existing in the language family, Przezdziecki (2005) studied whether dialects *without* high-vowel harmony nonetheless show phonetic trends in that direction.

What Przezdziecki (2005) found was that in Standard Yoruba and in the Mọba dialect of Yoruba, while the high vowels do not undergo harmony, there is nonetheless a variable but statistically significant trend toward the vowel [i] being more laxed when it precedes a lax vowel. Przezdziecki did not find such a trend for [u], concluding that "this leaves the dilemma of explaining how it is that /i/ and /u/ pattern together as targets for harmony [in Central Ede dialects], since they do not both exhibit harmony-like patterns in [the Mọba and Standard Yoruba] data" (2005, 225). As a result, it is not clear that the participation of the high vowels /i,u/ in harmony in Central Ede dialects such as Ijẹsa results from a simple thresholding/bootstrapping of an existing coarticulatory process into a phonologized pattern, as Przezdziecki had hoped to find.[1]

Rather, as I will show throughout this book, rules of vowel harmony are based on natural classes of symbolic phonological features, such as [+high]. These rules vary across dialects and languages in how they compute locality: in some cases, they treat segments as completely invisible to vowel harmony (e.g., /i,u/ in Ifẹ Yoruba); in others, as participating donors of vowel harmony (e.g., /i,u/ in Standard Yoruba); and in still others, as elements that themselves undergo vowel harmony (e.g., /i,u/ in Ijẹsa Yoruba). This variation is of a cognitive and symbolic nature that cannot be reduced to coarticulatory trends of varying strengths: even the most careful acoustic studies do not find evidence for these trends where they would be expected if all harmony ultimately corresponded to below-the-radar coarticulation. Microvariation in vowel harmony found between closely related dialects of the same language is the result of how locality is computed, and it can be modeled by a small set of parametric options that restrict the possible variation in what counts as relevant.

1.3 Locality Is Not Measured by Pure Distance in Syntax Either

Another case where locality is not measured in terms of distance alone is found among syntactic dependencies. Anaphoric noun phrases such as *himself* and *herself* mean nothing on their own; their defining property is that they must find another noun phrase within the same sentence to fix their reference. In a sentence such as *Mary thinks that John is proud of himself*, we understand *himself* to mean *John*, the closest noun phrase that can fix the reference of this anaphor. Thus, a reasonable description of an anaphor like *himself* is that it requires a nearby referential element (with matching gender and number) in order to license its presence.

We can minimally change this sentence by flipping the first and second noun phrases, yielding *John thinks that Mary is proud of himself*. The result, we find, is ungrammatical. Our intuition is that in this case the word *John* is "too far" from *himself* in order to fix its reference. The measuring-tape theory of locality can produce this result. There is another noun phrase closer to *himself*, since *Mary* is only four words away, while *John* is seven words away. In terms of absolute distance, *Mary* is closer, but since *himself* is specified as masculine, the goal closest to it is of the wrong gender. The sentence thus "crashes": the search for a closest goal in terms of absolute distance has failed to find a noun phrase matching in gender.

But the measuring-tape theory immediately makes a wrong prediction. Consider *Mary thinks that a sister of John is proud of himself*. As in *Mary thinks that John is proud of himself,* here the word *John* is four words away from *himself* and so should by all rights be the closest element for purposes of fixing its reference. But this sentence is ungrammatical. The reason is, natural language doesn't count distance in terms of number of words. As in our Boston subway system example, it is the distance *relevant within a structure* that matters. In the internal structure of *Mary thinks that a sister of John is proud of himself,* *a sister of John* is the subject of the predicate *proud,* and it turns out that what's relevant for anaphoric distance is being an argument of the predicate. Since it's a sister of John who's proud, it's the phrase *a sister of John* that's considered as the closest noun phrase to *himself*—and indeed, it's *a sister of John* that fails to match the gender of *himself* and causes the search to fail and the sentence to crash. What's relevant in determining the closest noun phrase for fixing the referent of *himself* is, yet again, not absolute distance, but distance as relativized to being an argument of the same two-place predicate *proud* that the anaphor *himself* is an argument of.[2] This fact about human language is one that never ceases to cause problems for strictly word-by-word models of syntax: the relevant distance to determine anaphoric locality is not computed as the crow flies, but relativized to certain properties borne by the elements being measured. In the chapters that follow, I explore a number of somewhat more intricate cases from the domain of vowel harmony to demonstrate that this basic principle is universal across seemingly different levels of linguistic structure.

1.4   Overview of the Major Claims

The inspiration for this book began in part with the suspicion that a casual remark made by Noam Chomsky in the fall of 2000 might be incorrect—namely, the remark that there was little indication that the strong minimalist thesis (that language provides optimal solutions to linking interfaces) could hold for phonology. A central objective of this book is to demonstrate that subsegmental phonology can indeed be insightfully modeled according to the core tenets of the Minimalist Program: (1) an emphasis on interface-driven computations, (2) a principle of minimal search and efficient computation, and (3) an attempt to derive crosslinguistic variation from the structure of the inventory rather than from violable principles. The principal empirical focus of syntactic theory is on long-distance dependencies, such as the agreement relation (*Agree* in Chomsky 2000 et seq.) between a verbal predicate (the *probe*) and an argument noun phrase (the *goal*).

Vowel harmony provides one of the best opportunities within phonology to explore the calculus of the Agree relation, as vowel harmony typically involves cases of a long-distance dependency between the dependent vowel (typically, an alternating suffixal vowel) and the determiner of its harmonic value (the closest eligible leftward vowel within the root). In fact, alternating suffixal vowels, which by definition have no stable underlying value, may be modeled as underlyingly unvalued; however, an interface requirement (namely, phonetic convergence) requires full specification for these values.

Vowel harmony emerges as a computational operation whose purpose is to provide a solution for valuing this "uninterpretable" suffixal vowel through the principle of minimal search for the closest goal to act as a feature-source. Importantly, I argue that applying the Agree model to asymmetric dependencies among subsegmental features in phonology goes far beyond simple resemblance to applying it in syntax: for example, the perplexing phenomena of "parasitic harmony" within phonology (whereby a goal providing a value for a feature F bears a prerequisite value for a feature G) are argued to receive a unified analysis under the rubric of *defective intervention* developed for the Agree system by Chomsky (2000) and Hiraiwa (2001). Finally, I argue that the model of vowel harmony, necessarily "target-centric" (i.e., one in which the suffixal vowel initiates the search and in which locality is defined from the perspective of the value-copying, rather than value-providing, element), is empirically superior to traditional "trigger-centric" accounts of vowel harmony for cases of nonconstituent copying in Turkish and bidirectional copying in Woleaian.

In comparing the execution of interface-driven feature-copying at the levels of syntactic structure and phonological structure, I introduce the notion of *Crossmodular Structural Parallelism*, a hypothesis about the nature of human language that seeks to minimize differences between levels that do not follow from a difference in alphabet. I will argue that the core locality computation driving Agree and vowel harmony differs only in the alphabet of data structures to which it applies. This is an unorthodox hypothesis, driven by the goal of a higher-order synthesis between linguistic phenomena; a similar hypothesis has been pursued to some extent by Anderson (1992). The attempt to track as closely as possible the syntactic phenomena of locality in tandem with the conditions on long-distance vowel harmony is a unique effort, and one whose success will ultimately be measured in terms of its empirical accuracy.

The data structures adopted in this book follow the tradition of generative phonology (see Odden 2003 for an introduction) in employing binary features as the basic currency of intersegmental relations. The theoretical framework adopted in this book is the principles-and-parameters approach (Chomsky 1981) to linguistic universals and variation, in which a core set of invariant principles holds across all languages and a limited set of parameters restricts the possible variation. The book is typologically oriented, drawing on a large number and a wide range of languages from diverse families, selected to demonstrate the limits of crosslinguistic variation in locality effects on vowel harmony.

There are a few things this book does not cover. In particular, the cases studied here are ones in which the relation between two vowels is clearly a phonotactic dependency. Cases of "morphemic harmony," in which vowels or consonants undergo "mutations" as the exponent of a morphological process, are not handled. While phonological harmony is about featural identity *between* elements, morphemic harmony requires that a feature be realized across a certain domain. For example, in Kanembu, the distinction between two types of aspectual interpretation requires that all vowels in the word be [+ATR] or [−ATR], even though there is no visible affix for completive or incompletive aspect.

(7) *Kanembu completive is [+ATR] and incompletive is [−ATR] (Akinlabi 1996)*
    a. gɔnəkɪ   gonʌki   'I took / I am taking'
    b. dalləkɪ   dʌllʌki   'I got up / I am getting up'
    c. barɛnəkɪ   bʌrenʌki   'I cultivated / I am cultivating'

Kanembu instantiates what is called "featural affixation" (Akinlabi 1996), in which the relevant affix is only expressed by a single phonological feature, which is then realized on specific elements of the word to which it attaches. Such cases of morphological exponence represent a wholly different type of process than phonological vowel harmony (see Cole 1987 and Finley 2009 for a thorough comparison).

Vowel harmony of the type exemplified in the Altaic, Finno-Ugric, Niger-Congo, and Bantu languages, among others studied in this book, is a locality computation initiated by a single morpheme, which copies features from a single source. Morphemic harmony, by contrast, appears to be a globally sensitive process of realizing a single feature, such as [+nasal], sometimes on as many segments in the word as possible, as the exponent of a morphological category that does not have its own segmental content. For example, in Terena (Piggott 1988), the 1st person possessor is grammatically realized by a [+nasal] feature showing up on every possible segment of the word.

(8) *Terena nasalization*
    a. ajo   ãjõ   'his / my brother'
    b. arine   ãrĩnẽ   'his / my sickness'
    c. owoku   õw̃õⁿgu   'his / my house'

Similarly, in Mixtec (Piggott 1992), inflection for 2nd person is achieved by nasalizing as many segments as possible from the final segment leftward. While phonological vowel harmony may fail to occur altogether for a given morpheme if the vowel fails to find a source of harmony within the bounds permitted by locality, morphemic harmony always occurs in order to realize a morphological category; the only thing that varies is how many segments it will get a chance to apply to in a given word. In Korean ideophone harmony, used only to express 'light' and 'dark' senses of ideophones, both [±ATR] and [±high] sometimes change just the initial vowel of a word (e.g., [minduŋ]~[mɛnduŋ] 'bald'), while sometimes they change both the initial and the final vowel (e.g., [umullək]~[omullak] 'chewing'). These processes are related to exponence of "floating" features via mutation of the edges of a word.

Morphemic harmony can also require that a class of vowels appear only in the presence of a particular morpheme. For example, [−ATR] vowels occur only in the presence of the masculine singular suffix [-ʊ] in Pasiego: "Lax vowels may not occur in a word without this suffix" (McCarthy 1984, 294). When the masculine singular morpheme is added, every vowel possible becomes [−ATR]; but this change never takes place outside of the highly specific inflectional category of the masculine singular.

Such processes are well accounted for by the literal notion of a "floating" feature that associates to one or both edges of the word and attempts to express itself on as many segments as possible within some bounded range (Akinlabi 1996; Zoll 1996; Wolf 2007). Vowel harmony, however, is not: I will argue that it is crucially needy-vowel-centric, rather than being computed from the point of view of the donor. The omission of morphemic harmony from the present study is a principled exclusion.

A second topic, fascinating in its own right, but outside the aims of the current study, concerns the functional motivations or "benefits" of vowel harmony. This book focuses on the formal rather than substantive properties of this phonological process, attempting to characterize what is a possible or impossible vowel harmony system. This is an independent line of inquiry from how useful such a system might be in terms of its auditory-perceptual properties. Illuminating experimental work such as that of Suomi, McQueen, and Cutler (1997), Vroomen, Tuomainen, and deGelder (1998), and Mintz and Walker (2006) has demonstrated that vowel harmony can be used as a heuristic in word segmentation, providing cues to the listener for where one word stops and the next word begins—in much the same way that a fontsizechangecanbeused as a replacement for white space to help readers separate words in text (Kaye 1989). The question of what vowel harmony may be useful for will be left to other ambitious researchers: I will focus here on the procedures and constraints responsible for the way that harmony is executed and computed within a word, and on how the notion of closest vowel is measured, rather than how harmony is used in connected speech. This methodological narrowing of focus is parallel to the choices that are made within syntactic theorizing to explore restrictions on the locality of agreement relations independently from what verbal agreement may be used for.

The narrative of the rest of this book is broadly as follows. I will introduce how the Search procedure works for harmony and why the locality of harmony should be computed from the point of view of the needy segment. I will then show how locality is computed in a relativized manner and how languages may differ in terms of what is considered relevant. Elements considered "irrelevant" form a theory of what are traditionally called *transparent* elements. Next, I will provide a number of cases where harmony fails to occur. Elements that interfere with the locality of vowel harmony form a theory of what are traditionally called *blocking* elements. I will argue that the right way to model all of these effects is in terms of a Search procedure whose locality instantiates many of the same principles and parameters that determine locality of syntactic dependencies. The algorithm developed for vowel harmony will ultimately provide a bridge between phonological theory and syntactic theory.

Section 1.5 provides an overview of two existing classes of theories of vowel harmony, one of which has minimal locality requirements (hence is too weak) and one of which allows only strictly adjacent locality (hence is too strong). The discussion sets the stage for the Search procedure, parametric visibility, and defective intervention; I outline the key aspects of the new model for vowel harmony I propose, foreshadowing the detailed exposition in the following chapters.

Chapter 2 introduces the core mechanism of vowel harmony: the Search procedure, in which a search is conducted from a point of origin (such as Harvard Square in our subway example above) to find the closest element that satisfies a certain need (such as setting the value of harmony). The main demonstration will be that locality is best modeled in terms of measuring from the dependent element (the recipient of a feature-value) rather than in terms of measuring from the donor element.[3] Illustrating the application of the Search procedure in Turkish, Woleaian, and Barra Gaelic harmony, this chapter situates vowel harmony within the rubric of *search for closest element* that has become a key focus of inquiry in the minimalist approach to linguistic computation (Chomsky 1995).

Chapter 3 introduces an important source of crosslinguistic variation: the definition of *relevant* that is important in pinning down the *closest relevant element* as discussed above. Different settings of this parameter may yield dramatically different surface behavior in harmony, as demonstrated in the contrast between Ifẹ Yoruba and Standard Yoruba. The main demonstration of this chapter is that locality may be relativized to certain types of properties of phonological features, namely, the contrastive or marked status of the features in the segment that bears them.[4] This exclusion of irrelevant segments subsumes the locality effects called "transparency" in the traditional literature on vowel harmony. In illustrating the parametric variation in how feature-sensitive locality may be relativized in Finnish, in the Turkic and Tungusic language families (Karaim, Sibe, and Sanjiazi Manchu), and in dialectal variation within Kirghiz, Yoruba, and Finnish, this chapter draws important formal parallels between vowel harmony and the tradition of relativized minimality that prescribes a theory of *closest relevant element* within syntax (Rizzi 1990).

Chapter 4 explores what happens when the search fails because an intervening segment stands between the value-seeking recipient and its donor in the search domain. This subsumes the locality effects called "blocking" or "opaqueness" in the traditional literature on vowel harmony. A certain segment, because of an intrinsic property such as its value for a feature orthogonal to the one being searched for, is a "defective" value-source. Since the Search procedure has no lookahead, as soon as the search encounters a defective element in the domain, it ends in failure, even if there is a potentially eligible value-source further downstream. In illustrating the effects of failed copying due to minimality in Nawuri, Kisa, Khalkha Mongolian, and Jingulu, this chapter draws important parallels with syntactic agreement—where an inappropriately case-marked noun phrase with plural number blocks agreement between a verb and a postverbal subject noun phrase, yielding a defective intervention effect in which the verb can look no further than the intervening element that caused the search to fail.

Chapter 5 introduces a final source of parametric variation: how far a search can go before it gives up. Extrinsic barriers on search yield a type of locality, sometimes called "islandhood" (Ross 1967), by which certain extrinsically defined domains limit the extent of dependency relations, even where relativized closeness is kept constant. The chapter demonstrates how crosslinguistic and even within-language variation in harmony can result from different settings of "how far a vowel is able to look"—where the search must end, whether something is found or not.[5] In illustrating the parametric variation in the extent of the search domain in Hungarian and Gikuyu, this chapter draws important parallels with the role of closed domains of computation in barrier-based (Chomsky 1986) or impenetrability-based (Chomsky 2001) formalizations of limits on syntactic dependency. The second half of the chapter explores the ways in which high-sonority elements may also close off a search domain, acting as "hurdles," and establishes an implicational generalization about sonority, based on Wolof, Classical Manchu, Hungarian, and Finnish low vowels.

The broader consequences of this principles-and-parameters approach are that the vowel harmony systems of the world can be essentially reduced to one basic principle, with some parametric variables that can be filled in on a language-specific basis, and that what appear to be different, nuanced harmony systems from language to language reduce to variations on a core theme. The analysis of diverse harmony patterns in terms of a limited set of parametric options adds to the growing body of evidence (e.g., from stress systems in phonology and from *wh*-movement in syntax) that the diversity of human languages is not the result of every imaginable Babelian divergence from one to the next. Crosslinguistic and within-language variation results from easily isolated parametric choices (in this case, what's in the search domain and how far it extends) supplied as input to a fundamental algorithm of human cognition. The implications of a single principle of locality, and its consequences for our understanding of the structural parallels between phonology and syntax within the human language faculty, are discussed in chapter 6.

1.5 The Need for a New Model of Vowel Harmony

Existing models of vowel harmony can be broadly classified into two types: declarative identity-enforcement and sharing-by-spreading.

Examining these in turn, with reference to various vowel harmony patterns, we will conclude that neither type is sufficient to model the locality of vowel harmony, as identity-enforcement models are too permissive (in that they undesirably allow patterns of vowel harmony that do not exist) and sharing-by-spreading models are too restrictive (in that they undesirably disallow patterns of vowel harmony that do exist).

The distinction between these two types of models has been well-characterized by Rose and Walker (2004, 520), who propose that natural language actually contains both mechanisms for harmony: declarative identity-enforcement for processes that show no locality constraints at all (i.e., any two eligible vowels in a word must be identical for the harmonic feature, regardless of their distance), and sharing-by-spreading for processes that are strictly local and allow no skipping of elements between harmonizing vowels.

Under declarative identity-enforcement (e.g., relations of surface *correspondence* between vowels (see, e.g., Baković 2000; Hansson 2001; Krämer 2003)), it is straightforward to model the long-distance nature of vowel harmony. Given constraints on what types of vowels need to be identical for which features, there is no issue of locality: the harmonizing vowels are simply subject to a requirement of identity for roundness or whatever the harmonic feature is. Thus, in Ifẹ Yoruba, the requirement might be ALL MID VOWELS MUST BEAR THE SAME VALUE OF LAXNESS. A word like [èlùbɔ́] would satisfy this requirement, whereas a hypothetical Ifẹ word like [èlùbó] or [èlùbɔ́] would not. The issue of the nonlax [u] in the middle of these two vowels would simply not arise, as the constraint on identity does not mention high vowels.

Under sharing-by-spreading (e.g., autosegmental spreading or Firthian prosodies (Palmer 1970; Goldsmith 1976; Gafos 1996)), vowel harmony involves the spreading of a single featural specification (e.g., [+round]) across an entire word, where spreading may be halted by vowels that are incompatible with the spreading feature or are already specified for the opposite value. Thus, in Standard Yoruba, the laxness feature in a word like [èlùbɔ́] would begin spreading from the rightmost vowel and would be stopped by the tenseness value on the medial vowel, which would then spread its own tenseness value to the left.

If we only considered these two types of models, we might say that Ifẹ Yoruba employs declarative identity-enforcement, while Standard Yoruba employs sharing-by-spreading. Different dialects would then exhibit different locality restrictions because they employ different mechanisms for achieving vowel harmony.

The issue becomes more complicated, however, when we consider languages in which some vowels are treated nonlocally and others locally. Consider the pattern of [±round] harmony in Khalkha Mongolian that is responsible for alternations in the form of the reflexive suffix as either [a] or round [o,ɔ], depending on the roundness values of vowels to its left (where the further distinction between [o] and [ɔ] is due to an additional tense/lax harmony).

(9) *Khalkha Mongolian (Svantesson et al. 2005, 50)*
    a. poor-ig-o   'kidney-ACC-REFL'
    b. xɔɔlʒ-ig-ɔ   'food-ACC-REFL'
    c. mʊʊr-ig-a   'cat-ACC-REFL'
    d. suulʒ-ig-e   'tail-ACC-REFL'

As (9a–b) show, the intervening vowel /i/ is not counted in determining the suffix's harmony: even though /i/ is unround, it is irrelevant for computing the closest vowel. This might lead one to think that Khalkha vowel harmony is the result of declarative identity-enforcement. However, as (9c–d) show, the high vowels /u,ʊ/ cannot provide a value for round harmony, even though they are round. Now, one might counter that /u,ʊ/ are simply not part of the relevant constraint, which is instead ALL NONHIGH VOWELS MUST BEAR THE SAME VALUE FOR ROUNDNESS. In this case, there is simply no identity requirement that would cause [mʊʊr-ig-a] to become [mʊʊr-ig-ɔ].

As it turns out, however, /u,ʊ/ *are* involved in the computation of locality, because they "prevent" rounding harmony between nonhigh vowels. In (10), we see that the perfect suffix harmonizes with round /o,ɔ/ in (10a–b), but not when the closest vowel is round /u,ʊ/, as in (10c–d).

(10) *Defective intervention in Khalkha rounding harmony*
    a. tor-oːd   'be.born-PERF'
    b. ɔr-ɔːd   'enter-PERF'
    c. tor-uːl-eːd   'be.born-CAUS-PERF'
    d. ɔr-ʊːl-aːd   'enter-CAUS-PERF'

We must conclude that declarative identity-enforcement cannot account for Khalkha rounding harmony, as it is "blocked" by vowels of the wrong height. At the same time, the strictly local spreading-by-sharing model cannot account for Khalkha either, as the vowel /i/ is "transparent" and not part of the locality computation.

The spreading-by-sharing proposal of Rose and Walker (2004) is one in which all feature-sharing is strictly local, and Gafos (1996, 77–81) demonstrates that the autosegmental formalism actually requires all spreading to be strictly local, given an interpretation of autosegmental association lines as temporal overlap. Indeed, the very intuition of sharing-by-spreading theories is an intuition of articulatory "persistence" of a particular gesture from one vowel to the next, a notion that is very difficult to square with the data in (10c–d), in which two round vowels in a row nevertheless do not induce lip rounding in a third vowel that follows both of them.

The intuition underlying the central proposal in this book is that the autosegmental formalism on which sharing-by-spreading is based is not the best way to model the locality of vowel harmony, and that a target-centric, relativized search makes an empirically tighter set of predictions. The autosegmental formalism was developed for tonal phenomena, which display very different locality effects from vowel harmony, as tonal phenomena essentially show no instances of "blocking" of long-distance spreading.[6] In addition, tonal phenomena often involve the existence of independent "melodies," such as HL in Kukuya (Zoll 2003) that must be mapped to accommodate monomoraic, bimoraic, and trimoraic stems as H͡L, HL, and HLL, respectively; there is no obvious analogue to this word-length-invariant "melody" in any sequence of subsegmental features. I find it entirely plausible that tonal interactions and subsegmental feature-copying might employ different grammatical mechanisms, and I will remain largely agnostic on the question of whether long-distance tone spreading can be assimilated to the target-centric model proposed in this book, or whether traditional autosegmental accounts for tone should be maintained. (Interestingly, William Leben (2006), one of the founders of autosegmental approaches to tone, has recently discussed the possibility that alternative formalisms for tone realization are superior to autosegmental theory.) In any event, the phenomena of vowel harmony themselves demand a new model that strikes a balance between being overly restrictive and being overly permissive.

The present book offers a new theory of vowel harmony, the Search-and-Copy procedure, which views crosslinguistic variation in locality as the result of different *parameters* on a search procedure. Under this model, harmony is a search initiated by a "needy" vowel for the features (e.g., laxness, roundness) that it requires. Variations in locality (e.g., between Ifẹ Yoruba and Standard Yoruba) are determined by parameters that cut certain vowels out of the search domain, rendering them irrelevant in computing "closest." Some languages may relativize their search only to vowels that are *contrastive* for the harmonic feature; as a result, in

Ifẹ Yoruba the high vowels are pruned from the search domain and not counted in determining "closest" (see analysis in chapter 3). Other languages may relativize their search only to vowels that are *marked* for the harmonic feature; as a result, in Khalkha Mongolian the high front vowel /i/ is irrelevant for the search and not counted in determining "closest" (see analysis in chapter 4).

Yet other languages may determine that, even though the principle of searching for the closest relativized element is crosslinguistically invariant, once the closest relevant vowel is found, additional parameters prevent it from being copied from. Thus, even though Khalkha /ʊ/ is the closest vowel to the perfect suffix in [ɔr-ʊːl-aːd], it differs in height from the suffix vowel and hence cannot be copied from. The search, however, is over, and even though an eligible vowel is just further upstream, no harmony happens in this case. In the chapters that follow, I argue that patterns of transparency and opacity of intervening vowels can be predicted from a restricted set of parameters based on properties of the languages' inventory and requirements on boundedness, sonority, and orthogonal identity.

In the Search-and-Copy procedure, the computation of locality in vowel harmony is target-driven, as it involves a procedural search initiated by the needy vowel. In a sharing-by-spreading model of harmony, the harmonic value must extend throughout the domain, and failure of a potential target to undergo harmony is treated as a lexical exception. As a result, random occurrences of harmonizing and nonharmonizing affixes are not predicted. However, an important claim in this book is that morphemes that acquire a harmony value must be morphologically specified as needing such a value. This specification is what is crucial for needy morphemes to initiate a search; morphemes that do not harmonize simply lack it.

This asymmetric computation of locality (in which "closest" is counted from the perspective of the feature-seeker, rather than the feature-provider) is defended in chapter 2. It marks a significant departure from sharing-by-spreading theories, in which locality is computed from the perspective of the feature-provider, and from static/declarative theories, in which vowels must simply be identical for the relevant feature. These approaches to locality are empirically distinguishable, and I argue that the right fit between predictions and data is achieved by the target-initiated model.

It is perhaps most broadly interesting that the algorithm developed for vowel harmony based on the empirical demand of coverage that is neither too restrictive nor too permissive results in a model that closely mirrors the way locality is computed for syntactic dependencies such as verbal agreement. Previous models of vowel harmony, of both the sharing-by-spreading and declarative identity-enforcement varieties, bear no obvious relation to considerations that have led to the development of the Agree procedure in syntax, with its emphasis on efficient, interface-driven, no-lookahead, relativized search as a method for providing feature-values. The present model allows comparison of the computational systems of syntax and phonology, as discussed in chapter 6.

In the chapters that follow, successive presentations of the vowel harmony algorithm are accompanied by pseudocode representations of the Search procedure. This algorithm has been implemented in python and is available, along with case studies, at http://mitpress.mit.edu/vowel_harmony. It is my hope that interested readers will verify the predictions made by the principles and parameters of the locality of vowel harmony proposed here by experimenting with this software.

2 The Search Principle

Natura semper agit per vias brevissimas.
(Nature always acts through the shortest pathways.)
—Edwin A. Burtt

2.1 Harmony and Agree Are Both a Process of Finding a Value

Assimilation refers to any process whereby features from one segment are copied to another, making the recipient segment "more like" the donor segment. For example, the casual pronunciation of *in Boston* is *im Boston*, where the expected nasal consonant with an alveolar place of articulation is instead pronounced with a bilabial place of articulation. Within phonological theory, assimilation processes (in this case, the nasal consonant copying the place of articulation of the following segment) are analyzed as the result of copying a feature from one segment to another. Phonological features specify and constitute the articulatory instructions that make up segments. Thus, "N" is really just a shorthand for the cluster of features including [+nasal], [coronal], and so forth.[1] The assimilatory process of copying the bilabial property of "B" to a nasal, turning an "N" into an "M," is the result of copying [labial] from one segment to another.

Vowel harmony is a special kind of assimilation that differs in two ways from the case above. First, it operates specifically between vowels; as a result, it does not simply occur between strictly adjacent segments. Second, it often affects or involves all vowels within a word, rather than simply the two segments at the juncture between, say, preposition and noun.

One of the reasons why assimilation of vowel features is called "harmony" is that it instantiates a kind of dependency relation, in which a newly added suffix is forced to "harmonize" with the stem it attaches to.

A musical analogy could be made, perhaps, to an open-mic jazz session: a trumpet player who walks into an ongoing tune has to play in the key that's already been established.

With vowels, there are only four or five features along which this kind of harmonizing can be required. Three of them have to do with dimensions of tongue movement: [±back] determines whether the tongue body is fronted or backed, [±high] determines whether the tongue body is raised or not (while [±low] determines whether it is lowered or not), and [±advanced tongue root] (abbreviated *ATR*) determines whether the root of the tongue (which anchors it toward the pharynx) is advanced or not. In addition, the feature [±round] determines whether or not the lips are rounded during the production of a vowel or consonant (distinguishing, for example, French /i/ and /ü/), and the feature [±nasal] determines whether or not airflow through the nose occurs (distinguishing, for example, Portuguese /a/ and /ã/). In principle, harmony can be required among any of these features.

A straightforward and well-known example where harmony is required is found in Turkish. Turkish does not employ the features [±ATR] or [±nasal] in the phonology of its vowels; [±high, ±back, ±round] are sufficient to uniquely determine each of the language's eight vowels. As in the example of our trumpet player, when a new suffix waltzes up to an existing root, it must engage in harmony. A newly added accusative case suffix is forced to harmonize with the existing "key" set by the root for the features [±back] and [±round]. Since there are two possible values for [±back] and two possible values for [±round], the suffix can show four different forms: /i/ is [−back, −round], /ü/ is [−back, +round], /ɨ/ is [+back, −round], and /u/ is [+back, +round].[2] Which form will surface depends on what values the root has for these features. While the accusative suffix brings its own height feature [+high] to the table, it must agree with the root for the other two features. (This is a specific aspect of the way the morphology-phonology interface works in Turkish: specific morphemes participate in harmony, while others do not, a distinction that must be learned.)

(1) *Turkish vowel harmony of accusative suffix*
    a. ip   ip-i   'rope / rope-ACC.SG'
    b. kɨz   kɨz-ɨ 'girl / girl-ACC.SG'
    c. yüz yüz-ü 'face / face-ACC.SG'
    d. pul   pul-u 'stamp / stamp-ACC.SG'
    e. el   el-i   'hand / hand-ACC.SG'

f. sap³   sap-i̇   'stalk / stalk-ACC.SG'
g. köy   köy-ü   'villa / villa-ACC.SG'
h. son   son-u   'end / end-ACC.SG'

This type of dependency relation, in which one element's form depends on features of another's, is quite common across varying levels of linguistic structure. Consider verb agreement in Italian: in *Tu sei andato* 'You have gone', *Gioia è andata* 'Gioia has gone', and *I ragazzi sono andati* 'The boys have gone', the verb shows a masculine singular, feminine singular, or masculine plural ending, depending on what the gender feature of the subject noun phrase is. Clearly we would not say that the gender or number of *Gioia* or *i ragazzi* depends on the ending of *andato/andati/andata*; rather, it's an asymmetric dependency relation in which the verbal element depends on the subject for its identity.

(2) *Italian auxiliary and participle agreement*

Dependent element	Copies person	Copies number	Copies gender
a. sei	2nd	[−plural]	none
b. è	3rd	[−plural]	none
c. sono	3rd	[+plural]	none
d. andato	none	[−plural]	[−fem]
e. andata	none	[−plural]	[+fem]
f. andati	none	[+plural]	[−fem]

Within syntactic theory, the agreements found on the auxiliary (*è* vs. *sono* vs. *sei*) and the participle (*andata* vs. *andati* vs. *andato*) are modeled as asymmetric dependency relations. With these verbs of motion in the present perfect tense, the auxiliary copies the person and number features from the subject noun phrase, and the participle copies the number and gender features from the subject noun phrase. Notice that the auxiliary does not agree in gender, and that the participle does not agree in person. The auxiliary "needs" person and number, but not gender, whereas the participle "needs" gender and number, but not person. Agreement is viewed as a process in which recipient nodes find and copy the features that they need.

The goal of this chapter is to present a model of vowel harmony processes like (1) as the result of a Search-and-Copy procedure that is formally identical to verbal agreement as illustrated in (2), with the obvious difference that syntactic structure defines closeness in terms of hierarchical c-command whereas phonological structure defines closeness in terms of linear precedence. Irrespective of syntactic or phonological structure, the core principles are identical between the Agree operation defined in syntactic theory and the *Harmonize* operation, whose preliminary formulation is this:

(3) *Statement of Harmonize as a procedure like syntactic Agree*
A recipient needs a value for a feature F. Search is always initiated *from* the target/recipient of assimilation. Once the target encounters a donor, it copies the value of a feature F.

Crucial to the model will be the notion that the segments of a word are in a total order, so that for any x and y that are segments in the word, either x will precede y or y will precede x.[4] The notion of precedence permits us to derive the relation *closer*.

(4) *Definition of* closer
Given a, b, c: b is *closer* to a than c if either (i) a precedes b and b precedes c or (ii) b precedes a and c precedes b, where a, b, c are segments.

The Search procedure for vowel harmony begins with a recipient and looks for the closest donor in a certain direction δ, which can be either to the left or to the right (or in both directions simultaneously).

(5) *Harmonic Search-and-Copy procedure, in two steps: (τ, δ, F)*
 a. Find: $x =$ the closest τ to the recipient y in the direction δ
 b. Copy: the value of F on x onto y, where x, y are segments, F is a feature, τ is a predicate over segments.

When there is more than one feature to copy, these are all looked for on the same search. With Turkish suffixal high vowels, for example, Back-Harmonize and Round-Harmonize occur on the same search; that is, the same pointer is tracking positions backward, searching simultaneously for each independently and valuing each as soon as possible. The Search procedure is formalized in the algorithm in figure 2.1, where variables named with *my* represent the values updated during search.

That's the core of the Search algorithm: a forced march leftward and/or rightward that stops at each potential donor segment, sees whether there is a [±back] and/or [±round] value to copy, and if there is, takes it. The Search-and-Copy procedure is simple and minimalist, but this particular formulation will turn out to have important consequences in the empirical cases examined in the following sections.

The Search Principle

myVals V
myPosition P
myFeatsneeded F

while F is not empty:
- Go in direction δ and update P
- **if** P has a value for any $f, f \in F$:
  - Copy Val(P, f) to V
  - Remove f from F

Figure 2.1
Single-pass search with all features harmonized

2.2 Back Harmony and Round Harmony in Turkish Suffixes

Let's observe this process in action by returning to the Turkish accusative suffix. The suffix vowel is merged with the root, and it needs a value for [±back] and a value for [±round]. It conducts a Search-and-Copy procedure for each of these values simultaneously, looking at possible vowel donors.

(6) *Turkish accusative case morpheme suffix must:*
Back- and Round-Harmonize: δ = left, F = [±back, ±round]

The procedure is illustrated for [ip-i] 'rope-ACC'. The X-slots above each feature-matrix in (7)–(9) represent the Root node, over which precedence relations are defined, and the arrow represents the direction of search δ. The arrow ← represents the current segment being traversed through the search as the needy vowel seeks a licit value-source. When copying occurs, ↰ indicates an element being copied from.

(7) *Accusative suffix begins Back-Harmonize in [ip-i]*

$$\begin{array}{ccc} x_1 & x_2 \leftarrow & x_3 \\ \begin{bmatrix} +\text{voc} \\ +\text{high} \\ -\text{back} \\ -\text{rd} \end{bmatrix} & \begin{bmatrix} -\text{voc} \\ \text{lab} \\ -\text{cont} \\ -\text{nas} \end{bmatrix} & \begin{bmatrix} +\text{voc} \\ +\text{high} \end{bmatrix} \end{array}$$

(8) *Accusative suffix finds [−back] on x_1 and finds [−round] on x_1*

$$\begin{array}{ccc} x_1 \leftarrow & x_2 & x_3 \\ \begin{bmatrix} +\text{voc} \\ +\text{high} \\ \mathbf{-back} \\ \mathbf{-rd} \end{bmatrix} & \begin{bmatrix} -\text{voc} \\ \text{lab} \\ -\text{cont} \\ -\text{nas} \end{bmatrix} & \begin{bmatrix} +\text{voc} \\ +\text{high} \end{bmatrix} \end{array}$$

(9) *Accusative suffix copies [−back] and [−round] to itself*

$$x_1 \quad \uparrow \quad x_2 \quad x_3$$

$$\begin{bmatrix} +\text{voc} \\ +\text{high} \\ -\text{back} \\ -\text{rd} \end{bmatrix} \begin{bmatrix} -\text{voc} \\ \text{lab} \\ -\text{cont} \\ -\text{nas} \end{bmatrix} \begin{bmatrix} +\text{voc} \\ +\text{high} \\ -\text{back} \\ -\text{rd} \end{bmatrix}$$

$$\quad\; i \qquad\qquad p \qquad\quad\; i$$

This basic principle of Search-and-Copy underlies all vowel harmony, though as we will see in chapters 3, 4, and 5, the items that are searched for and the extent of the search are subject to varying parametric conditions.

2.3 Harmony Can Iterate from Morpheme to Morpheme

Harmony occurs whenever a new morpheme that needs a value is added (as well as when a new vowel is added to a morpheme by epenthesis), and what makes the process iterative is that a morpheme M_j that has found a value for harmony can then in turn provide a value for a linearly subsequent morpheme M_{j+1}. This iterative process is illustrated below in the interaction of harmony in Turkish with both a genitive case morpheme and a plural number morpheme.

(10) *Turkish genitive case morpheme suffix must:*
Back- and Round-Harmonize: δ = left, F = [±back, ±round]

(11) *Turkish plural morpheme suffix must:*
Back-Harmonize: δ = left, F = [±back]

(10) says that the genitive case must find values for both [±back] and [±round], while (11) says that the plural must find a value for [±back]. The plural suffix is inherently [−round]. (In fact, all noninitial [−high] vowels in Turkish are [−round], unless lexically specified otherwise.) An important consequence of the plural's failure to undergo harmony for [±round] is that any harmonically dependent element that immediately follows the plural will be [−round].

(12) *Harmony in Turkish nouns plus plural plus genitive*
    a. ip   ip-ler-in   'rope / rope-PL-GEN'
    b. kiz   kiz-lar-in   'girl / girl-PL-GEN'
    c. el   el-ler-in   'hand / hand-PL-GEN'
    d. sap sap-lar-in 'stalk / stalk-PL-GEN'
    e. yüz yüz-ler-in 'face / face-PL-GEN'

f. pul   pul-lar-ın   'stamp / stamp-PL-GEN'
g. köy   köy-ler-in   'villa / villa-PL-GEN'
h. son   son-lar-ın   'end / end-PL-GEN'

Observing (12), one might think that the genitive suffix is limited to alternating between [-ın] and [-in]. However, this is not the case: the form of the genitive singular (i.e., just the genitive suffix) is not equal to just taking [-lar]/[-ler] away and subtracting it to get the result. The relationship between the suffix and the root is not direct: it is mediated by the harmony that the intervening plural suffix happened to (not) undergo. The following examples show that the noun plus the genitive alone is distinct from subtracting the plural from (12):

(13) *Harmony in Turkish nouns plus genitive alone*
     a. ip   ip-in   'rope / rope-GEN'
     b. kız   kız-ın   'girl / girl-GEN'
     c. el   el-in   'hand / hand-GEN'
     d. sap   sap-ın   'stalk / stalk-GEN'
     e. yüz   yüz-ün   'face / face-GEN'
     f. pul   pul-un   'stamp / stamp-GEN'
     g. köy   köy-ün   'villa / villa-GEN'
     h. son   son-un   'end / end-GEN'

Compare, for example, the form of the genitive suffix in [pul-un] and in [pul-lar-ın]. There is a round vowel in the genitive when it immediately follows the root, and there is an unround vowel in the genitive when it immediately follows the plural. There is a simple explanation for this behavior, and it is in fact exactly what we would expect given a principle of closest-source defined in terms of leftward precedence.

(14) *Plural begins Back-Harmonize in [pul-lar]*

$$\begin{bmatrix} +\text{voc} \\ +\text{high} \\ +\text{rd} \\ +\text{back} \end{bmatrix}_{x_1} \begin{bmatrix} -\text{voc} \\ +\text{son} \\ -\text{nas} \\ +\text{lat} \end{bmatrix}_{x_2} \begin{bmatrix} -\text{voc} \\ +\text{son} \\ -\text{nas} \\ +\text{lat} \end{bmatrix}_{x_3} \leftarrow \begin{bmatrix} +\text{voc} \\ -\text{high} \\ -\text{rd} \\ \end{bmatrix}_{x_4} \begin{bmatrix} -\text{voc} \\ +\text{son} \\ -\text{nas} \\ -\text{lat} \end{bmatrix}_{x_5}$$

(15) *Plural finds and copies [+back]*

$$\begin{bmatrix} +\text{voc} \\ +\text{high} \\ +\text{rd} \\ +\textbf{back} \end{bmatrix}_{x_1} \curvearrowright \begin{bmatrix} -\text{voc} \\ +\text{son} \\ -\text{nas} \\ +\text{lat} \end{bmatrix}_{x_2} \begin{bmatrix} -\text{voc} \\ +\text{son} \\ -\text{nas} \\ +\text{lat} \end{bmatrix}_{x_3} \begin{bmatrix} +\text{voc} \\ -\text{high} \\ -\text{rd} \\ +\textbf{back} \end{bmatrix}_{x_4} \begin{bmatrix} -\text{voc} \\ +\text{son} \\ -\text{nas} \\ -\text{lat} \end{bmatrix}_{x_5}$$

     u   l   l   a   r

Added next is the genitive suffix, next in line in terms of the morphological structure.

(16) *Genitive begins Back- and Round-Harmonize in [pul-lar-in]*

x_1	x_2	x_3	x_4	x_5 ←	x_6
$\begin{bmatrix} +\text{voc} \\ +\text{high} \\ +\text{rd} \\ +\text{back} \end{bmatrix}$	$\begin{bmatrix} -\text{voc} \\ +\text{son} \\ -\text{nas} \\ +\text{lat} \end{bmatrix}$	$\begin{bmatrix} -\text{voc} \\ +\text{son} \\ -\text{nas} \\ +\text{lat} \end{bmatrix}$	$\begin{bmatrix} +\text{voc} \\ -\text{high} \\ -\text{rd} \\ +\text{back} \end{bmatrix}$	$\begin{bmatrix} -\text{voc} \\ +\text{son} \\ -\text{nas} \\ -\text{lat} \end{bmatrix}$	$\begin{bmatrix} +\text{voc} \\ +\text{high} \end{bmatrix}$

(17) *Genitive finds and copies [+back] and [−round]*

x_1	x_2	x_3	x_4 ↱	x_5	x_6
$\begin{bmatrix} +\text{voc} \\ +\text{high} \\ +\text{rd} \\ +\text{back} \end{bmatrix}$	$\begin{bmatrix} -\text{voc} \\ +\text{son} \\ -\text{nas} \\ +\text{lat} \end{bmatrix}$	$\begin{bmatrix} -\text{voc} \\ +\text{son} \\ -\text{nas} \\ +\text{lat} \end{bmatrix}$	$\begin{bmatrix} +\text{voc} \\ -\text{high} \\ \mathbf{-rd} \\ \mathbf{+back} \end{bmatrix}$	$\begin{bmatrix} -\text{voc} \\ +\text{son} \\ -\text{nas} \\ -\text{lat} \end{bmatrix}$	$\begin{bmatrix} +\text{voc} \\ +\text{high} \\ \mathbf{-rd} \\ \mathbf{+back} \end{bmatrix}$
u	l	l	a	r	ɨ

We can observe that this process is iterative. The key is, there is no relation between the genitive suffix and the root in (16), and, more generally, there is never any relation stated as "between the genitive suffix and the root." Rather, there is a relationship between the genitive suffix and the immediately preceding vowel, *whatever morpheme it is contained in.*

2.4 Turkish Vowel Harmony Reflects a Phonological Computation

As specified in the δ parameter of its vowel harmony pattern, Turkish copies vowel features from left to right. One interesting question is whether there is any relationship between the algorithmic procedure of copying feature-values from left to right and the articulatory production trends for vowel sequences in the language that do not display harmony. For example, one might expect that if vowel harmony somehow represents the crystallization or discretizing threshold of existing articulatory patterns of tongue body backing or fronting in the language (an existing hypothesis among some researchers, as mentioned in section 1.2), then even words without this thresholded rule might show low-level, transient traces of left-to-right effects of coarticulation. If, on the other hand, vowel harmony is a symbolic phonological computation, as formalized here, then it should be possibly independent of what happens with the coarticulation of vowels in their phonetic implementation.

In a study of Turkish disharmonic sequences of the form [iCa], [iCe], [eCa], and [iCa] (where *C* represents a consonant between the two vowels), Beddor and Yavuz (1995) measured the amounts of anticipatory (i.e., right-to-left) and carryover (i.e., left-to-right) coarticulation affecting the fronting or backing of the vowels. They found that all three vowels exhibited effects of anticipatory coarticulation (e.g., [i,e] were reliably more backed when followed by [a], and [a] was more fronted when followed by [i,e]), but that the effects of carryover coarticulation were much more restricted—essentially, they found only an effect of fronting of [a] when preceded by [i]. They conclude:

> If the primary left-to-right phonological pattern of vowel harmony in Turkish were to reflect active phonetic patterns of vowel-to-vowel coarticulation, then carryover should exceed anticipatory coarticulation in Turkish disharmonic roots. However, the reverse phonetic pattern holds for the set of roots tested here, in that anticipatory coarticulation was found to be a much more general phenomenon than carryover coarticulation.... One interpretation to be considered is that perhaps this outcome should cause us to question our underlying assumption of a cause-and-effect relation between vowel-to-vowel coarticulation and vowel harmony.... The alternative interpretation that we offer is that once a phonetic behavior is phonologized, it becomes largely distinct from the behavior which gave rise to it. (1995, 49).

This is an important finding about the modular division between phonological computation and phonetic exigencies. Perhaps a useful analogy is that of the rules of etiquette for holding a wineglass: all epicurean reference guidelines assert that one must hold a wineglass by the stem. While this rule clearly has a functional origin in laws of thermodynamics, in that holding a wineglass by the bowl can raise the temperature of chilled white wines, it has been generalized and formalized beyond its original context to places where it no longer serves a functional need at all, such as with red wines, or mulled wines served warm. While the original cause-and-effect relationship between the gradient, variable laws of heat transfer and the rule of etiquette is clear, once formalized as a hard-and-fast rule, it remains distinct from the rules of physics that gave rise to it. Indeed, having your hand down on the stem still does in fact transmit minor amounts of heat to the wine bowl above it, but this is okay in terms of etiquette as long as the rule is categorically followed.

Returning to the fact that Turkish vowel harmony is a phonological computation that proceeds from left to right, whereas its transient coarticulatory patterns are stronger from right to left, we note that Modern Turkish stress falls on the final syllable. Phonetic coarticulation effects are often stronger from stressed vowels to unstressed vowels (Fowler 1981), which may explain the directionality of the right-to-left coarticulatory pattern that Beddor and Yavuz (1995) found. Interestingly, Proto-Turkic is posited to have had stress on the initial syllable (Poppe 1960), and the location of initial stress is thought to have given rise to left-to-right vowel harmony in Turkish (Barnes 2006). Once the rules of vowel harmony became an entrenched phonological computation in Turkish, even when the stress pattern of the language changed and the pattern of vowel-to-vowel phonetic coarticulation changed, the harmony pattern remained the same, an autonomous search-and-copy computation of the kind specified in (11).

2.5 Nonundergoing Morphemes Can Still Be Donors

Up to this point, we have formulated harmony as essentially a statement about a phonological process that a certain morpheme must undergo upon entering the phonological computation. Just as it is a listed fact in the speaker's mental representation of lexical items that sometimes a grammatical morpheme may not receive any phonological content (such as the plural of *sheep* in English), it is also a property of some morphemes that they must or must not undergo some type of vowel harmony. We thus might expect another suffix in Turkish that has overall phonological properties similar to those of the plural suffix (i.e., being a CVC syllable with a [−high] and [−round] vowel), but does not have to undergo harmony. A suffix like this indeed exists: the nominalizing morpheme /-gen/. The instruction label for harmony in this case would read as follows:

(18) *Turkish nominalizing morpheme suffix must:*
 (empty)

In other words, while it is a property of the plural morpheme that it must Back-Harmonize, showing up as either [-lar] or [-ler] depending on the value of the closest source to its left, this is not a property of the nominalizing morpheme /-gen/. It does not harmonize and is not a phonologically "needy" element, and little more needs to be said in the lexicon than that.

In one possible way of looking at it, /-gen/ is an "exception" to vowel harmony, that is, a suffix that does not "need" to undergo it. But being exceptional with respect to harmony means only that. It is an automatic consequence of the asymmetrically dependent recipient-centric nature of vowel harmony that:

(19) *A morpheme might not need to search for harmony, but it still must be a donor.* While a suffix might be "exceptional" in not undergoing harmony, no suffix is listed as "exceptional in not triggering harmony."

The Search Principle

Finley (2007) argues for the same point: crosslinguistically, there are a number of exceptionally nonsearching morphemes, but there are no exceptionally nondonating morphemes. Thus, of the two logically possible types of exceptions in generative phonology distinguished by Coats (1970), exceptionally not-undergoing a phonological process or exceptionally not-providing the features/environment needed for a phonological process, in vowel harmony only the former type of exceptions are found. This is exactly what we would expect if harmony is a process initiated by the searching, "needy" morpheme, in which the donor is merely a passive source of a value to be copied.

Morphemes that don't participate in vowel harmony aren't like noble gases in molecular chemistry: it's not as though these morphemes completely fail to interact in harmony with the other morphemes around them. It's just that *they* don't need a value. While /-gen/ does not need to undergo harmony itself, the exception does not affect whether other morphemes will have such a need or not. We can actually stack the harmonizing plural suffix right next to its stoic foil, the nominalizer, and the result is that *the plural's harmony is determined as usual*, by the value of [−back] immediately to its left, namely, the lexical and unalternating value of that feature borne by /-gen/.

(20) *Turkish nonharmonizing nominalizer plus harmonizing plural suffix*

	Stem		Stem+NMLZ	
a.	üč	'three'	üč-gen-ler	'triangles'
b.	altɨ	'five'	altɨ-gen-ler	'pentagons'
c.	sek^{j}iz	'eight'	sek^{j}iz-gen-ler	'octagons'
d.	čok	'many'	čok-gen-ler	'polygons'

(21) *Turkish plural suffix initiates leftward search in [čok-gen-ler]*

$$\begin{bmatrix} +\text{voc} \\ -\text{high} \\ +\text{rd} \\ +\text{back} \end{bmatrix}_{x_1} \begin{bmatrix} -\text{voc} \\ +\text{vel} \\ -\text{cont} \\ -\text{voi} \end{bmatrix}_{x_2} \begin{bmatrix} -\text{voc} \\ +\text{vel} \\ -\text{cont} \\ +\text{voi} \end{bmatrix}_{x_3} \begin{bmatrix} +\text{voc} \\ -\text{high} \\ -\text{rd} \\ -\text{back} \end{bmatrix}_{x_4} \begin{bmatrix} -\text{voc} \\ \text{cor} \\ +\text{nas} \end{bmatrix}_{x_5} \begin{bmatrix} -\text{voc} \\ +\text{son} \\ -\text{nas} \\ +\text{lat} \end{bmatrix}_{x_6} \leftarrow \begin{bmatrix} +\text{voc} \\ -\text{high} \\ -\text{rd} \end{bmatrix}_{x_7} \begin{bmatrix} -\text{voc} \\ +\text{son} \\ -\text{nas} \\ -\text{lat} \end{bmatrix}_{x_8}$$

(22) *Turkish plural suffix finds and copies [−back] from nominalizer*

$$\begin{bmatrix} +\text{voc} \\ -\text{high} \\ +\text{rd} \\ +\text{back} \end{bmatrix}_{x_1} \begin{bmatrix} -\text{voc} \\ +\text{vel} \\ -\text{cont} \\ -\text{voi} \end{bmatrix}_{x_2} \begin{bmatrix} -\text{voc} \\ +\text{vel} \\ -\text{cont} \\ +\text{voi} \end{bmatrix}_{x_3} \begin{bmatrix} +\text{voc} \\ -\text{high} \\ -\text{rd} \\ \mathbf{-back} \end{bmatrix}_{x_4} \begin{bmatrix} -\text{voc} \\ \text{cor} \\ +\text{nas} \end{bmatrix}_{x_5} \begin{bmatrix} -\text{voc} \\ +\text{son} \\ -\text{nas} \\ +\text{lat} \end{bmatrix}_{x_6} \begin{bmatrix} +\text{voc} \\ -\text{high} \\ -\text{rd} \\ \mathbf{-back} \end{bmatrix}_{x_7} \begin{bmatrix} -\text{voc} \\ +\text{son} \\ -\text{nas} \\ -\text{lat} \end{bmatrix}_{x_8}$$

o　　k　　g　　e　　n　　l　　e　　r

As shown above, a needy suffix is a greedy suffix: it will copy from the suffix immediately to its left, even though the source from which it copies does not itself need to harmonize.

2.6 "Exceptionally" Nonseeking Vowels in Turkish

The phenomenon of nonseeking elements in vowel harmony languages might at first blush look like a property of a whole morpheme: that the morpheme as a whole is lexically indexed to avoid harmony. However, it turns out that languages have fine-grained specifications of which vowels within a morpheme must undergo vowel harmony and which ones need not, and this is best represented as a property of each vowel. Let's examine the phenomenon first with the disyllabic suffix used to express the progressive in Turkish.

(23) *Turkish "half-harmonizing" progressive suffix*
    a. gʲelʲ-ijor-um   'come-PROG-1SG'
    b. koʃ-ujor-um   'run-PROG-1SG'
    c. gülʲ-üjor-um   'laugh-PROG-1SG'
    d. bak-ijor-um   'look-PROG-1SG'

The first vowel of the suffix /-ijor/ harmonizes, but the second one does not. Only the first vowel is required to undergo Back- and Round-Harmonize, which yields a surface form incorporating one of [u,ü,i,ɨ]. The second vowel is eternally fixed as /o/. Importantly, the next suffix to its right, whatever it is (1sg in the case above), will harmonize with this /o/, the closest segment to it. Thus, it is possible that only a single vowel within a morpheme needs to harmonize.

We have seen that Turkish suffixes differ from each other in that some require back harmony and round harmony, some require back harmony and round harmony for only one of their vowels, and some require no harmony at all. In chapter 6, we will return to the question of whether and how learners generalize from the harmonic requirements of one suffix to predict the patterning of classes of suffixes in the language as a whole, concluding that relevant insights may come from both first- and second-language acquisition. Importantly, once the lexically specified harmony requirements for each affix are set, however this may occur through the learning process, the Search-and-Copy procedure operates as described here.

2.7 Nonharmonizing Root Vowels in Turkish and Finnish and Their Nonfate in Language Games

This brings us to a discussion of whether noninitial vowels in roots need to harmonize. All of the cases of harmony considered thus far take place only across morpheme boundaries. However, in a computation over the lexicon, Harrison, Thomforde, and O'Keefe (2004) determined that 73% of Turkish unsuffixed stems are harmonic; in other words, the number of roots whose vowels agree in backness and roundness is higher than would be expected from chance combinatorial shuffling without determinants of allowable cooccurrence. The question is ripe to ask, then, whether harmony is going on inside single morphemes.

This question is often difficult to pose, because the primary evidence for vowel harmony in the affixes we considered above comes from the fact that they alternate: for example, the Turkish accusative suffix has four different surface variants, determined by the vowel immediately to its left, and dependent only on what noun is being put in the accusative case. However, since Turkish has no prefixes that would provide a variety of leftward vowels from which the root itself could copy,[5] roots themselves do not show alternations—not necessarily because they are immune from harmony, but because the environments in which the effects of harmony could be detected are absent ... save for one very revealing process.

Somewhat like the formation of English binomial compounds *dilly-dally, knick-knack, ping-pong, pitter-patter*, Turkish has a language game in which a root is doubled but the nonce copy has an initial back vowel. This is accomplished by "overwriting" the initial vowel in the nonce copy with [a], as in [moloz-maloz] 'debris'. What's crucially different about forming these compounds in Turkish, in contrast to English, is that the *second vowel* within the nonce copy undergoes harmony, as in (24b–c) (Harrison and Kaun 2001).

(24) *Turkish overwriting reduplication game: Replace initial vowel with [a]*

	Input	Second word of output	
a.	moloz	maloz	'debris'
b.	kibrit	kabrit	'match'
c.	bütün	batin	'whole'

While the first vowel of the nonce copy is always [a], the noninitial vowels in the reduplicant stem completely harmonize for back and round with the newly encountered [a] to their left. This is shown for [kibrit-kabrɨt] in (25)–(28).

(25) *Second vowel of [kibrit] seeks round and back harmony*

$$\begin{matrix} x_1 & x_2 & x_3 & \leftarrow & x_4 & x_5 \\ \begin{bmatrix} +\text{voc} \\ +\text{high} \\ -\text{rd} \\ -\text{back} \end{bmatrix} & \begin{bmatrix} -\text{voc} \\ \text{lab} \\ -\text{cont} \\ +\text{voi} \end{bmatrix} & \begin{bmatrix} -\text{voc} \\ +\text{son} \\ -\text{nas} \\ -\text{lat} \end{bmatrix} & & \begin{bmatrix} +\text{voc} \\ +\text{high} \\ \\ \end{bmatrix} & \begin{bmatrix} -\text{voc} \\ \text{cor} \\ -\text{cont} \\ -\text{voi} \end{bmatrix} \end{matrix}$$

(26) *Second vowel of root [kibrit] copies from closest leftward vowel*

$$\begin{matrix} x_1 & \leftharpoonup & x_2 & x_3 & & x_4 & x_5 \\ \begin{bmatrix} +\text{voc} \\ +\text{high} \\ \mathbf{-rd} \\ \mathbf{-back} \end{bmatrix} & & \begin{bmatrix} -\text{voc} \\ \text{lab} \\ -\text{cont} \\ +\text{voi} \end{bmatrix} & \begin{bmatrix} -\text{voc} \\ +\text{son} \\ -\text{nas} \\ -\text{lat} \end{bmatrix} & & \begin{bmatrix} +\text{voc} \\ +\text{high} \\ \mathbf{-rd} \\ \mathbf{-back} \end{bmatrix} & \begin{bmatrix} -\text{voc} \\ \text{cor} \\ -\text{cont} \\ -\text{voi} \end{bmatrix} \\ i & & b & r & & i & t \end{matrix}$$

(27) *Second vowel of nonce /kabr_t/ seeks round and back harmony*

$$\begin{matrix} x_1 & x_2 & x_3 & \leftarrow & x_4 & x_5 \\ \begin{bmatrix} +\text{voc} \\ -\text{high} \\ -\text{rd} \\ +\text{back} \end{bmatrix} & \begin{bmatrix} -\text{voc} \\ \text{lab} \\ -\text{cont} \\ +\text{voi} \end{bmatrix} & \begin{bmatrix} -\text{voc} \\ +\text{son} \\ -\text{nas} \\ -\text{lat} \end{bmatrix} & & \begin{bmatrix} +\text{voc} \\ +\text{high} \\ \\ \end{bmatrix} & \begin{bmatrix} -\text{voc} \\ \text{cor} \\ -\text{cont} \\ -\text{voi} \end{bmatrix} \end{matrix}$$

(28) *Second vowel of nonce /kabr_t/ copies from closest leftward vowel*

$$\begin{matrix} x_1 & \leftharpoonup & x_2 & x_3 & & x_4 & x_5 \\ \begin{bmatrix} +\text{voc} \\ -\text{high} \\ \mathbf{-rd} \\ \mathbf{+back} \end{bmatrix} & & \begin{bmatrix} -\text{voc} \\ \text{lab} \\ -\text{cont} \\ +\text{voi} \end{bmatrix} & \begin{bmatrix} -\text{voc} \\ +\text{son} \\ -\text{nas} \\ -\text{lat} \end{bmatrix} & & \begin{bmatrix} +\text{voc} \\ +\text{high} \\ \mathbf{-rd} \\ \mathbf{+back} \end{bmatrix} & \begin{bmatrix} -\text{voc} \\ \text{cor} \\ -\text{cont} \\ -\text{voi} \end{bmatrix} \\ a & & b & r & & ɨ & t \end{matrix}$$

The second root vowel in the compound word /k_br_t/ shows the alternation pattern we were looking for: it is [i] in [kibrit] and [ɨ] in [kabrɨt]. Harmony is in fact found when one rearranges a string of segments into a novel configuration by overwriting the first vowel of a root.

One response to characterizing the reharmonization of roots in this way might be that the reduplication game has simply created a new sequence of segments, [kabrɨt], and that this form therefore doesn't tell us anything about root-internal harmony per se—one might think that in real words, the speaker faithfully reproduces the root stored in memory and that the root involves no harmony, but that whenever segments are shuffled or replaced as in a language game, a wholly new string results, where no faithfulness to that stored form of an existing word need apply.

A striking confirmation that root-internal harmony really is a process in which *each vowel* is specified for whether it needs to harmonize or not comes from what happens in this game with disharmonic roots: they don't reharmonize (Harrison and Kaun 2001). For example, consider the disharmonic root /butik/ 'boutique', in which the first and second root vowels are not identical in backness or roundness. If root-internal harmony as an active Search-and-Copy procedure really is the regular state of affairs, this word, like the second vowel of the progressive suffix /-ijor/ encountered above, simply is marked as exceptionally not-undergoing harmony. As a result, even when the first root vowel is over-written in binominal compound formation, the second root vowel stays nonneedy.

(29) *Turkish overwriting reduplication game: No harmony with disharmonic roots*

	Input	Second word of output	
a.	butik	batik	'boutique'
b.	bordür	bardür	'edge ornamentation'
c.	kuvvet	kavvet	'strength'

The formal difference in behavior between the second root vowel in /kibrit/ and the second root vowel in /butik/ is the result of whether or not there is a requirement that this vowel must undergo harmony.[6]

(30) *Harmony requirements of root /kibrit/*
2nd vowel must: Back-Harmonize and Round-Harmonize

(31) *Harmony requirements of root /butik/*
2nd vowel must: (empty)

The failure of disharmonic roots such as /butik/ to reharmonize (say, as [butik-batik]) is evidence that the game of binomial compound formation preserves the second root vowel's lexical requirement of undergoing or not undergoing harmony. The results allow us to conclude that even in nongame utterances of /kibrit/, this second root vowel really is undergoing a Search-and-Copy procedure with the vowel to its left. By examining the root in isolation, we could not determine whether harmony was occurring or not. But in the special circumstance of overwriting the initial root vowel and observing harmonic alternation, we derive evidence that 73% of Turkish roots do show harmony between their noninitial and their initial vowels within a morpheme as the result of an active harmony process of the same type that occurs across morpheme boundaries. The remaining 27%, the disharmonic roots, have a representation like that of the progressive suffix /-ijor/, in which a particular vowel of a morpheme is specified as not needing to undergo harmony.

This pattern, in which disharmonic roots fail to "reharmonize," is specific neither to this game nor just to Turkish. At this point I will briefly introduce Finnish vowel harmony, although a full treatment awaits the next chapter. Finnish also has [±back] harmony, in which, for example, the [+back] [o] cannot cooccur with the [−back] [ö]. Finnish speakers play a game called *kontti kieli* (Campbell 1980, 1986), which involves overwriting the first CV of a stem with /ko-/. This causes reharmonization of [−back] vowels, like /ö,ü,ä/, as shown in (32).

(32) *Harmony of root vowels in Finnish* kontti kieli *game*
    Input   First word
                   of output
    a. nähnüt   kohnut   'seen'
    b. mitä   kota   'what'
    c. nälässänsäkö kolassansako 'in his hunger'

In disharmonic Finnish words, root-internal reharmonization does not occur, as shown in (33). This is because by hypothesis any disharmonic or nonharmonic vowel is one that does not need a value. The absence of a requirement to copy a value will hold even when the vowel is put in a different context.

(33) *Lack of harmony in* kontti kieli *for nonneedy vowels*
    Input   First word
                   of output
    jonglööri   ko+nglööri 'juggler'

No matter whether the game that provides the evidence for harmony is an overwriting game of binomial compound formation or a game where the initial CV sequence is replaced, all root vowels to the right of the newly introduced vowel will undergo harmony as usual if they are in a harmonic root, and will not undergo harmony if they are in a disharmonic root. The representation of harmonic and disharmonic roots can therefore be captured using the same leftward Search-and-Copy procedure for needy vowels that is independently found in suffixes. We conclude that vowel harmony occurs in Turkish and Finnish roots using this procedure. (Also see the appendix to this chapter, where I argue that non-final sibilant consonants in a word—including those within a root—must undergo harmony in Chumash.)

2.8 Bidirectional Harmony in Woleaian

Thus far, we have seen one important empirical argument for representing harmony as a recipient-initiated search, rather than a donor-initiated process: the empirical generalization (19), repeated here.

(34) *A morpheme might not need to search for harmony, but it still must be a donor*. While a suffix might be "exceptional" in not undergoing harmony, no suffix is listed as "exceptional in not triggering harmony."

This generalization is natural to derive in the present model: the Search-and-Copy procedure is either initiated or not by a particular vowel. There is simply no way to designate a particular closest leftward vowel to the recipient as exceptionally unwilling to be copied from: the Search algorithm is greedy and will opportunistically copy from the first vowel it finds.

As further evidence that harmony is a recipient-initiated process, we will examine a second case in which the opposite view, that harmony is donor-initiated, would by comparison be needlessly cumbersome. Rather than being viewed as "an imperative to spread," initiated by the donor, in cases where there is *more than one donor* it becomes immediately clear that harmony should be modeled from the perspective of the recipient.

In the Turkish cases discussed above, the direction of search was specified as leftward. In the case of a suffix, of course, it is somewhat natural to expect search to proceed to the left, as in the limiting case there will be no material to the right. Similarly, one might expect that when prefixes undergo harmony, they will search for a harmonic value to the right. This prediction is confirmed by the pattern of [±ATR] harmony in Akan prefixes. For example, the 3rd person prefix varies between [+ATR] [o] and and [−ATR] [ɔ] in harmony with the leftmost stem vowel (O'Keefe 2003).

(35) *Akan [±ATR] prefixal harmony contrast*
 a. ɔ-bɛkʊ '3sg-fight'
 b. o-betu '3sg-dig'

(36) *Akan 3rd person singular morpheme must:*
   ATR-Harmonize: δ = right, F = [±ATR]

When a past tense suffix is added, this suffix will search to its left for harmony.

(37) *Akan [±ATR] suffixal harmony contrast*
   a. ɔ-bɛkʊ-ɪ   '3SG-fight-PAST'
   b. o-betu-i   '3SG-dig-PAST'

(38) *Akan past tense morpheme must:*
   ATR-Harmonize: δ = left, F = [±ATR]

Thus, when a sole suffix is searching, it will look to the left, and when a sole prefix is searching, it will look to the right. However, as will be discussed in chapter 4, languages may also contain root vowels that copy harmonic features from suffixes to the right. Direction thus must be a free parameter of search. As mentioned previously, there is the possibility that the search direction could be simultaneously left and right.

Woleaian, a language spoken throughout the Woleai atoll (Micronesia), has a process of vowel assimilation (Sohn 1971; Howard 1972) applying to a thematic formative affix that occupies a position between the verbal stem and the agreement suffix. Woleaian has three levels of vowel heights, with both long and short versions of each vowel.

(39) *Woleaian vowel inventory*

[−rd]	[+back, −rd]	[+back, +rd]	
i	ü	u	[+high, −low]
e	ö	o	[−high, −low]
a		ɔ	[−high, +low]

The features distinguishing Woleaian vowels are [±high], [±low], [±back], and [±round].[7] The harmonizing suffix in question is always [−high, −round], but it is dependent on the surrounding vowels for its feature of [±low]. In Woleaian, this search is not set to be strictly leftward or strictly rightward. As a result, in the harmonizing suffix's search for [±low] valuation, determined by the closest value-source, it turns out that *both* flanking vowels are equally close. As a consequence, only when both vowels are [−low] will /a/ be raised to [e]; otherwise, a default value of [+low] will have to be inserted.[8]

(40) *Woleaian theme vowel must:*
   Low-Harmonize: δ = left and right, F = [±low]

The results of this harmony are shown in (41). A number of other phonological processes affect the form of nouns in Woleaian, such as deletion of final vowels and changes in palatal consonants; for that reason, both the underlying representation (UR) and the surface representation (SR) are shown here.

(41) *Woleaian bidirectional [±low] harmony*

	UR	SR	
a.	ülüm	üːl	'drinking object' (independent form)
b.	ülüm-a-ji	ülümej	1SG
c.	ülüm-a-mu	ülümem^w	2SG
d.	ülüm-a-la	ülümal	3SG
e.	ülüm-a-ca	ülümaʃ	1PL.INCL
f.	ülüm-a-mii	ülümemi	2PL
g.	ülüm-a-jire	ülümeːr	3PL

Importantly, the determinants for this process may be *deleted on the surface*, as seen in, for example, the form in (41b). The "two-sided" nature of the determining environment cannot be attributed to surface coarticulation. Moreover, as shown in (42), a nonlow vowel on the right is not sufficient to trigger raising. (There is an orthogonal process of low-vowel dissimilation, by which an /a/ before another /a/ changes to [e], as in the stem in (42).)

(42) *Woleaian failure of harmony when leftward and rightward vowels have different values for [±low]*

	UR	SR	
a.	mata-ji	metaj	'eye-1SG'
b.	mata-mu	metam^w	'eye-2SG'
c.	mata-mii	metami	'eye-2PL'
d.	mata-la	metal	'eye-3SG'
e.	mata-ca	metaʃ	'eye-1PL.INCL'

In a donor-initiated theory, there would need to be two rules for Woleaian low harmony in (41), one spreading [−low] leftward and one spreading [−low] rightward, plus the condition that *each could only apply if the other did*. A recipient-initiated *Search-and-Copy-from-closest*, on the other hand, provides an effective way to model *multiple-source valuation* of this sort without additional stipulations about resolving the application of two-sided spreading rules.

The Search-and-Copy procedure for the relevant portions of /ülüm-a-mii/ (resulting in [ülümemi]) is illustrated in (43)–(45), where ← and →

represent stepwise progressions of the bidirectional search, and ↶ and ↷ represent successful copying.⁹

(43) *Woleaian theme vowel begins Low-Harmonize in [ülümemi]*

$$x_1 \quad x_2 \leftarrow x_3 \rightarrow x_4 \quad x_5$$

$$\begin{bmatrix} +\text{voc} \\ +\text{rd} \\ +\text{high} \\ -\text{low} \\ -\text{back} \end{bmatrix} \begin{bmatrix} -\text{voc} \\ \text{lab} \\ -\text{cont} \\ +\text{nas} \end{bmatrix} \begin{bmatrix} +\text{voc} \\ -\text{rd} \\ -\text{high} \end{bmatrix} \begin{bmatrix} -\text{voc} \\ \text{lab} \\ -\text{cont} \\ +\text{nas} \end{bmatrix} \begin{bmatrix} +\text{voc} \\ -\text{rd} \\ +\text{high} \\ -\text{low} \\ -\text{back} \end{bmatrix}$$

(44) *Woleaian theme vowel finds [−low] on x_1 and on x_5*

$$x_1 \leftarrow x_2 \quad x_3 \quad x_4 \rightarrow x_5$$

$$\begin{bmatrix} +\text{voc} \\ +\text{rd} \\ +\text{high} \\ \mathbf{-low} \\ -\text{back} \end{bmatrix} \begin{bmatrix} -\text{voc} \\ \text{lab} \\ -\text{cont} \\ +\text{nas} \end{bmatrix} \begin{bmatrix} +\text{voc} \\ -\text{rd} \\ -\text{high} \end{bmatrix} \begin{bmatrix} -\text{voc} \\ \text{lab} \\ -\text{cont} \\ +\text{nas} \end{bmatrix} \begin{bmatrix} +\text{voc} \\ -\text{rd} \\ +\text{high} \\ \mathbf{-low} \\ -\text{back} \end{bmatrix}$$

(45) *Woleaian theme vowel copies [−low] from x_1 and from x_5*

$$x_1 \;\curvearrowright\; x_2 \quad x_3 \quad x_4 \;\curvearrowleft\; x_5$$

$$\begin{bmatrix} +\text{voc} \\ +\text{rd} \\ +\text{high} \\ \mathbf{-low} \\ -\text{back} \end{bmatrix} \begin{bmatrix} -\text{voc} \\ \text{lab} \\ -\text{cont} \\ +\text{nas} \end{bmatrix} \begin{bmatrix} +\text{voc} \\ +\text{rd} \\ -\text{high} \\ \mathbf{-low} \end{bmatrix} \begin{bmatrix} -\text{voc} \\ \text{lab} \\ -\text{cont} \\ +\text{nas} \end{bmatrix} \begin{bmatrix} +\text{voc} \\ +\text{rd} \\ +\text{high} \\ \mathbf{-low} \\ -\text{back} \end{bmatrix}$$

ü   m   e   m   i

The central phenomenon illustrated here by Woleaian is bidirectional harmony. As with the Turkish and Akan harmony processes discussed above, this type of harmony applies to a specific morpheme; thus, the fact that the relevant morphemes participate in bidirectional harmony is explicitly listed as a lexically specific aspect of their representation.

(46) *Woleaian thematic formative morpheme must:*
    Low-Harmonize: δ = left and right, F = [±low]

One aspect of the formalization in (46) is that it effectively states that copying of a [−low] feature depends on a "tie" in which the closest vowel in both directions bears [−low].¹⁰ Given (46), when both the immediately closest preceding and the immediately closest following vowel to the thematic formative are [αlow] (where α is either + or −, and both sides have the same value for α), the thematic formative will successfully copy [αlow]. However, if one side is [+low] and the other is [−low], there is *no way to copy the value from the closest donor(s)*. The uniqueness presupposition of "*the* value" in this statement fails, since it's impossible to copy + from one side and − from the other side. Nothing can be copied at all, and the search terminates in failure.

(47) *Woleaian theme vowel begins Low-Harmonize*

$$x_1 \quad\quad x_2 \quad \leftarrow \quad x_3 \quad \rightarrow \quad x_4 \quad\quad x_5$$

$$\begin{bmatrix} +\text{voc} \\ -\text{rd} \\ -\text{high} \\ +\text{low} \end{bmatrix} \begin{bmatrix} -\text{voc} \\ \text{cor} \\ -\text{cont} \\ -\text{nas} \\ -\text{voi} \end{bmatrix} \begin{bmatrix} +\text{voc} \\ -\text{rd} \\ -\text{high} \end{bmatrix} \begin{bmatrix} -\text{voc} \\ \text{cor} \\ +\text{del.rel} \\ -\text{nas} \\ +\text{voi} \end{bmatrix} \begin{bmatrix} +\text{voc} \\ -\text{rd} \\ +\text{high} \\ -\text{low} \\ -\text{back} \end{bmatrix}$$

(48) *Woleaian theme vowel finds [+low] on x_1 and [−low] on x_5*

$$x_1 \quad \leftarrow \quad x_2 \quad\quad x_3 \quad\quad x_4 \quad \rightarrow \quad x_5$$

$$\begin{bmatrix} +\text{voc} \\ -\text{rd} \\ -\text{high} \\ \mathbf{+low} \end{bmatrix} \begin{bmatrix} -\text{voc} \\ \text{cor} \\ -\text{cont} \\ -\text{nas} \\ -\text{voi} \end{bmatrix} \begin{bmatrix} +\text{voc} \\ -\text{rd} \\ -\text{high} \end{bmatrix} \begin{bmatrix} -\text{voc} \\ \text{cor} \\ +\text{del.rel} \\ -\text{nas} \\ +\text{voi} \end{bmatrix} \begin{bmatrix} +\text{voc} \\ -\text{rd} \\ +\text{high} \\ \mathbf{-low} \\ -\text{back} \end{bmatrix}$$

(49) *Woleaian theme vowel fails to copy a value*

$$x_1 \quad \leftarrow \quad x_2 \quad\quad x_3 \quad\quad x_4 \quad \rightarrow \quad x_5$$

$$\begin{bmatrix} +\text{voc} \\ -\text{rd} \\ -\text{high} \\ +\text{low} \end{bmatrix} \begin{bmatrix} -\text{voc} \\ \text{cor} \\ -\text{cont} \\ -\text{nas} \\ -\text{voi} \end{bmatrix} \begin{bmatrix} +\text{voc} \\ -\text{rd} \\ -\text{high} \end{bmatrix} \begin{bmatrix} -\text{voc} \\ \text{cor} \\ +\text{del.rel} \\ -\text{nas} \\ +\text{voi} \end{bmatrix} \begin{bmatrix} +\text{voc} \\ -\text{rd} \\ +\text{high} \\ -\text{low} \\ -\text{back} \end{bmatrix}$$

a   t   j   i

No feature can be copied in (49), because there are two different values. This is actually identical to what happens in verbal agreement when a conjoined subject consists of noun phrases with different values for some category. In the Italian sentence with a conjoined subject *Gli uccelli e le farfalle sono andati* 'The birds and the butterflies have gone', the participle cannot simultaneously agree with both masculine plural *uccelli* and feminine plural *farfalle*. From a hierarchical perspective, the two parts of this conjunction are equally close to the participle, as (50) illustrates.

(50) *Mixed-gender conjunct in agreement configuration*

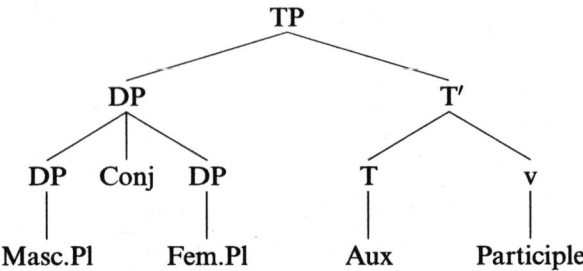

The case of mixed-gender conjunctions and verb agreement in Italian is formally identical to that of Woleaian bidirectional harmony: when two sources of features are equally close but disagree in their feature-value, the otherwise straightforward procedure of copying fails. All cases of search-based dependencies that seek the closest feature-value to copy must include some "Plan B"—what to do when search fails. Search can fail either because it finds no value to copy or because it finds no unique value to copy. We will return to syntactic cases in which there is no nominative argument in chapter 4.

Lest this sound like an esoteric case of feature-purgatory in phonological limbo, consider the fact that verbal agreement, itself modeled as a search-and-copy procedure, may end up with a failed search and no value copied as a result of the process. Yet this failed search does not result, for example, in the option to pronounce the Italian participle as *andat*, with no gender or number encoding whatsoever. There are "default" settings: last-resort feature-values that can be cheaply inserted without ruffling too many feathers. What these values turn out to be for a given feature in a given language depends in large part on what is called *markedness theory*, essentially a grammatical statement of which value for a given phonological or morphological feature (say, + or −) is considered to be the preferred or otherwise assumed one (we will return to this issue in chapter 3).

A Plan B is needed because a speaker of Woleaian cannot pronounce a vowel that is [−high, −round] but has no value for [±low]: at the interface between phonological representations and phonetic implementation, such a representation is illegible and cannot be properly interpreted. All vowel features that are active in a given language must be fully specified on all vowels as an interface requirement. Similarly, a Plan B is needed because a speaker of Italian cannot pronounce a participle with no value for gender: at the interface between abstract syntactic features and morphological realization, such a representation is illegible. The

Plan B in both cases is insertion of the default value in these contexts: [+low] for Woleaian [−high, −round] vowels, and [−feminine] for Italian participles.

(51) *Woleaian thematic formative morpheme must:*
    a. Low-Harmonize: δ = left and right, F = [±low]
    b. Failure results in default insertion of [+low]

While the clause in (51b) has not been previously encountered in our model, it is necessary when harmony fails: the "plain vanilla" value of [±low] in Woleaian, [+low], is what is chosen for the thematic formative.[11] In chapter 3, we will further discuss default value-insertion when harmonic search fails.

We've covered a lot of ground in these examples of vowel harmony. The important lesson from Woleaian for the theory of locality comes when we consider how naturally the recipient-initiated model of search explains what happens in cases of bidirectionally dependent harmony. Any theory of vowel harmony must deal with the fact that the height of the Woleaian thematic formative is determined by leftward and rightward dependencies. When these two search-based dependencies cannot both resolve to the same value, the result is a default value.

2.9 Directionality in Kalenjin "Dominant/Recessive" Harmony

Directionality is often taken as a property of vowel harmony that can be predicted from the morphological structure of the language: in a wide set of patterns, suffixes copy from the left and prefixes copy from the right. However, as we have seen, this is not always the end of the story: vowels within the root also initiate harmonic search under certain conditions, the direction of search not being predictable by general morphological structure; and in Woleaian, the thematic vowel searches bidirectionally. Finally, as will be discussed in section 4.7.2, languages such as Jingulu show root vowels copying from suffixes but not vice versa. The latter kinds of examples establish that directionality of search must be a property of roots, and that affixes may search in both roots and suffixes.

One of the apparent challenges to the notion of directionality as an independent parameter of vowel harmony comes from the existence of patterns described as "dominant/recessive," which are often characterized as entirely nondirectional, in the sense that a single feature value "anywhere within the word" can cause all other vowels to change, regardless of direction or morphological status.

However, upon closer scrutiny, the nature of δ as a free parameter of search specified on individual harmonizing morphemes is perhaps best observed in the interaction of directionality and needy morphemes in the [±ATR] harmony of Kalenjin, a Nilotic language of Kenya claimed to be dominant/recessive. In the discussion below, I present an analysis of Kalenjin's vowel harmony system that demonstrates how dominant/recessive systems can be reanalyzed in terms of directionality specifications, and with positive consequences. The discussion follows the description of Kalenjin by Hall et al. (1974), on which many analyses in terms of a dominant/recessive pattern are based. Kalenjin has a symmetric [±ATR] contrast at three heights.

(52) *Kalenjin vowel inventory*

[−back, −rd]	[+back, −rd]	[+back, +rd]	
i		u	[+high, −low, +ATR]
ɪ		ʊ	[+high, −low, −ATR]
e		o	[−high, −low, +ATR]
ɛ		ɔ	[−high, −low, −ATR]
	ʌ		[−high, +low, +ATR]
	a		[−high, +low, −ATR]

A property of Kalenjin vowel harmony that has attracted special attention is that harmony may affect not only prefixes and suffixes, but also roots. As the following examples show, prefixes and roots copy [±ATR] from their right, while suffixes copy [±ATR] from their left. However, some prefixes, such as /ma-/ in (53d), and some suffixes, such as /kɛː/ in (53e), do not copy.

(53) *Kalenjin [±ATR] harmony affects prefixes, roots, and suffixes (Hall et al. 1974, 247; Lodge 1995, 32)*
    a. ki-   ʌ-   keːr- in
       DIST.PAST- 1SG- see- 2SG.OBJ
       'I saw you'
    b. kɪ-   a-   par- ɪn
       DIST.PAST- 1SG- kill- 2SG.OBJ
       'I killed you'
    c. ki-   ʌ-   ker- e
       DIST.PAST- 1SG- shut- NONCOMPL
       'I was shutting it'
    d. ka-   ma- ʌ-   keːr- ʌk
       REC.PAST- NEG- 1SG- see- 2PL
       'I didn't see you (PL)'

e. ki- ɐ- un- kɛː
   DIST.PAST- 1SG- wash- REFL
   'I was washing myself'
f. keːr- un
   see- DIR
   'see it from here'
g. kʊt- ʊn
   blow- DIR
   'blow it here'

As mentioned above, a dominant/recessive system is commonly ascribed to Kalenjin, which in intuitive terms means that the value [+ATR] "anywhere in the word" should cause all morphemes in the word to become [+ATR]. Dominant/recessive systems are claimed to be nondirectional, featurally asymmetric, and nonlocal, as summarized in the statement "The presence of a dominant vowel in a word changes the vowels of the nondominant series" (Aoki 1968, 143). Authors such as Baković (2000) explicitly adopt a dominant/recessive analysis for Kalenjin, whereby [+ATR] values are seen as asymmetrically controlling vowel harmony regardless of directionality.

However, as many cases in (53) reveal, exceptionally nonundergoing morphemes are not hard to come by (e.g., the negative, the reflexive); in fact, these seem to be as much the rule as the exception. Moreover, prefixes may copy either [+ATR] or [−ATR], depending on what is immediately to their right, regardless of whether a [+ATR] morpheme is found in the root. Summing up, no prefixes cause roots to harmonize, and when prefixes search for a value to copy, they do so on the basis of locality, instead of "dominance."

In fact, once the nonharmonizing morphemes, such as the negative prefix /ma-/, are taken into account in the locality and directionality of vowel harmony, the pattern of Kalenjin harmony reduces to the same directionally specified Search-and-Copy algorithm developed throughout this chapter. As Lodge (1995) points out, the most straightforward characterization of Kalenjin harmony is not as a dominant/recessive system, but as a system with a three-way contrast: morphemes that are inherently [+ATR], morphemes that are inherently [−ATR], and morphemes that need to find a value for [±ATR] through directionally specified harmony. The specifications for the morphemes in (53a–g) are thus as follows:

(54) *Harmonic specifications of Kalenjin morphemes*
   a. *Kalenjin distant past morpheme must:*
      ATR-Harmonize: δ = right, F = [±ATR]
   b. *Kalenjin recent past morpheme must:*
      ATR-Harmonize: δ = right, F = [±ATR]
   c. *Kalenjin subject agreement morpheme must:*
      ATR-Harmonize: δ = right, F = [±ATR]
   d. *Kalenjin object agreement morpheme must:*
      ATR-Harmonize: δ = left, F = [±ATR]
   e. *Kalenjin directional morpheme must:*
      ATR-Harmonize: δ = left, F = [±ATR]
   f. *Kalenjin negative morpheme must:*
      (none; inherently [−ATR])
   g. *Kalenjin noncompletive morpheme must:*
      (none; inherently [+ATR])
   h. *Kalenjin reflexive morpheme must:*
      (none; inherently [−ATR])
   i. *Kalenjin roots* BLOW, SHUT, KILL *must:*
      ATR-Harmonize: δ = right, F = [±ATR]
   j. *Kalenjin roots* SEE, WASH *must:*
      (none; inherently [+ATR])

In other words, Kalenjin is *not* a "fully bidirectional" system. Roots are specified to copy from the right, and suffixes are specified to copy from the left. Roots do not copy from prefixes, and prefixes never copy from their left (e.g., [-ɐ-] in [ka-ma-ɐ-keːr-ɐk]). If no value is found (e.g., in a sequence of a set of entirely unspecified morphemes, as in [kʊt-ʊn] 'blow-DIR'), then a default value will be supplied as a last resort.

Harmonization in Kalenjin will be illustrated with three types of root suffix combinations, the result of which will be combined with prefixes afterward in the derivations; this later order of prefix harmony is adopted only for the sake of expository ease. We will consider the following configurations: a needy root and a specified suffix, a specified root and a needy suffix, and a needy root and a needy suffix.

The first case is that of a needy root concatenated with a specified suffix. The derivation for [ki-ɐ-ker-e] 'DIST.PAST-1SG-shut-NONCOMPL' is shown in (55)–(58), with the root copying from the suffix, followed by the prefixes copying from the root.

The Search Principle

(55) *Kalenjin root begins ATR-Harmonize in [ker-e]*

$$x_4 \quad x_5 \quad \rightarrow \quad x_6 \quad x_7$$

$$\begin{bmatrix} -\text{voc} \\ \text{dors} \\ -\text{cont} \\ -\text{voi} \end{bmatrix} \begin{bmatrix} +\text{voc} \\ -\text{high} \\ -\text{low} \\ -\text{rd} \\ +\text{back} \end{bmatrix} \begin{bmatrix} -\text{voc} \\ \text{cor} \\ +\text{son} \\ -\text{nas} \\ -\text{lat} \end{bmatrix} \begin{bmatrix} +\text{voc} \\ -\text{high} \\ -\text{low} \\ -\text{rd} \\ +\text{back} \\ +\text{ATR} \end{bmatrix}$$

(56) *Kalenjin root finds and copies [+ATR] in [ker-e]*

$$x_4 \quad x_5 \quad x_6 \quad \curvearrowleft \quad x_7$$

$$\begin{bmatrix} -\text{voc} \\ \text{dors} \\ -\text{cont} \\ -\text{voi} \end{bmatrix} \begin{bmatrix} +\text{voc} \\ -\text{high} \\ -\text{low} \\ -\text{rd} \\ +\text{back} \\ +\text{ATR} \end{bmatrix} \begin{bmatrix} -\text{voc} \\ \text{cor} \\ +\text{son} \\ -\text{nas} \\ -\text{lat} \end{bmatrix} \begin{bmatrix} +\text{voc} \\ -\text{high} \\ -\text{low} \\ -\text{rd} \\ +\text{back} \\ +\text{ATR} \end{bmatrix}$$

(57) *Kalenjin prefix begins ATR-Harmonize in [ʊ-ker-e]*

$$x_3 \quad \rightarrow \quad x_4 \quad x_5 \quad x_6 \quad x_7$$

$$\begin{bmatrix} +\text{voc} \\ -\text{high} \\ +\text{low} \\ -\text{rd} \\ +\text{back} \end{bmatrix} \begin{bmatrix} -\text{voc} \\ \text{dors} \\ -\text{cont} \\ -\text{voi} \end{bmatrix} \begin{bmatrix} +\text{voc} \\ -\text{high} \\ -\text{low} \\ -\text{rd} \\ +\text{back} \\ +\text{ATR} \end{bmatrix} \begin{bmatrix} -\text{voc} \\ \text{cor} \\ +\text{son} \\ -\text{nas} \\ -\text{lat} \end{bmatrix} \begin{bmatrix} +\text{voc} \\ -\text{high} \\ -\text{low} \\ -\text{rd} \\ +\text{back} \\ +\text{ATR} \end{bmatrix}$$

(58) *Kalenjin prefix finds and copies [+ATR] in [ʊ-ker-e]*

$$x_3 \quad x_4 \quad \curvearrowleft \quad x_5 \quad x_6 \quad x_7$$

$$\begin{bmatrix} +\text{voc} \\ -\text{high} \\ +\text{low} \\ -\text{rd} \\ +\text{back} \\ +\text{ATR} \end{bmatrix} \begin{bmatrix} -\text{voc} \\ \text{dors} \\ -\text{cont} \\ -\text{voi} \end{bmatrix} \begin{bmatrix} +\text{voc} \\ -\text{high} \\ -\text{low} \\ -\text{rd} \\ +\text{back} \\ +\text{ATR} \end{bmatrix} \begin{bmatrix} -\text{voc} \\ \text{cor} \\ +\text{son} \\ -\text{nas} \\ -\text{lat} \end{bmatrix} \begin{bmatrix} +\text{voc} \\ -\text{high} \\ -\text{low} \\ -\text{rd} \\ +\text{back} \\ +\text{ATR} \end{bmatrix}$$

$$\text{ʊ} \quad \text{k} \quad \text{e} \quad \text{r} \quad \text{e}$$

The second case is that of a specified root concatenated with a needy suffix, exemplified with [ka-ma-ʊ-keːr-ʊk] 'REC.PAST-NEG-1SG-see-2PL'. The suffix will copy from its left, as in [ʊ-keːr-ʊk]. Prefixes will copy from their right.

(59) *Kalenjin suffix begins ATR-Harmonize in [ka-ma-ʋ-keːr-ʋk]*

x_6 $\quad x_7 \quad\quad x_8 \quad\quad \leftarrow \quad x_9 \quad\quad x_{10}$

$$\begin{bmatrix} -\text{voc} \\ \text{dors} \\ -\text{cont} \\ -\text{voi} \end{bmatrix} \begin{bmatrix} +\text{voc} \\ -\text{high} \\ -\text{low} \\ -\text{rd} \\ +\text{back} \\ +\text{ATR} \end{bmatrix} \begin{bmatrix} -\text{voc} \\ \text{cor} \\ +\text{son} \\ -\text{nas} \\ -\text{lat} \end{bmatrix} \begin{bmatrix} +\text{voc} \\ -\text{high} \\ +\text{low} \\ -\text{rd} \\ +\text{back} \end{bmatrix} \begin{bmatrix} -\text{voc} \\ \text{dors} \\ -\text{cont} \\ -\text{voi} \end{bmatrix}$$

(60) *Kalenjin suffix finds and copies [+ATR] in [keːr-ʋk]*

$x_6 \quad\quad x_7 \quad\quad \bar{\text{↶}} \quad x_8 \quad\quad x_9 \quad\quad x_{10}$

$$\begin{bmatrix} -\text{voc} \\ \text{dors} \\ -\text{cont} \\ -\text{voi} \end{bmatrix} \begin{bmatrix} +\text{voc} \\ -\text{high} \\ -\text{low} \\ -\text{rd} \\ +\text{back} \\ +\text{ATR} \end{bmatrix} \begin{bmatrix} -\text{voc} \\ \text{cor} \\ +\text{son} \\ -\text{nas} \\ -\text{lat} \end{bmatrix} \begin{bmatrix} +\text{voc} \\ -\text{high} \\ +\text{low} \\ -\text{rd} \\ +\text{back} \\ +\text{ATR} \end{bmatrix} \begin{bmatrix} -\text{voc} \\ \text{dors} \\ -\text{cont} \\ -\text{voi} \end{bmatrix}$$

k $\quad$ e $\quad$ r $\quad$ ʋ $\quad$ k

(61) *Kalenjin prefix searches for [±ATR] in [ʋ-keːr-ʋk]*

$x_5 \quad \rightarrow \quad x_6 \quad\quad x_7 \quad\quad x_8$

$$\begin{bmatrix} +\text{voc} \\ -\text{high} \\ +\text{low} \\ -\text{rd} \\ +\text{back} \end{bmatrix} \begin{bmatrix} -\text{voc} \\ \text{dors} \\ -\text{cont} \\ -\text{voi} \end{bmatrix} \begin{bmatrix} +\text{voc} \\ -\text{high} \\ -\text{low} \\ -\text{rd} \\ +\text{back} \\ +\text{ATR} \end{bmatrix} \begin{bmatrix} -\text{voc} \\ \text{cor} \\ +\text{son} \\ -\text{nas} \\ -\text{lat} \end{bmatrix}$$

(62) *Kalenjin prefix finds and copies [+ATR] in [ʋ-keːr-ʋk]*

$x_5 \quad\quad x_6 \quad \text{↶} \quad x_7 \quad\quad x_8$

$$\begin{bmatrix} +\text{voc} \\ -\text{high} \\ +\text{low} \\ -\text{rd} \\ +\text{back} \\ +\text{ATR} \end{bmatrix} \begin{bmatrix} -\text{voc} \\ \text{dors} \\ -\text{cont} \\ -\text{voi} \end{bmatrix} \begin{bmatrix} +\text{voc} \\ -\text{high} \\ -\text{low} \\ -\text{rd} \\ +\text{back} \\ +\text{ATR} \end{bmatrix} \begin{bmatrix} -\text{voc} \\ \text{cor} \\ +\text{son} \\ -\text{nas} \\ -\text{lat} \end{bmatrix}$$

ʋ $\quad$ k $\quad$ eː $\quad$ r

In a sequence of two or more prefixes, each one copies from its right. If a needy prefix precedes a [−ATR] specified prefix, it will copy from it, even if a [+ATR] affix is further downstream, showing that the "dominant/recessive" system is constrained by closest-source locality, just like any other.

The Search Principle

(63) *Kalenjin prefix searches for [±ATR] in [ka-ma-ɛ-]*

$$x_1 \quad x_2 \quad \rightarrow \quad x_3 \quad x_4 \quad x_5$$

$$\begin{bmatrix} -\text{voc} \\ \text{dors} \\ -\text{cont} \\ -\text{voi} \end{bmatrix} \begin{bmatrix} +\text{voc} \\ -\text{high} \\ +\text{low} \\ -\text{rd} \\ +\text{back} \end{bmatrix} \begin{bmatrix} -\text{voc} \\ \text{lab} \\ +\text{son} \\ +\text{nas} \end{bmatrix} \begin{bmatrix} +\text{voc} \\ -\text{high} \\ +\text{low} \\ -\text{rd} \\ +\text{back} \\ -\text{ATR} \end{bmatrix} \begin{bmatrix} +\text{voc} \\ -\text{high} \\ -\text{low} \\ -\text{rd} \\ +\text{back} \\ +\text{ATR} \end{bmatrix}$$

(64) *Kalenjin prefix finds and copies [−ATR] in [ka-ma-ɛ-]*

$$x_1 \quad x_2 \quad x_3 \quad \uparrow \quad x_4 \quad x_5$$

$$\begin{bmatrix} -\text{voc} \\ \text{dors} \\ -\text{cont} \\ -\text{voi} \end{bmatrix} \begin{bmatrix} +\text{voc} \\ -\text{high} \\ +\text{low} \\ -\text{rd} \\ +\text{back} \\ -\text{ATR} \end{bmatrix} \begin{bmatrix} -\text{voc} \\ \text{lab} \\ +\text{son} \\ +\text{nas} \end{bmatrix} \begin{bmatrix} +\text{voc} \\ -\text{high} \\ +\text{low} \\ -\text{rd} \\ +\text{back} \\ -\text{ATR} \end{bmatrix} \begin{bmatrix} +\text{voc} \\ -\text{high} \\ -\text{low} \\ -\text{rd} \\ +\text{back} \\ +\text{ATR} \end{bmatrix}$$

$$\text{k} \quad\quad \text{a} \quad\quad \text{m} \quad\quad \text{a} \quad\quad \text{ɛ}$$

Finally, consider the case of a needy root concatenated with a needy suffix, as in [kɪ-ɛ-par-ɪn] 'DIST.PAST-1SG-kill-2SG.OBJ', which begins with the root+suffix. After the suffix fails to find any specified value, default insertion will supply the value [−ATR] for the suffix.

(65) *Kalenjin suffix begins ATR-Harmonize in [par-ɪn]*

$$x_4 \quad x_5 \quad x_6 \quad \leftarrow \quad x_7 \quad x_8$$

$$\begin{bmatrix} -\text{voc} \\ \text{lab} \\ -\text{cont} \\ -\text{voi} \end{bmatrix} \begin{bmatrix} +\text{voc} \\ -\text{high} \\ +\text{low} \\ -\text{rd} \\ +\text{back} \end{bmatrix} \begin{bmatrix} -\text{voc} \\ \text{cor} \\ +\text{son} \\ -\text{nas} \\ -\text{lat} \end{bmatrix} \begin{bmatrix} +\text{voc} \\ +\text{high} \\ -\text{low} \\ -\text{rd} \\ +\text{back} \end{bmatrix} \begin{bmatrix} -\text{voc} \\ \text{cor} \\ +\text{son} \\ +\text{nas} \end{bmatrix}$$

(66) *Kalenjin suffix continues search for [±ATR] in [par-ɪn]*

$$x_4 \quad x_5 \quad \leftarrow \quad x_6 \quad x_7 \quad x_8$$

$$\begin{bmatrix} -\text{voc} \\ \text{lab} \\ -\text{cont} \\ -\text{voi} \end{bmatrix} \begin{bmatrix} +\text{voc} \\ -\text{high} \\ +\text{low} \\ -\text{rd} \\ +\text{back} \end{bmatrix} \begin{bmatrix} -\text{voc} \\ \text{cor} \\ +\text{son} \\ -\text{nas} \\ -\text{lat} \end{bmatrix} \begin{bmatrix} +\text{voc} \\ +\text{high} \\ -\text{low} \\ -\text{rd} \\ +\text{back} \end{bmatrix} \begin{bmatrix} -\text{voc} \\ \text{cor} \\ +\text{son} \\ +\text{nas} \end{bmatrix}$$

(67) *Kalenjin suffix continues search for [±ATR] in [par-ɪn]*

$$x_4 \leftarrow x_5 \quad x_6 \quad x_7 \quad x_8$$

$$\begin{bmatrix} -\text{voc} \\ \text{lab} \\ -\text{cont} \\ -\text{voi} \end{bmatrix} \begin{bmatrix} +\text{voc} \\ -\text{high} \\ +\text{low} \\ -\text{rd} \\ +\text{back} \end{bmatrix} \begin{bmatrix} -\text{voc} \\ \text{cor} \\ +\text{son} \\ -\text{nas} \\ -\text{lat} \end{bmatrix} \begin{bmatrix} +\text{voc} \\ +\text{high} \\ -\text{low} \\ -\text{rd} \\ +\text{back} \end{bmatrix} \begin{bmatrix} -\text{voc} \\ \text{cor} \\ +\text{son} \\ +\text{nas} \end{bmatrix}$$

(68) *Kalenjin suffix fails (↔) to ATR-Harmonize in [par-ɪn]*

$$\leftarrow\!\!\!\!\!\!\!\!\!\!\!\!\!| \quad x_4 \quad x_5 \quad x_6 \quad x_7 \quad x_8$$

$$\begin{bmatrix} -\text{voc} \\ \text{lab} \\ -\text{cont} \\ -\text{voi} \end{bmatrix} \begin{bmatrix} +\text{voc} \\ -\text{high} \\ +\text{low} \\ -\text{rd} \\ +\text{back} \end{bmatrix} \begin{bmatrix} -\text{voc} \\ \text{cor} \\ +\text{son} \\ -\text{nas} \\ -\text{lat} \end{bmatrix} \begin{bmatrix} +\text{voc} \\ +\text{high} \\ -\text{low} \\ -\text{rd} \\ +\text{back} \end{bmatrix} \begin{bmatrix} -\text{voc} \\ \text{cor} \\ +\text{son} \\ +\text{nas} \end{bmatrix}$$

(69) *Kalenjin suffix undergoes default [−ATR] insertion in [par-ɪn]*

$$x_4 \quad x_5 \quad x_6 \quad x_7 \quad x_8$$

$$\begin{bmatrix} -\text{voc} \\ \text{lab} \\ -\text{cont} \\ -\text{voi} \end{bmatrix} \begin{bmatrix} +\text{voc} \\ -\text{high} \\ +\text{low} \\ -\text{rd} \\ +\text{back} \end{bmatrix} \begin{bmatrix} -\text{voc} \\ \text{cor} \\ +\text{son} \\ -\text{nas} \\ -\text{lat} \end{bmatrix} \begin{bmatrix} +\text{voc} \\ +\text{high} \\ -\text{low} \\ -\text{rd} \\ +\text{back} \\ -\text{ATR} \end{bmatrix} \begin{bmatrix} -\text{voc} \\ \text{cor} \\ +\text{son} \\ +\text{nas} \end{bmatrix}$$

(70) *Kalenjin root begins rightward [±ATR] search in [par-ɪn]*

$$x_4 \quad x_5 \rightarrow x_6 \quad x_7 \quad x_8$$

$$\begin{bmatrix} -\text{voc} \\ \text{lab} \\ -\text{cont} \\ -\text{voi} \end{bmatrix} \begin{bmatrix} +\text{voc} \\ -\text{high} \\ +\text{low} \\ -\text{rd} \\ +\text{back} \end{bmatrix} \begin{bmatrix} -\text{voc} \\ \text{cor} \\ +\text{son} \\ -\text{nas} \\ -\text{lat} \end{bmatrix} \begin{bmatrix} +\text{voc} \\ +\text{high} \\ -\text{low} \\ -\text{rd} \\ +\text{back} \\ -\text{ATR} \end{bmatrix} \begin{bmatrix} -\text{voc} \\ \text{cor} \\ +\text{son} \\ +\text{nas} \end{bmatrix}$$

The Search Principle   53

(71) *Kalenjin root finds and copies [−ATR] in [par-ın]*

$$
\begin{array}{ccccc}
x_4 & x_5 & x_6 & x_7 & x_8 \\
\begin{bmatrix} -\text{voc} \\ \text{lab} \\ -\text{cont} \\ -\text{voi} \end{bmatrix} & \begin{bmatrix} +\text{voc} \\ -\text{high} \\ +\text{low} \\ -\text{rd} \\ +\text{back} \\ -\text{ATR} \end{bmatrix} & \begin{bmatrix} -\text{voc} \\ \text{cor} \\ +\text{son} \\ -\text{nas} \\ -\text{lat} \end{bmatrix} \overset{\curvearrowleft}{} & \begin{bmatrix} +\text{voc} \\ +\text{high} \\ -\text{low} \\ -\text{rd} \\ +\text{back} \\ -\text{ATR} \end{bmatrix} & \begin{bmatrix} -\text{voc} \\ \text{cor} \\ +\text{son} \\ +\text{nas} \end{bmatrix} \\
p & a & r & ı & n
\end{array}
$$

To summarize, the patterns of Kalenjin [±ATR] harmony based on Hall et al.'s (1974) description show that the language's computation of vowel harmony is determined by directionality and locality, instead of "dominance" as a factor trumping all else. Prefixes copy from the closest local source to their right, regardless of its value, and the interaction of suffixes and roots is determined by which is needy, as shown in the three derivations above.

Kalenjin's system of [±ATR] harmony requires no special devices beyond the theory of locality already developed. It differs from the Akan pattern, in which prefixes copy from roots and suffixes copy from roots, only in the fact that some roots may also copy from suffixes.

Before concluding, I will mention that one of the challenges in conducting research on putative dominant/recessive systems is the great range of morphological combinations that are needed to confirm all of the potential directionality effects. In particular, for Kalenjin, arbitrating between certain analytic possibilities depends on what cases of multiple suffixes are possible, and what value will be computed for a needy suffix flanked by a [+ATR] root to its left and a [−ATR] suffix to its right. Nonfinal suffixes of this sort may have δ set either rightward or bidirectionally.[12]

We have seen that an application of harmony, whereby needy suffixes harmonize first, followed by needy roots, followed by needy prefixes, accounts for all of the patterns noted by Hall et al. (1974) without any need to appeal to nonlocal "dominant/recessive" principles. Kalenjin has a variety of needy and nonneedy morphemes, and the needy morphemes specify their directionality of search.

2.10 Split-Source Harmony: When a Consonant and a Vowel Are Each Copied From in Turkish

Thus far, we have devised a relatively simple model, one in which harmony takes place with a given direction of search, starting with the recipient segment "in need." As soon as the closest value of the harmonic feature is found, it is copied to the recipient. Yet if search really is driven in terms of an efficient computation to find the closest source of a harmonic feature, we might expect that in certain configurations, some rather unexpected players could furnish the value for harmony, provided they are closest to the recipient.

One important case, which provides striking confirmation for the recipient-centric model of search, occurs in Turkish vowel harmony. Besides the patterns we looked at earlier, Turkish has an extra twist: three pairs of *consonants*—/k,kʲ/, /g,gʲ/, /l,lʲ/—may participate in vowel harmony.

In the Turkish consonant inventory, /k,g,l/ have [−back] counterparts (Clements and Sezer 1982, 233); thus, in /k∼kʲ/, /g∼gʲ/, /l∼lʲ/, the feature [±back] is contrastive (and cannot be predicted allophonically).

(72) *Contrastive [±back] in Turkish consonants*
    a. bol   'abundant'   bolʲ   'cocktail'
    b. kalp   'counterfeit'   kalʲp   'heart'
    c. kar   'snow'   kʲar   'profit'
    d. gaz   'gas'   gʲavur   'infidel'

What is interesting is that these consonants, which show a contrastive and unpredictable [±back] specification, "participate" in vowel harmony. /k,g,l/ are contrastively [+back], and hence vowels added after them will find these consonants as the closest source and copy [+back]. Even in a word whose last vowel is [+back], if the last *segment* is contrastively [−back], then the suffixal alternant will be [−back].

(73) *Effect of [−back] liquid on harmony of following vowels in Turkish*
    a. usulʲ   usulʲ-ü   'system / system-ACC.SG'
    b. petrolʲ   petrolʲ-ü   'petrol / petrol-ACC.SG'
    c. sualʲ   sualʲ-i   'question / question-ACC.SG'
    d. okul   okul-u   'school / school-ACC.SG'
    e. karakol   karakol-u   'police station / police.station-ACC.SG'
    f. tʃatal   tʃatal-ɨ   'fork / fork-ACC.SG'
    g. petrolʲ   petrolʲ-de   'petrol / petrol-LOC.SG'
    h. meʃgulʲ   meʃgulʲ-düm   'busy / busy-PAST.1SG'

Importantly, (73g–h) show that the vowel undergoing valuation and the palatalized liquid need not be strictly adjacent for [−back] valuation to "unexpectedly" occur.

Conversely, in a word whose last vowel is [−back], where we would expect the suffix vowel to be [−back], if an intervening consonant is contrastively [+back], this consonant will determine the harmonic alternant instead (Clements and Sezer 1982; Levi 2004). We can see this with the [+back] velar, which yields [+back] suffix vowels in an otherwise [−back] harmonic sequence.

(74) *Participation of Turkish [k] in [+back] harmony*
    a. ʃevk   ʃevk-ɨ   'desire / desire-ACC'
    b. haːlʲik haːlʲik-i 'creator / creator-ACC'

These examples clearly show that a consonant may "intercept" [±back] harmony. What is most interesting from the point of view of theoretical models of phonological locality is what happens when both [±back] and [±round] harmony are operative in high-voweled suffixes and find their values from different sources. In a form such as [meʃgulʲ-düm] in (73), the [ü] of the suffix receives its [+round] value from the preceding root vowel /u/, while it receives its [−back] value from the preceding root consonant /lʲ/.

The intuition to be captured in these Turkish cases is that there are *two sources* of valuation for the needy affix in [meʃgulʲ-düm]. In most cases of vowel harmony, both features, [±back] and [±round], are found in the same source, namely, the preceding vowel. However, given that search is opportunistically "greedy," if one feature can be valued immediately, it will be.

(75) *Turkish accusative case morpheme must:*
    Back-Harmonize: δ = left, F = [±back]
    Round-Harmonize: δ = left, F = [±round]

Not just vowels but any segment that bears [±back] can be a potential donor. In fact, parametric variation in what can be a possible donor will occupy most of the next chapter. For now, we will continue to focus on the Search procedure and the fact that once the set of segments bearing the needed feature is delimited, the Search procedure will literally terminate with the closest copy-source.

From the perspective of the needy suffix vowel in [meʃgulʲ-düm], the /lʲ/ is a closer potential source for [±back] valuation than the preceding /u/. Hence, in the leftward search for a value-source, once /lʲ/ is encountered, [−back] is copied to the suffix and the search for [±back] ends. As /lʲ/ does not provide a value for [±round], the search for [±round] continues, until /u/ is encountered. This is schematized in (76)–(80):

(76) *Turkish accusative suffix searches leftward for [±back] and [±round] in [meʃgulʲ-düm]*

$$x_1 \quad\quad x_2 \quad\quad x_3 \;\leftarrow\; x_4$$

$$\begin{bmatrix} +\text{voc} \\ +\text{high} \\ +\text{back} \\ +\text{rd} \end{bmatrix} \begin{bmatrix} -\text{voc} \\ +\text{son} \\ -\text{nas} \\ +\text{lat} \\ -\text{back} \end{bmatrix} \begin{bmatrix} -\text{voc} \\ \text{cor} \\ -\text{cont} \\ -\text{nas} \\ +\text{voi} \end{bmatrix} \begin{bmatrix} +\text{voc} \\ +\text{high} \end{bmatrix}$$

(77) *Turkish accusative suffix finds [−back]*

$$x_1 \quad\quad x_2 \;\leftarrow\; x_3 \quad\quad x_4$$

$$\begin{bmatrix} +\text{voc} \\ +\text{high} \\ +\text{back} \\ +\text{rd} \end{bmatrix} \begin{bmatrix} -\text{voc} \\ +\text{son} \\ -\text{nas} \\ +\text{lat} \\ \mathbf{-back} \end{bmatrix} \begin{bmatrix} -\text{voc} \\ \text{cor} \\ -\text{cont} \\ -\text{nas} \\ +\text{voi} \end{bmatrix} \begin{bmatrix} +\text{voc} \\ +\text{high} \end{bmatrix}$$

(78) *Turkish accusative suffix copies [−back]*

$$x_1 \quad\quad x_2 \quad\quad x_3 \quad\quad x_4$$

$$\begin{bmatrix} +\text{voc} \\ +\text{high} \\ +\text{back} \\ +\text{rd} \end{bmatrix} \begin{bmatrix} -\text{voc} \\ +\text{son} \\ -\text{nas} \\ +\text{lat} \\ \mathbf{-back} \end{bmatrix} \begin{bmatrix} -\text{voc} \\ \text{cor} \\ -\text{cont} \\ -\text{nas} \\ +\text{voi} \end{bmatrix} \begin{bmatrix} +\text{voc} \\ +\text{high} \\ \mathbf{-back} \end{bmatrix}$$

(79) *Turkish accusative suffix finds [+round]*

$$x_1 \;\leftarrow\; x_2 \quad\quad x_3 \quad\quad x_4$$

$$\begin{bmatrix} +\text{voc} \\ +\text{high} \\ +\text{back} \\ \mathbf{+rd} \end{bmatrix} \begin{bmatrix} -\text{voc} \\ +\text{son} \\ -\text{nas} \\ +\text{lat} \\ -\text{back} \end{bmatrix} \begin{bmatrix} -\text{voc} \\ \text{cor} \\ -\text{cont} \\ -\text{nas} \\ +\text{voi} \end{bmatrix} \begin{bmatrix} +\text{voc} \\ +\text{high} \\ -\text{back} \end{bmatrix}$$

(80) *Turkish accusative suffix copies [+round]*

$$x_1 \quad\quad x_2 \quad\quad x_3 \quad\quad x_4$$

$$\begin{bmatrix} +\text{voc} \\ +\text{high} \\ +\text{back} \\ \mathbf{+rd} \end{bmatrix} \begin{bmatrix} -\text{voc} \\ +\text{son} \\ -\text{nas} \\ +\text{lat} \\ -\text{back} \end{bmatrix} \begin{bmatrix} -\text{voc} \\ \text{cor} \\ -\text{cont} \\ -\text{nas} \\ +\text{voi} \end{bmatrix} \begin{bmatrix} +\text{voc} \\ +\text{high} \\ -\text{back} \\ \mathbf{+rd} \end{bmatrix}$$

$$\text{u} \quad\quad \text{l}^{\text{j}} \quad\quad \text{d} \quad\quad \text{ü}$$

When inflectional suffixes are added in Turkish, they take their specification for [±back] from the *closest* source of valuation, which is, in these cases, a consonant. Again, we see confirmation that the search procedure is greedy: even though both [±back] and [±round] could be copied together from the further-away root vowel, [±back] is copied as soon as it is encountered, it is removed from the list of needed values, and the search inexorably proceeds until all remaining values (in this case, [±round]) are furnished.

2.11 Lack of Lookahead in Barra Gaelic Epenthesis Harmony

We have just considered the participation of contrastive [±back] consonants in vowel harmony to illustrate multiple-source valuation. In some configurations in which multiple sources value multiple features, the set of outcomes is even more restricted than we might expect. Moreover, it provides justification for a stepwise derivational account of the feature-valuing steps as the search proceeds leftward.

Barra Gaelic (Borgstrom 1937; Sagey 1987) displays a scenario quite similar to that of Turkish: palatalized consonants "intercept" featural valuation that is otherwise determined by a vocalic source.

In Barra Gaelic, an epenthetic vowel is inserted to break up consonant clusters composed of sonorant+consonant. This epenthetic vowel is often a full copy of *all* vocalic features of the preceding vowel.

(81) *Barra Gaelic vowel harmony with full copying of the preceding vowel*
UR   SR
a. tʲimxʲal   tʲimixʲal   'round about'
b. æmsʲirʲ   æmæsʲirʲ   'time'

Whenever a consonant specified as [±back] intervenes, what is actually copied from the vowel must be characterized as a "deficient" constituent: all features *except* [±back]. A distinguishing feature of the consonantal inventory in Barra Gaelic is that *all* consonants in the inventory are contrastive for [±back] except labials (/m,p,b/) and /n/. The vowel system of Barra Gaelic is as follows:

(82) *Barra Gaelic vowel system*

[−back, −rd]	[+back, −rd]	[+back, +rd]	
i	ɨ	u	[+high, −low]
e	ʌ	o	[−high, −low]
æ	a	ɔ	[−high, +low]

While Barra Gaelic exhibits contrastive [±back] extensively among the consonants, it lacks front round vowels such as /ü/. Nonetheless, [±round] is contrastive for /u/, as it distinguishes /u/ from /i/; hence, [±round] will be copied to an epenthetic vowel from /u/, as we will presently observe.

Barra Gaelic exhibits the phenomenon of leftward *multiple-source valuation* for epenthetic vowels that arise in order to break up sonorant+consonant clusters.

(83) *Barra Gaelic vowel harmony*

	UR	SR	
a.	alpə	alapə	'Scotland'
b.	sʲærv	sʲærav	'bitter'
c.	urpel	urupel	'tail'
d.	ɔrm	ɔrɔm	'on me'
e.	færk	færak	'anger'
f.	mʌrʲv	mʌrʲev	'the dead'
g.	bulʲkʲ	bulʲikʲ	'bellows.GEN.SG'
h.	merʲkʲ	merʲekʲ	'rust'

In (83a–d), the intervening consonant has the same [±back] value as the preceding vowel. Hence, the epenthetic vowel is surface-identical to the preceding vowel, even though, on the account developed here, its [±back] value is furnished by the consonant. This divergence in value-sources is most apparent in (38e–h), where the epenthetic vowel and the preceding vowel are identical for all features *except* back. The intervening consonant bears a different value for [±back] than the preceding vowel, and since the consonant is a *closer* value-source, it is encountered immediately in the leftward search.[13]

The steps involved are the same as those outlined above for Turkish [meʃgulʲ-düm], except that there are more features to be valued. In Barra Gaelic, a vowel must bear specifications for [±high], [±low], [±back], and [±round] in order to be lexically distinct. On the view that the epenthesis process furnishes only a timing slot with the feature [+vocalic], the potential vowel must conduct a dynamic search in order to find values for its four vocalic features.

(84) *Barra Gaelic epenthetic vowel must:*
Back-Harmonize: δ = left, F = [±back]
Round-Harmonize: δ = left, F = [±round]
High-Harmonize: δ = left, F = [±high]
Low-Harmonize: δ = left, F = [±low]

The Search Principle

A representative case, [bulʲikʲ], reveals an important aspect of the computation: that the closest source is immediately copied from, *without lookahead*. Recall that the inventory lacks front round vowels, such as /ü/. Similarly to the vowel in the Turkish example discussed above, the Barra Gaelic epenthetic vowel copies [±back] from a preceding consonant and the rest of its feature-values from a preceding vowel. Consider [bulʲikʲ]: if full vowel copy *did* take place, we would expect an [u] in the second syllable. However, what we find is [i]. Let us see how the directional search proceeds.

Barra Gaelic vowels require full specification for [±high], [±low], [±back], and [±round]. As mentioned, the feature combination [−back, +round] is banned from the inventory; we may understand this in terms of either an inviolable constraint or an implicational statement, [−back] → [−round]. For concreteness of illustration, I adopt the latter (though this implementation is a secondary-level assumption). Now consider the steps involved in valuing the epenthetic vowel in [bulʲikʲ].

(85) *Barra Gaelic epenthetic vowel's search begins*

$$\begin{matrix} x_1 & x_2 & x_3 \end{matrix}$$
$$\begin{bmatrix} +\text{voc} \\ +\text{back} \\ +\text{rd} \\ +\text{high} \\ -\text{low} \end{bmatrix} \begin{bmatrix} -\text{voc} \\ +\text{son} \\ -\text{nas} \\ +\text{lat} \\ -\text{back} \end{bmatrix} \begin{bmatrix} +\text{voc} \\ \\ \\ \\ \end{bmatrix}$$

(86) *Barra Gaelic epenthetic vowel finds and copies [−back]*

$$\begin{matrix} x_1 & x_2 & \qquad x_3 \end{matrix}$$
$$\begin{bmatrix} +\text{voc} \\ +\text{back} \\ +\text{rd} \\ +\text{high} \\ -\text{low} \end{bmatrix} \begin{bmatrix} -\text{voc} \\ +\text{son} \\ -\text{nas} \\ +\text{lat} \\ \mathbf{-back} \end{bmatrix} \begin{bmatrix} +\text{voc} \\ \mathbf{-back} \\ \\ \\ \end{bmatrix}$$

(87) *Barra Gaelic default insertion of [−round] when [+vocalic, −back]*

$$\begin{matrix} x_1 & x_2 & \leftarrow & x_3 \end{matrix}$$
$$\begin{bmatrix} +\text{voc} \\ +\text{back} \\ +\text{rd} \\ +\text{high} \\ -\text{low} \end{bmatrix} \begin{bmatrix} -\text{voc} \\ +\text{son} \\ -\text{nas} \\ +\text{lat} \\ -\text{back} \end{bmatrix} \begin{bmatrix} +\text{voc} \\ -\text{back} \\ -\text{rd} \\ \\ \end{bmatrix}$$

(88) *Barra Gaelic epenthetic vowel's search for other features continues*

$$x_1 \leftarrow x_2 \quad x_3$$

$$\begin{bmatrix} +\text{voc} \\ +\text{back} \\ +\text{rd} \\ +\text{high} \\ -\text{low} \end{bmatrix} \begin{bmatrix} -\text{voc} \\ +\text{son} \\ -\text{nas} \\ +\text{lat} \\ -\text{back} \end{bmatrix} \begin{bmatrix} +\text{voc} \\ -\text{back} \\ -\text{rd} \end{bmatrix}$$

(89) *Barra Gaelic epenthetic vowel finds and copies values for [+high, −low]*

$$x_1 \leftarrow x_2 \quad x_3$$

$$\begin{bmatrix} +\text{voc} \\ +\text{back} \\ +\text{rd} \\ \mathbf{+high} \\ \mathbf{-low} \end{bmatrix} \begin{bmatrix} -\text{voc} \\ +\text{son} \\ -\text{nas} \\ +\text{lat} \\ -\text{back} \end{bmatrix} \begin{bmatrix} +\text{voc} \\ -\text{back} \\ -\text{rd} \\ \mathbf{+high} \\ \mathbf{-low} \end{bmatrix}$$

$$\text{u} \qquad \text{l}^j \qquad \text{i}$$

Importantly, the resulting epenthetic vowel is [i], not [u] or [ü]. Clearly, neither /lʲ/ nor /u/ alone could yield a high front unround vowel. It is crucial here that there are two potential contrastive sources for valuing the vowel. If both of them completely got their way, the result would be a front round vowel, which is banned by the implicational rule. But consider possible outputs with a front unround vowel or with a back round vowel: [bulʲikʲ] or the unattested *[bulʲukʲ]. The principle of dynamic, directional valuation will always guarantee the former, because [−back] is encountered first in the search, in derivational terms.

By contrast, in a donor-centric model, or a theory of global optimization of subsegmental agreement, nothing would guarantee this result. Although principles could be formulated to guarantee that the potential sources of copying are the palatalized liquid and the preceding vowel, such constraints alone will not choose between the attested and unattested outputs. What is required is a statement that the closest contrastive value must be copied and must be kept, regardless of what might ultimately lead to a better choice from a "global" perspective.[14] Even though in some imaginable grammars, copying all features from the *same* source might lead to a "less polygamous" set of copying relationships, this consideration never seems to matter.[15] Regardless of multiple-source harmony's ultimate implementation in terms of rules or constraints, all research into this phenomenon must reckon with the fact that valuation is a "greedy" operation and will copy the first value that it can.

The Search Principle

In the *Search-and-Copy* procedure developed here, this search is initiated *by the recipient*, and upon each match with a contrastive source for the feature in question, valuation occurs. When a contrastively (non)palatalized consonant is the first segment to the left of the epenthetic vowel, the vowel will copy its value for [±back] and commit to that value henceforth, then proceeding to search for the remaining unvalued features.

2.12 General Conclusion: Search Must Be Recipient-Initiated

This chapter has presented the essential Search algorithm: harmony is a Search-and-Copy procedure initiated by a needy vowel in order to find itself one or more feature-values. The search procedure operates directionally to find the closest value-source; and it is greedy, in the sense that it operates without lookahead but will copy a value as soon as it finds one. The resulting model bears a striking similarity to the Agree process posited in syntactic theory, in which a value-seeking element (such as a Tense node) engages in a downward search for the closest noun phrase from which to copy person and number features.

We have considered three main arguments for the recipient-initiated process of vowel harmony. The first is that in a recipient-centric model, it is a property of the Turkish plural morpheme [-lar/-ler] but not the nominalizing morpheme /-gen/ that it needs to copy feature-values from its closest leftward source. The fact that some morphemes may exceptionally not undergo harmony, but no morpheme may exceptionally not furnish harmony, requires no modification to the general Search procedure. In contrast, in a donor-centric theory, the absence of exceptional nontriggers is surprising.

The second argument is that in a recipient-centric model, when the search is bidirectional, the result of copying-from-closest will require identical feature-values on both sides in case of a literal tie in closeness. In Woleaian theme-vowel harmony, only when both flanking vowels are high will harmony occur, a result that requires no modification to the general Search procedure. In a donor-centric theory, by contrast, this situation would require serious negotiation between two separate spreading rules.

The third main argument is that when more than one feature-value is needed on the harmonizing vowel, the search will copy from the first source it finds, even if in global terms there might be a better choice downstream. In Barra Gaelic vowel harmony, [−back] is copied from a consonant, even though this prevents subsequent copying of [+round] from the next vowel over because the language lacks the front round vowel /ü/. This result is natural given the directional leftward march of the search procedure, but additional principles would be required to guarantee it in a system that considers multiple feature-value-source candidates in parallel.

These empirical considerations strongly establish the need for a recipient-centric model of vowel harmony. This chapter has established the basic Search procedure that accomplishes this goal; namely, it requires copying from the closest element in the domain. The fact that search halts with the closest element of the relevant type finds strong parallels within other modules of linguistic computation. The Search procedure has direct syntactic analogues in cases such as the locality of head movement. Consider the C node in an interrogative question, which must attract a contentful head as its sister: it always attracts the closest head (90b) (Travis 1984) and cannot skip the closest element to attract a more distant one instead (90c).

(90) a. [$_{CP}$ C [$_{IP}$ they could have left]]
 b. [$_{CP}$ Could [$_{IP}$ they t_{could} have left]]?
 c. *[$_{CP}$ Have [$_{IP}$ they could t_{have} left]]?

While the Search procedure for vowel harmony has a broad applicability across languages, however, there are a number of parametric options that determine the nature of the *search domain* itself, to which we turn in subsequent chapters. For example, in both the Turkish case of [meʃgul^{j}düm] and the Barra Gaelic case of [bul^{j}ik^j], harmony was accomplished with a [−back] consonant. These patterns required revising the statement that the possible donors of harmony to be changed to "any segment" rather than "vowel." What is traditionally called "back vowel harmony" in fact is harmony with any eligible source of a [−back] value. However, even this statement does not really paint the full picture, since there are some segments that are phonetically [−back] (such as the glide /j/) but do not participate in harmony at all. What is a possible donor in both of these cases is not actually "any segment," but "any segment contrastive for [±back]." I begin the next chapter by spelling out exactly what this means.

Appendix: Harmony Necessitated by Deletion

In this appendix, I will demonstrate that the Search algorithm developed in this chapter can be extended to cases of harmony that result from deletion processes. While the harmony algorithm is ordinarily used in phonological computations to supply a value for a needy segment requiring a feature-value because it lacks one in its memorized representation, the same algorithm can be used for segments that lack a feature-value because of a deletion rule that applies later in the phonology. For example, in Chumash, an isolate language of California, certain coronal fricatives require harmony for the feature [±distributed] (affecting tongue tip orientation), not because they lack an underlying value for it, but because a postcyclic rule deletes their values.

Chumash has a process of leftward [±distributed] harmony affecting its coronal fricatives (henceforth "sibilants") /s/ and /ṣ/, as described in Poser 1982. Since the contrast between laminal /s/ and apical /ṣ/ in Chumash rests on [±distributed] (see Mithun 1998, 221; Hansson 2001, 58), I will transcribe Poser's š as [−distributed] /ṣ/. The apical consonants /d,t,l,n/ in Chumash are [−distributed].

What is unique about Chumash's [±distributed] harmony is that all nonfinal sibilants harmonize with the sibilant to their right, regardless of their morphological affiliation, morphological constituency, or underlying value of [±distributed].

(91) *Chumash sibilant harmony (Poser 1982, 132)*

	UR	SR	
a.	k+sunon+us	ksunonus	'I obey him'
b.	k+sunon+ṣ	kṣunotṣ	'I am obedient'
c.	su+wayan	suwayan	'cause to hang'
d.	k+su+ṣoyin	kṣuṣoyin	'I darken it'
e.	s+ixut	sixut	'it burns'
f.	s+ilakṣ	ṣilakṣ	'it is soft'
g.	s+kuti+waṣ	ṣkutiwaṣ	'he saw'
h.	s+apitṣʰo+it	ṣapitṣʰolit	'I have a stroke of good luck'
i.	s+apitṣʰo+us+waṣ	ṣapitṣʰoluṣwaṣ	'they had a stroke of good luck'

As this type of harmony affects prefixes, roots, and suffixes alike, without regard to the order of morphological structure, the harmony process is not a cyclic rule of supplying a value for newly added morphemes. Poser (1982, 134) shows for (91i), for example, that no morphological bracketing of [[3SUBJ [[good+luck] 3OBJ]] PAST] would result in morpheme-by-morpheme copying of [−distributed] all the way through to every coronal fricative. The distinction between cyclic and postcyclic processes (see, e.g.,

Halle and Vergnaud 1987) is that cyclic processes apply in a single pass through the word, without regard to morphological constituency, and that postcyclic processes apply after all cyclic processes have applied.

Chumash [±distributed] harmony occurs after the morphological structure of a word is completely built and all of its feature-values are complete. It is therefore somewhat unusual from the point of view of other types of agglutinative-morphology harmony, and it has been treated as a postcyclic process that *changes* rather than supplies feature-values.

In a word such as /s+apits̯ʰo+us+waṣ/, let us assume that there is no harmony upon affixation and that the subject agreement, object agreement, and tense affixes are underlyingly fully specified for [±distributed]. Prior to the application of the postcyclic process of harmony, they have the following representations (for convenience, only the coronal fricatives are shown):

(92) *Representation of fricatives in /s+apits̯ʰo+us+waṣ/ before the postcyclic block*

$$
\begin{array}{cccc}
f_1 & f_2 & f_3 & f_4 \\
\begin{bmatrix} +\text{cons} \\ \text{cor} \\ +\text{cont} \\ -\text{voi} \\ -\text{asp} \\ +\text{distr} \end{bmatrix} &
\begin{bmatrix} +\text{cons} \\ \text{cor} \\ +\text{cont} \\ -\text{voi} \\ +\text{asp} \\ -\text{distr} \end{bmatrix} &
\begin{bmatrix} +\text{cons} \\ \text{cor} \\ +\text{cont} \\ -\text{voi} \\ -\text{asp} \\ +\text{distr} \end{bmatrix} &
\begin{bmatrix} +\text{cons} \\ \text{cor} \\ +\text{cont} \\ -\text{voi} \\ -\text{asp} \\ -\text{distr} \end{bmatrix} \\
s & s^h & s & \underset{\cdot}{s}
\end{array}
$$

Following Poser's original proposal, what is particular to Chumash is that all nonfinal coronal fricatives have their [±distributed] specification *deleted* from the representation.[16]

(93) *Representation of fricatives in /s+apits̯ʰo+us+waṣ/ after deletion of nonfinal [±distributed]*

$$
\begin{array}{cccc}
f_1 & f_2 & f_3 & f_4 \\
\begin{bmatrix} +\text{cons} \\ \text{cor} \\ +\text{cont} \\ -\text{voi} \\ -\text{asp} \end{bmatrix} &
\begin{bmatrix} +\text{cons} \\ \text{cor} \\ +\text{cont} \\ -\text{voi} \\ +\text{asp} \end{bmatrix} &
\begin{bmatrix} +\text{cons} \\ \text{cor} \\ +\text{cont} \\ -\text{voi} \\ -\text{asp} \end{bmatrix} &
\begin{bmatrix} +\text{cons} \\ \text{cor} \\ +\text{cont} \\ -\text{voi} \\ -\text{asp} \\ -\text{distr} \end{bmatrix}
\end{array}
$$

This postcyclic deletion rule is all that is unique about Chumash's feature-changing harmony. The subsequent harmony process follows the same algorithm adopted in this chapter, with the Search-and-Copy procedure occurring on each element from right to left. All elements contrastive for [±distributed] (e.g., the coronal fricatives) within the postcyclic word must harmonize.

(94) *Chumash postcyclic word must:*
Distr-Harmonize: δ = right, F = [contrastive: ±distr]

The application of Distr-Harmonize to each nonfinal fricative, from right to left, is shown in (95)–(97).

(95) *First nonfinal fricative searches for [±distributed]*

$$f_1 \quad f_2 \quad f_3 \quad \stackrel{\curvearrowleft}{} \quad f_4$$

$$\begin{bmatrix} +\text{cons} \\ \text{cor} \\ +\text{cont} \\ -\text{voi} \\ -\text{asp} \end{bmatrix} \begin{bmatrix} +\text{cons} \\ \text{cor} \\ +\text{cont} \\ -\text{voi} \\ +\text{asp} \end{bmatrix} \begin{bmatrix} +\text{cons} \\ \text{cor} \\ +\text{cont} \\ -\text{voi} \\ -\text{asp} \\ -\textbf{distr} \end{bmatrix} \begin{bmatrix} +\text{cons} \\ \text{cor} \\ +\text{cont} \\ -\text{voi} \\ -\text{asp} \\ -\textbf{distr} \end{bmatrix}$$

(96) *Second nonfinal fricative searches for [±distributed]*

$$f_1 \quad f_2 \quad \stackrel{\curvearrowleft}{} \quad f_3 \quad f_4$$

$$\begin{bmatrix} +\text{cons} \\ \text{cor} \\ +\text{cont} \\ -\text{voi} \\ -\text{asp} \end{bmatrix} \begin{bmatrix} +\text{cons} \\ \text{cor} \\ +\text{cont} \\ -\text{voi} \\ +\text{asp} \\ -\textbf{distr} \end{bmatrix} \begin{bmatrix} +\text{cons} \\ \text{cor} \\ +\text{cont} \\ -\text{voi} \\ -\text{asp} \\ -\textbf{distr} \end{bmatrix} \begin{bmatrix} +\text{cons} \\ \text{cor} \\ +\text{cont} \\ -\text{voi} \\ -\text{asp} \\ -\text{distr} \end{bmatrix}$$

(97) *Third nonfinal fricative searches for [±distributed]*

$$f_1 \quad \stackrel{\curvearrowleft}{} \quad f_2 \quad f_3 \quad f_4$$

$$\begin{bmatrix} +\text{cons} \\ \text{cor} \\ +\text{cont} \\ -\text{voi} \\ -\text{asp} \\ -\textbf{distr} \end{bmatrix} \begin{bmatrix} +\text{cons} \\ \text{cor} \\ +\text{cont} \\ -\text{voi} \\ +\text{asp} \\ -\textbf{distr} \end{bmatrix} \begin{bmatrix} +\text{cons} \\ \text{cor} \\ +\text{cont} \\ -\text{voi} \\ -\text{asp} \\ -\text{distr} \end{bmatrix} \begin{bmatrix} +\text{cons} \\ \text{cor} \\ +\text{cont} \\ -\text{voi} \\ -\text{asp} \\ -\text{distr} \end{bmatrix}$$

$$\quad \text{ṣ} \quad\quad\quad \text{ṣ} \quad\quad\quad \text{ṣ} \quad\quad\quad \text{ṣ}$$

Thus, Chumash feature-changing harmony can be incorporated into the basic Search-and-Copy algorithm of this chapter, provided a postcyclic process of deleting all nonfinal [±distributed] specifications is included. Indeed, other phonological processes of feature-changing copying have been treated with deletion of features on nonfinal elements; Cho (1990) treats [±voice] assimilation in consonant clusters in Serbo-Croatian (e.g.,

[rob]~[ro**pst**avo] 'slave, slavery'; [svat]~[sva**db**a] 'wedding guest, wedding') as the result of deletion of voicing on nonfinal consonants in an adjacent sequence, followed by assimilation. In Chumash, since all representations must exit the phonology with a specification for [±distributed], the harmony procedure is enlisted to provide a value for elements that lost theirs via deletion.

Another process of interest in Chumash [±distributed] harmony is its interaction with apicalization (called "precoronal palatalization" in Poser 1982), which supplies a [−distributed] value for a sibilant that immediately precedes a [−distributed] segment (i.e., /t,l,n/). Since this process only occurs under immediate adjacency, I will call it *local apicalization*, distinguishing it from the unbounded [±distributed] harmony between sibilants contrastive for the feature.

(98) *Chumash local apicalization (Poser 1982, 152)*

	UR	SR	
a.	s+nit^{h}oy	ṣnit^{h}oy	'he goes'
b.	s+tumun	ṣtumun	'its egg'
c.	s+lok'in	ṣlok'in	'he cuts it'

Following Poser (1993), I assume that the rule of local apicalization precedes any initiation of the Search-and-Copy procedure for harmony.[17] Local apicalization is a process that occurs only under immediate precedence, with additional morphological restrictions, and it can be clearly separated from the harmony process. In addition, as /s/ and /ṣ/ are contrastive for [±distributed] while /t,l,n/ are not, local apicalization must clearly be distinct from harmony, since neither /n/ in [ksunonus] induces apicalization of the sibilant to its left.

Given the greedy and local character of the Search procedure, every sibilant will copy [±distributed] from the sibilant source immediately to its right, regardless of whether that value comes from an underlying specification (as in final sibilants), from local apicalization, or from the result of harmony itself. Thus, a sibilant enacting a harmonic search for [±distributed] may copy it from another sibilant that has itself acquired it via local apicalization.

(99) *Interaction of locally apicalized segments in [±distributed] harmony (Poser 1982, 153)*

	UR	SR	
a.	s+is+tiʔ	ṣiṣtiʔɨ	'he finds it'
b.	s+ti+yep+us	ṣtiyepus	'he tells him'
c.	s+iṣ+lu+sisin	ṣiṣlusisin	'they two are gone awry'

The Search Principle

The form in (99c), [şişlusisin], has three nonfinal sibilants. The first nonfinal sibilant copies [±distributed] from its closest rightward source, which bears an underlying value. The second nonfinal sibilant acquired [−distributed] via local apicalization. The third nonfinal sibilant copies [±distributed] from its closest rightward source. The derivation proceeds following deletion of [±distributed] on all nonfinal fricatives (for convenience, only the fricatives and the /l/ are represented).

(100) *Representation of fricatives in /s+iṣ+lu+sisin/ after deletion of all nonfinal [±distributed]*

f_1	f_2	l	f_3	f_4
$\begin{bmatrix} +\text{cons} \\ \text{cor} \\ +\text{cont} \\ -\text{voi} \end{bmatrix}$	$\begin{bmatrix} +\text{cons} \\ \text{cor} \\ +\text{cont} \\ -\text{voi} \end{bmatrix}$	$\begin{bmatrix} +\text{cons} \\ \text{cor} \\ +\text{cont} \\ +\text{lat} \\ -\text{distr} \end{bmatrix}$	$\begin{bmatrix} +\text{cons} \\ \text{cor} \\ +\text{cont} \\ -\text{voi} \end{bmatrix}$	$\begin{bmatrix} +\text{cons} \\ \text{cor} \\ +\text{cont} \\ -\text{voi} \\ +\text{distr} \end{bmatrix}$

(101) *Application of local apicalization*

f_1	f_2	l	f_3	f_4
$\begin{bmatrix} +\text{cons} \\ \text{cor} \\ +\text{cont} \\ -\text{voi} \end{bmatrix}$	$\begin{bmatrix} +\text{cons} \\ \text{cor} \\ +\text{cont} \\ -\text{voi} \\ -\textbf{distr} \end{bmatrix}$	$\begin{bmatrix} +\text{cons} \\ \text{cor} \\ +\text{cont} \\ +\text{lat} \\ -\text{distr} \end{bmatrix}$	$\begin{bmatrix} +\text{cons} \\ \text{cor} \\ +\text{cont} \\ -\text{voi} \end{bmatrix}$	$\begin{bmatrix} +\text{cons} \\ \text{cor} \\ +\text{cont} \\ -\text{voi} \\ +\text{distr} \end{bmatrix}$

(102) *First nonfinal fricative searches for [±distributed]*

f_1	f_2	f_3	↱	f_4
$\begin{bmatrix} +\text{cons} \\ \text{cor} \\ +\text{cont} \\ -\text{voi} \end{bmatrix}$	$\begin{bmatrix} +\text{cons} \\ \text{cor} \\ +\text{cont} \\ -\text{voi} \\ -\text{distr} \end{bmatrix}$	$\begin{bmatrix} +\text{cons} \\ \text{cor} \\ +\text{cont} \\ -\text{voi} \\ +\textbf{distr} \end{bmatrix}$		$\begin{bmatrix} +\text{cons} \\ \text{cor} \\ +\text{cont} \\ -\text{voi} \\ +\textbf{distr} \end{bmatrix}$

(103) *Initial fricative searches for [±distributed]*

f_1	↱	f_2	f_3	f_4
$\begin{bmatrix} +\text{cons} \\ \text{cor} \\ +\text{cont} \\ -\text{voi} \\ -\textbf{distr} \end{bmatrix}$		$\begin{bmatrix} +\text{cons} \\ \text{cor} \\ +\text{cont} \\ -\text{voi} \\ -\textbf{distr} \end{bmatrix}$	$\begin{bmatrix} +\text{cons} \\ \text{cor} \\ +\text{cont} \\ -\text{voi} \\ +\text{distr} \end{bmatrix}$	$\begin{bmatrix} +\text{cons} \\ \text{cor} \\ +\text{cont} \\ -\text{voi} \\ +\text{distr} \end{bmatrix}$
ş		ş	s	s

In conclusion, perhaps many cases of "feature-changing" harmony can be accounted for by an initial step of deletion. For example, iterative [±ATR] harmony in dialects of Canadian French (Poliquin 2006) affects all nonfinal high vowels within a word; this can be derived if deletion feeds harmony. The process of *ikan'e* in Russian changes unstressed /a/ to [i] when preceded by a [+high, −back] consonant. One way to derive this feature-change is to postcyclically delete features of all unstressed vowels (a kind of vowel reduction) and copy [±high, ±back] from the closest leftward source. Finally, as mentioned above, feature-changing [±voice] assimilation in languages such as Serbo-Croatian has been handled as the result of deleting [±voice] specifications on nonfinal consonants in a sequence, followed by feature-copying (Cho 1990).

The harmony algorithm developed in chapter 2 enables a theory of locality for segments that need a feature-value; whether they need this value because of an "innate" or "acquired" property of their representation is irrelevant to the computation employed to supply it.

3 Contrastiveness, Markedness, and Feature-Based Locality

The Search procedure introduced in chapter 2 finds and copies needed feature-values from the closest element in the search domain. An important source of crosslinguistic variation in delimiting the search domain results from language-specific reference to two paradigmatic properties defined by the inventory of sounds in the language. Once these two properties are defined, differences between languages reduce to use of the same Search algorithm over different sets of elements; these differences can be predicted by inspecting given languages' featural alphabets.

This chapter will explore crosslinguistic variation in what is excluded from the search domain and will conclude by summarizing how the range of "transparency" effects in harmony is limited by the grammatical options made available within a relativized-search-domain approach to feature-copying rules.

3.1 Contrastiveness Cuts Potential Donors in Finnish Harmony

We begin by examining Finnish, which has a [±back] harmony system similar to that observed for Turkish in chapter 2. The essive case suffix alternates between [-na] (with [+back] vowel) and [-nä] (with [−back] vowel) depending on the value of the vowel to its left. However, not all vowels count: in particular, the high front vowel /i/ and the mid front vowel /e/ act as if they were not there (Ringen 1975). To illustrate with /i/:

(1) *The high front vowel /i/ is invisible in Finnish harmony*
    a. pöütä-nä   'table-ESS'
    b. pouta-na   'fine.weather-ESS'
    c. koti-na   'home-ESS'
    d. pappi-na   'priest-ESS'

e. väkkärä-nä 'pinwheel-ESS'
f. makkara-na 'sausage-ESS'
g. tühmä-nä 'stupid-ESS'
h. tuhma-na 'naughty-ESS'

As examples (1a–b) show, the [−back] suffix [-nä] follows a root that is all [−back], and the [+back] suffix [-na] follows a root that is all [+back]. However, (1c–d) show that when the closest leftward vowel to the suffix is /i/, it is skipped, and the search continues leftward to the next vowel, which in these cases is [+back], eventually yielding the [+back] variant of the suffix.

What's going on here? Shouldn't the search halt immediately with the closest vowel in the domain? To answer this puzzle, we return to one of the central points raised in chapter 1: that humans often do not compute distance "as the crow flies," but rather within a system. Let's examine the properties of the Finnish vowel inventory. In the table in (2), I indicate "missing" vowels with ✗.[1]

(2) *Finnish vowel inventory*

[−back, −rd]	[−back, +rd]	[+back, +rd]	[+back, −rd]	
i	ü	u	✗	[+high, −low]
e	ö	o	✗	[−high, −low]
ä		a		[−high, +low]

As (2) shows, there are no [−low, +back, −round] vowels in the inventory, and thus, while /ü,ö,ä/ and /u,o,a/ differ only in [±back], the [−low, −back, −round] vowels /i,e/ have no harmonic counterpart. The notion of having or not having a harmonic counterpart can be formalized once we refer to features.[2]

(3) *Definition of* contrastive
A segment S with specification αF in position P is *contrastive* for F if there is another segment S′ in the inventory that can occur in P and is featurally identical to S, except that it is −αF.

This definition determines whether an element has a "twin" with respect to a certain feature-value. We are observing that a paradigmatic property of a vowel (whether it is contrastive or not) determines its syntagmatic behavior (whether it participates in vowel harmony or not). An easy mnemonic for this pattern might be "If you don't have a twin, you can't be a donor."

Since the vowels /i,e/ are noncontrastive for [±back] in Finnish, they pattern as invisible in [±back] harmony, not acting as donors and not

Contrastiveness, Markedness, and Feature-Based Locality

myVals V
myPosition P
myFeatsneeded F

while F is not empty:
- Go in direction δ and update P
- **if** P has a value for any $f, f \in F$:
  - **if** Val(f) is contrastive on P:
    - Copy Val(P, f) to V
    - Remove f from F

Figure 3.1
Search relativized to contrastive values

being included in the search. To put it differently, whether or not a vowel is contrastive for a harmonic feature determines whether or not it is included at all in what the search looks at.

The set of items that are potentially included in the search (based on, for example, whether they are contrastive or not) constitutes the *domain* of search. The modification of the Search algorithm to exclude non-contrastive items as potential donors is shown in figure 3.1.

Relativization prunes the search domain: in Finnish, it is not the closest vowel that is copied from, but the closest *contrastive* vowel.

(4) *Finnish essive case suffix must:*
    Back-Harmonize: δ = left, F = [contrastive: $\pm$back]

(5) *Essive suffix begins Back-Harmonize in [koti-na]*

$$\begin{array}{ccccc}
x_1 & x_2 & x_3 & \leftarrow x_4 & x_5 \\
\begin{bmatrix} +\text{voc} \\ -\text{high} \\ -\text{low} \\ +\text{rd} \\ +\text{back} \end{bmatrix} &
\begin{bmatrix} -\text{voc} \\ \text{cor} \\ -\text{cont} \\ -\text{voi} \end{bmatrix} &
\begin{bmatrix} +\text{voc} \\ +\text{high} \\ -\text{low} \\ -\text{rd} \\ -\text{back} \end{bmatrix} &
\begin{bmatrix} -\text{voc} \\ \text{cor} \\ +\text{nas} \end{bmatrix} &
\begin{bmatrix} +\text{voc} \\ -\text{high} \\ +\text{low} \\ -\text{rd} \end{bmatrix}
\end{array}$$

(6) *Essive suffix finds [+back] on x_1 and copies [+back] to itself*

$$\begin{array}{ccccc}
x_1 & x_2 & x_3 & x_4 & x_5 \\
\begin{bmatrix} +\text{voc} \\ -\text{high} \\ -\text{low} \\ +\text{rd} \\ \mathbf{+back} \end{bmatrix} &
\begin{bmatrix} -\text{voc} \\ \text{cor} \\ -\text{cont} \\ -\text{voi} \end{bmatrix} &
\begin{bmatrix} +\text{voc} \\ +\text{high} \\ -\text{low} \\ -\text{rd} \\ -\text{back} \end{bmatrix} &
\begin{bmatrix} -\text{voc} \\ \text{cor} \\ +\text{nas} \end{bmatrix} &
\begin{bmatrix} +\text{voc} \\ -\text{high} \\ +\text{low} \\ -\text{rd} \\ \mathbf{+back} \end{bmatrix} \\
\text{o} & \text{t} & \text{i} & \text{n} & \text{a}
\end{array}$$

A similar pattern of vowel harmony skipping /i/ and searching long-distance can be found in Classical Mongolian (Svantesson 1985), in which the vowel system also leaves /i/ noncontrastive for [±back].

(7) *Classical Mongolian vowel inventory*

[−back, −rd]	[−back, +rd]	[+back, +rd]	[+back, −rd]	
i	ü	u		[+high]
e	ö	o	a	[−high]

Classical Mongolian [−high, −round] suffixes copy the feature [±back] from the closest contrastive source, skipping /i/ (Svantesson 1985, 305).

(8) *Classical Mongolian suffixal harmony: Copies closest contrastive [±back]*
    a. ulus   ulus-ača   'nation / nation-ABL'
    b. aman   aman-ača   'mouth / mouth-ABL'
    c. üker   üker-eče   'ox / OX-ABL'
    d. mören   mören-eče   'river / river-ABL'
    e. morin   morin-ača   'horse / horse-ABL'

In summary, the pattern of transparent /i/ in the [±back] contrastive harmony systems of a number of languages exists because those languages lack [+high, +back, −round] /i/ (some having lost it from an earlier stage). This fact, coupled with the definition of contrastiveness, derives the rest.

3.2 Finnish Transparent Vowels Are Excluded from Harmony

As well as adopting a strict interpretation of the autosegmental view of harmony as spreading association lines—so that a single instance of a feature is shared among multiple segments—researchers such as Ní Chiosáin and Padgett (2001) hypothesize that all harmony is strictly local. (See Gafos 1996, 77–81, for a demonstration that interpreting the autosegmental formalism without underspecification inevitably leads to strict adjacency.)[3] Thus, Ní Chiosáin and Padgett (2001, 119) conjecture, "We assume that locality holds strictly, in two senses of 'strict'. First, spreading respects segmental adjacency. An essential result of this view is that segments are either blockers or participants in spreading: there is no transparency or skipping. Second, segmentally strict locality is inviolable."

The major claim of this book is that phonological locality is relativized, not strict, and that the model of harmony as spreading a feature from one segment to another is insufficient for capturing the invisibility of segments such as noncontrastive /i/. If strict locality were correct, it would mean that Finnish /i,e/ were actually not being skipped in harmony and that these vowels were in fact participating in harmony just as fully as any other vowels.

An important discovery of phonetic research (Öhman 1966; Butcher and Weiher 1976; Fowler 1981; Recasens 1984) is that coarticulation between vowels exists even in languages without vowel harmony, such as English, Swedish, and Catalan—and presumably universally. Vowel-to-vowel coarticulation refers to the process through which the phonetic targets of one vowel may be affected by the phonetic targets of a vowel that precedes or follows it. If vowel-to-vowel coarticulation can be found in languages without any vowel harmony to begin with, we should expect to find it in vowel harmony languages too, even for vowels not undergoing harmony.

If instances of [−back] vowels such as /i/ are found to be transiently backed when occurring between [+back]-harmonizing suffix and value-source in words such as [koti-na], how are we to know whether these effects are the result of a phonetic process of coarticulation, as opposed to the result of the vowel harmony process itself? The answer to this question bears directly on whether harmony is strictly local, or whether backing effects observed on noncontrastive /i/ are coarticulatory results independent of the phonology (and equally likely to be found in languages without harmony, as noted above).

Cohn (1990) synthesizes the distinctions between phonological and phonetic rules, as illustrated in (9).

(9) *Properties of phonological rules versus properties of phonetic rules (Cohn 1990, 26)*

Phonological rules	Phonetic rules
Categorical	Gradient/quantitative
Discrete & timeless segments	Continuous in time & space
Static effects	Segment may vary in quality continuously
Full segment affected	Part of a segment affected

With these distinctions in mind, we can outline the predictions for Finnish neutral vowels. The acoustic correlate of backness is the second formant, $F2$ (or $|F2 - F1|$), and so *backness* in what follows refers to these measurable formant values.

(10) *Effects of backing on Finnish /i,e/ in [+back] contexts*

If vowel harmony	If coarticulation
Effect of rule is categorical change in backness	Rule may vary with speech style
Backness values will cluster into bimodal distribution	Vowel backness may show broad unimodal distribution
Effects do not depend on properties of preceding vowel	Effects may vary in quality continuously
Whole vowel is affected	Only part of the vowel may be affected

Three phonetic studies have looked at effects on Finnish transparent /i,e/ in [+back] and [−back] contexts. The results of all three studies squarely place the effects in the right-hand column, allowing us to conclude that these vowels are affected by phonetic coarticulation, and not by a phonological process of vowel harmony.

Kim (2005) measured vowels that are transparent and participate in harmony. For categorical harmony, F2 values clustered around discrete values in [+back] and [−back] environments; their distributions showed a clear separation. On the other hand, for gradient coarticulation on /i,e/ (of the type observed since Öhman 1966), F2 values overlapped for [+back] and [−back] environments; the distributions showed no categorical separation. Moreover, Kim found that a given transparent vowel's F2 value varied directly as a function of the preceding vowel's F2 value, rather than as a function of its binary category. Finally, these lowered F2 values in [+back] contexts did not persist throughout the affected vowel; instead, they weakened throughout the duration of the vowel.

Like Kim, Gordon (1999) found that in the case of the transparent vowels, the phonetic difference between the variant occurring after front vowels and the variant occurring after back vowels is much smaller than the more salient differences found in the contrastive vowels. He concluded that "vowel harmony for the neutral vowels functions at a low phonetic level, unlike vowel harmony for non-neutral vowels" (p. 20).

Välimaa-Blum (1999) compared coarticulatory effects in two speech styles: casual and hyperarticulated (i.e., careful speech). She found a backing effect of neutral vowels in [+back] contexts during casual speech, but no effect at all under the careful speech register. On the other hand, true harmony did not vary with speech style. She concluded for the transparent vowels that "the differences between the formant means disappear in hyperarticulated speech, and this would mean that the assimilation [of

/i,e/], if there is one, is style dependent. And if it is style dependent, we propose that it is the result of some late phonetic assimilation rule applying in speech contexts which are less formal or require lesser clarity of presentation" (pp. 260–261).

One clear formulation of the difference between categorical feature-copying (of the type required in harmony) and phonetic interpolation (resulting from coarticulation) is offered by Keating (1996), who argues that in the phonological component, rules manipulate features and feature-values and use temporal chunking (parsing into discrete segments), while in the phonetic component, the objects of computation are continuous in time and space, allow overlap, and operate over quantitative values along multiple independent dimensions. Keating argues that "features specify 'targets' that the human articulators aim at, moving or 'interpolating' from target to target" (p. 264). Applying the notion of targets to vowel harmony, we can say that transparent vowels between harmonizing [+F] vowels do not copy [+F] in the phonology: they are [−F], but may allow for gradient interpolation between [+F] targets when implemented in the phonetics (see also Gick et al. 2006, 16, for this distinction applied to vowel harmony).

These comparisons can even be made between distinct processes within a single language, as shown by Zsiga (1997), who contrasts Igbo [±ATR] vowel harmony, a categorical and phonological process, with the process of adjacent vowel assimilation (e.g., /nwoke a/ → [nwoka a] 'man DEF'). Zsiga argues that "gradient processes such as Igbo vowel assimilation require reference to the specific temporal information that the gestural approach provides. Categorical alternations such as Igbo vowel harmony neither need nor benefit from detailed timing information. Their similarities are tantalizing, but they cannot be collapsed" (p. 266). Thus, both a module of featurally based phonological representations and one of inherently quantitative phonetic representation (implemented by Zsiga in terms of articulatory gestural scores) are needed, and neither can be reduced to the other. Igbo vowel harmony is categorical, obligatory, and independent of speech rate and speech style, while Igbo vowel assimilation between adjacent vowels (e.g., across word boundaries) is partial, gradient, variable throughout its time window, highly dependent on the duration of the two vowels, and conditioned by speech rate and speech style.

Thus, as Kim (2005, 2) concludes in her discussion of the truly transparent nature of phonological vowel harmony in Finnish [−low, −round] vowels, "Both vowel harmony *and* progressive front/back V-to-V coarticulation are independently needed to describe the behavior of harmonic (= non-neutral) vowels in Finnish. Of these two processes, neutral. Transparent vowels undergo coarticulation only." Relativized locality is able to compute harmony without involving them.

3.3 What If No Contrastive Source Exists?

When the search domain for a copy-source for a feature-value [±F] includes all potential donors, as with the Turkish examples in chapter 2, a donor will always be found. However, when the search domain is relativized to include only contrastive values of [±F] (and to exclude noncontrastive values), certain configurations will arise in which there is no donor to be copied from. Recall from (2) that the [−low, −back, −round] vowels /i,e/ are noncontrastive for the feature [±back] in Finnish. Since Finnish words can be composed in which noncontrastive vowels are the only vowels, an essive or other needy suffix searching for a value of [±back] will not be able to copy from them.

Nonetheless, a key premise of the model of vowel harmony proposed here is that all alternating suffixes come out of the lexicon lacking a value and that feature-copying from a sought donor is the way to supply them with one. When these suffixes are in the unfortunate situation of being concatenated with a root that contains only noncontrastive vowels, they must get a value somehow. As discussed in section 2.8, a last-resort option when harmonic search fails is insertion of the default value. We know already from syntactic theory that in certain configurations in which the verb searches for an argument to agree with, there may be no nominative argument at all, in which case the last resort is to insert a set of default feature-values.

(11) *Icelandic last-resort feature-insertion when there is no nominative argument*
Mig   vantar   peninga.
me.ACC lack.3SG.MASC money.ACC
'I lack money.'
(Andrews 1982)

Consider Finnish words that contain no contrastively [±back] values, such as those in (12).

(12) *Finnish default value in case of no donors is [−back]*
 a. tie   tie-nä   'road / road-ESS'
 b. veli   velje-nä 'brother / brother-ESS'

The attempted search in a word lacking contrastive values of [±back] is illustrated in (13)–(15). When the search fails at the leftmost edge of the word for lack of finding a value-source (indicated by ↔), the needy vowel undergoes last-resort default insertion.

(13) *Essive suffix begins Back-Harmonize in [tie-nä]*

$$x_1 \quad x_2 \quad x_3 \quad \leftarrow \quad x_4 \quad x_5$$

$$\begin{bmatrix} -\text{voc} \\ \text{cor} \\ -\text{cont} \\ -\text{voi} \end{bmatrix} \begin{bmatrix} +\text{voc} \\ +\text{high} \\ -\text{low} \\ -\text{rd} \\ -\text{back} \end{bmatrix} \begin{bmatrix} +\text{voc} \\ -\text{high} \\ -\text{low} \\ -\text{rd} \\ -\text{back} \end{bmatrix} \begin{bmatrix} -\text{voc} \\ \text{cor} \\ +\text{nas} \end{bmatrix} \begin{bmatrix} +\text{voc} \\ -\text{high} \\ +\text{low} \\ -\text{rd} \end{bmatrix}$$

(14) *Essive suffix fails (↔) to find contrastive donor in [tie-nä]*

$$\leftrightarrow \quad x_1 \quad x_2 \quad x_3 \quad x_4 \quad x_5$$

$$\begin{bmatrix} -\text{voc} \\ \text{cor} \\ -\text{cont} \\ -\text{voi} \end{bmatrix} \begin{bmatrix} +\text{voc} \\ +\text{high} \\ -\text{low} \\ -\text{rd} \\ -\text{back} \end{bmatrix} \begin{bmatrix} +\text{voc} \\ -\text{high} \\ -\text{low} \\ -\text{rd} \\ -\text{back} \end{bmatrix} \begin{bmatrix} -\text{voc} \\ \text{cor} \\ +\text{nas} \end{bmatrix} \begin{bmatrix} +\text{voc} \\ -\text{high} \\ +\text{low} \\ -\text{rd} \end{bmatrix}$$

(15) *Essive suffix undergoes last-resort [−back] insertion in [tie-nä]*

$$x_1 \quad x_2 \quad x_3 \quad x_4 \quad x_5$$

$$\begin{bmatrix} -\text{voc} \\ \text{cor} \\ -\text{cont} \\ -\text{voi} \end{bmatrix} \begin{bmatrix} +\text{voc} \\ +\text{high} \\ -\text{low} \\ -\text{rd} \\ -\text{back} \end{bmatrix} \begin{bmatrix} +\text{voc} \\ -\text{high} \\ -\text{low} \\ -\text{rd} \\ -\text{back} \end{bmatrix} \begin{bmatrix} -\text{voc} \\ \text{cor} \\ +\text{nas} \end{bmatrix} \begin{bmatrix} +\text{voc} \\ -\text{high} \\ +\text{low} \\ -\text{rd} \\ -\text{back} \end{bmatrix}$$

$$\text{t} \qquad \text{i} \qquad \text{e} \qquad \text{n} \qquad \text{ä}$$

In this Finnish derivation, when the search is relativized to exclude noncontrastive values, and the root to the left of the needy suffix contains only noncontrastive values, in order for the suffix to satisfy its requirement of possessing a [±back] value, a last-resort operation inserts the default value in this language, namely, [−back].

It is very important to note, however, that the default value for [±back] in cases in which harmonic search fails need not be the same as the value of [±back] in the noncontrastive vowels that failed to act as copy-sources. While in Finnish words such as [tie-nä] the root is [−back] and the suffix surfaces as [−back], it could have been the other way around. Indeed, if *the choice of last-resort value is independent of the vowels that are in the non-copied-from root*, we might expect a language displaying the effect opposite from that of Finnish.

Uyghur (a Turkic language of western China) possesses the same vowel inventory as Finnish, as shown in (16); crucially, therefore, the vowels /i,e/ are also noncontrastive in Uyghur.

(16) *Uyghur vowel inventory*

[−back, −rd]	[−back, +rd]	[+back, +rd]	[+back, −rd]	
i	ü	u		[+high, −low]
e	ö	o		[−high, −low]
ä			a	[−high, +low]

The plural suffix in Uyghur copies from the closest contrastive value, as illustrated in the straightforward cases in (17), which resemble the pattern in Turkish.

(17) *Uyghur plural suffix copies from contrastive [±back]*
    a. yol   yol-lar   'road / road-PL'
    b. pul   pul-lar   'money / money-PL'
    c. at   at-lar   'horse / horse-PL'
    d. köl   köl-lär   'lake / lake-PL'
    e. yüz   yüz-lär   'face / face-PL'
    f. xät   xät-lär   'letter / letter-PL'

Unlike Turkish harmony, Uyghur harmony is relativized to contrastive feature-values; as a result, there are cases in Uyghur in which search fails to supply a [±back] value. Unlike in Finnish, however, the last-resort value in Uyghur is [+back], *even though both languages possess identical vowel inventories.*

(18) *Uyghur default value in case of no donors is [+back]*
    a. til   til-lar   'tongue / tongue-PL'
    b. deniz   deniz-lar   'sea / sea-PL'

This last-resort value of [+back] in Uyghur is not limited to the plural suffix; Lindblad (1990) reports that this is a general phenomenon and provides examples for the dative, locative, and gerundive suffixes as well.

The conclusion we must draw from comparing Finnish and Uyghur is that there is indeed a last-resort process of inserting a default value for the harmonic feature when search fails. The reason search fails in these cases is that it is relativized to only contrastive values for the harmonic feature, and the root to which the alternating affix has been concatenated happens to be one that contains no contrastive value for the feature. This scenario is unavoidable, as there is no way to prevent an essive or plural suffix from attaching to a root that happens to lack vowels contrastive for

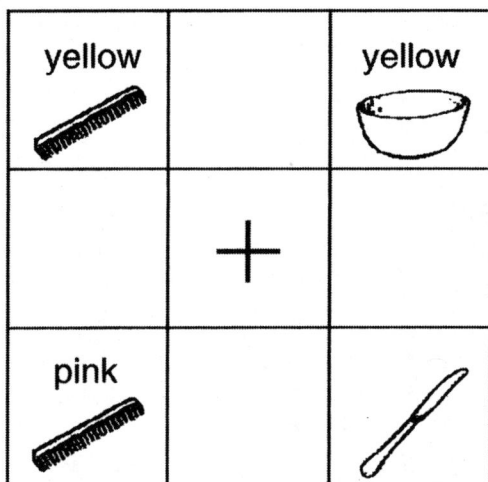

Figure 3.2
Visual setup in Sedivy et al.'s (1999) experiment. Hearing the request *Pick up the yellow comb*, subjects looked first at the object for which *yellow* was contrastive (i.e., the comb).

[±back]. Therefore, a "backup plan" is needed. This backup plan proceeds independently of what the nondonating root happens to look like.

3.4 Why Contrastiveness?

The importance of contrastiveness in the computation of motor planning and comparison has been established in interesting ways elsewhere in the study of human cognition. Sedivy et al. (1999) conducted an experiment with spoken language and visual contexts, using the real-time eye-tracking paradigm. Presented with a pink comb, a yellow comb, and a yellow bowl (see figure 3.2), subjects heard instructions such as *Pick up the yellow comb*. Importantly, the use of an eye tracker allowed Sedivy and her colleagues to measure where subjects looked in real time, as they heard each incoming word. They found that at the onset of the word *yellow*, subjects looked much faster and more frequently at the yellow *comb*, even before they had heard the head noun.

The only logical explanation is that subjects understood that their interlocutor would be more inclined to use the predicate *yellow* when it was *contrastive* for the object to be manipulated. That is, even though the predicate *yellow* was true of both the comb and the bowl, within 300 milliseconds the subjects preferred to interpret it in a contrastive way, only looking toward the object of which it was noncontrastively true much later (at 450 milliseconds). These results support the idea that preferring the contrastive use of a predicate (over a set of two or more objects for which it is true) may be a guiding principle in human cognition. Nobody would say that the bowl was "underspecified" for *yellow* and that is why subjects waited longer to look at it; rather, it seems that when humans search for something with a relevant feature, contrastive uses of that feature simply get priority.

When a noncontrastive vowel is adjacent to a vowel seeking specification, it is skipped, behaving as if it were invisible. In the present theory, the locality of harmony can largely be predicted from the structure of the inventory. The most direct source of inspiration for the current work is Calabrese (1995), who argues that "underspecification of feature values becomes an idiosyncratic property of individual rules" (p. 379). I will paraphrase this as follows for the case of Finnish, in which vowels not contrastive for [±back] are invisible in a search for harmonic values.

(19) *Parametric visibility*
A harmony rule R for the feature [F] may parameterize its search domain only to *contrastive* values for [F].

There is a different tradition for treating vowels invisible to harmony (e.g., Steriade 1987; Dresher 2003), in which vowels that do not participate in harmony for a feature [±F] (like Finnish /i/) literally lack a feature [−F] in the representation. This solution cannot be pursued for the invisibility of Finnish /i/ to [±back] harmony because the feature [−back] is independently needed on /i/ in order to explain the phenomenon of Finnish assibilation, whereby the coronal stop /t/ becomes a sibilant [s] when immediately preceding /i/.[4]

(20) *Finnish assibilation*
/t/ → [s] before [+high, −back] (Kiparsky 1973)
   a. halut-a 'want-INF'
   b. halus-i 'want-PAST'

Hall and Hamann (2006) characterize the assibilation process as a crucial result of the [+high, −back] features on the aerodynamic realization of obstruents. However, if Finnish /i/ literally lacks [−back], assibilation cannot be characterized in these terms, because the conditioning feature would have to be absent from the representation. While depriving /i/ of [−back] does work in making it invisible for harmony, such a representation leaves us puzzled as to why that same vowel should trigger assibilation. A rule-ordering solution, in which /i/ lacks [−back], then harmony happens, then /i/ becomes [+back], then assibilation happens, would be a possible account, but an explanation of why harmony comes first for all such processes would be lacking. In fact, there are instances of invisibility in harmony that cannot be solved by using underspecification algorithms based on predictability or redundancy (see section 3.12). The proper solution, then, is one in which /i/ is fully specified for [−back] *throughout* the phonology, but certain processes (e.g., harmony) are sensitive to what values of a feature are visible for their search domain.

As the phonology of Finnish requires /i/ to have a [−back] feature in its representation in order to describe assibilation, the right solution to the invisibility of /i/ in harmony must be that harmonic search—but not assibilation—is sensitive to contrastiveness. /i/ is "transparent" in Finnish vowel harmony because the affixes searching for a donor from which to copy have relativized their search so as to exclude noncontrastive values.

A similar argument that nonparticipating vowels must still be specified for the feature [−back] comes from Votic, in which /i/ is noncontrastive and transparent (e.g., [koːkkima] 'to dig', [kalli-łła] 'dear-ALLTV'). Blumenfeld and Toivonen (2009) show that while [+back] harmony that skips /i/ might suggest that /i/ has no [−back] feature, a second process of /l/-fronting before front vowels requires it to have one: compare [łuzikka] 'spoon' with [lidnaː] 'town'. Like Finnish assibilation, then, a nonharmonic process in Votic requires /i/ to be [−back], ruling out models in which it is invisible because it lacks specification.[5] Instead, the harmony process is relativized to *contrastive* values of [−back], thereby excluding /i/ from the search domain, while the adjacent consonant-vowel phonotactics are sensitive to all values of [−back].

Besides Finnish assibilation, there is another argument that invisibility of noncontrastive vowels to harmony must be due to the nature of the Search algorithm rather than to inherent properties of the vowels. This argument is based on Hungarian. Like Finnish, Hungarian has [±back] harmony in which /i/ is not contrastive for [±back].[6]

(21) *Hungarian vowel inventory (where "(ː)" indicates that a long version is also possible)*

[−back, −rd]	[−back, +rd]	[+back, +rd]	[+back, −rd]	
i(ː)	ü(ː)	u(ː)		[+high]
e(ː)	ö(ː)	o(ː)	a(ː)	[−high]

By the definition of contrastiveness established above, /i/ is noncontrastive in Hungarian. Because it is relativized to contrastive sources only, it is thereby transparent in [±back] harmony, in a manner parallel to /i/ in Finnish.

(22) *Hungarian dative suffix harmony: [-nak]/[-nek]*
    a. **bikaː**-nak   'bull-DAT'
    b. **kostüm**-nek   'costume-DAT'
    c. **kavit͡ʃ**-nak   'pebble-DAT'
    d. **aktiːv**-nak   'active-DAT'

The invisibility of /i/ in (22c–d) appears to show that, as in Finnish, this vowel is transparent to harmony in Hungarian. However, Farkas and Beddor (1987) and Ringen and Kontra (1989) discovered that when there is *more than one noncontrastive vowel in a row*, speakers exhibit variation in what they produce. While a one-/i/ word such as *aktiːv* always takes a [+back] suffix, a two-/i/ word such as *aszpirin* shows variation between *-nek* and *-nak*.

(23) *Hungarian "vacillating" stems with more than one noncontrastive vowel*
    ✓aszpirin-nak, ✓aszpirin-nek
    (*compare* ✓aktiːv-nak, *aktiːv-nek)

The fact that one instance of the vowel /i/ does not provide a [−back] value for harmony, but two instances seem to do so, suggests that we cannot simply state that /i/ has no value for [−back] throughout the language, because if this were the case we should expect no difference between one and two instances of "nothingness." In chapter 5, we will return to the reason that words with one noncontrastive vowel differ from words with two noncontrastive vowels, in the context of the role of prosodic constituents in "bounding" the extent of a harmony domain. At this point in the discussion, we can infer that Hungarian /i/ must have a representation beyond total invisibility in order for it to rear its head in cases like [ɒspirin-nɒk, ɒspirin-nɛk].

Taking the arguments from Finnish assibilation and Hungarian multiple-noncontrastive-vowel words together, we can see that the correct representation of noncontrastive vowels such as /i/ must include the feature [−back], since we can find evidence for its phonological activity outside the more elementary cases of harmony.

The existence of transparent vowels in harmony systems does not require revising the fundamental Search algorithm—merely relativizing its domain. Much of the observed crosslinguistic variation in grammatical processes results from variation not in the core computational procedure employed, but in the set of elements it operates over. Finnish vowel harmony is a clear case in which the basic algorithm for [±back] harmony (described for Turkish in chapter 2) remains the same, but in which the algorithm's effects differ once we move to a language with a less symmetric vowel inventory. In particular, Turkish has the [+high, +back, −round] vowel /ɨ/, while Finnish does not, and this makes all the difference.

The discussion above and in chapter 2 would seem to suggest that Turkish and Finnish differ in that the former has a process of copying [±back] from the closest vowel while the latter has a process of copying [±back] from the closest *contrastive* vowel. Since all vowels in Turkish are contrastive for [±back], the Turkish case is ambiguous between relativizing to only-contrastive vowels and not doing so. Several considerations will lead us to conclude that both languages actually relativize to only segments contrastive for [±back].

We have already seen evidence that Turkish suffixes sometimes copy their value from a consonant, as in the case of palatalized liquids. This is precisely because these segments are contrastive for [±back] as well. If indeed [±back] harmony in Turkish (and throughout the Turkic language family) therefore is relativized to contrastive values of [±back], we make two predictions: (1) any consonant in Turkic that is contrastive for [±back] will be included in the search domain, and (2) any vowel in Turkic that is not contrastive for [±back] will not be included in the search domain. We now turn to a Turkic language with a very unusual segmental inventory that confirms both predictions and, in doing so, provides welcome support for the central role of contrastiveness in delimiting the search domain.

3.5 Contrastiveness Determines Karaim (Consonant) Harmony

Karaim (Kowalski 1929; Hamp 1976; Csató and Nathan 2002) is an endangered Turkic language (spoken in Lithuania) similar to Turkish in its formulation of the harmony process but, because of its consonant inventory, radically different in terms of the surface effects of harmony. Geographically, Karaim is an outlier language within the Turkic family, and it has been embedded in a Baltic- and Slavic-speaking environment and subject to extensive language contact persisting over many centuries. In the late fourteenth century, a sizable population of Karaim were relocated from their original homeland on the Crimean peninsula to the town of Trakai (near Vilnius, Lithuania). An important factor in the development of *consonant* harmony and the loss of vowel harmony has been prolonged contact with neighboring Slavic and Baltic languages, where palatalization is contrastive in consonants and [±back] is not independently contrastive in vowels. (The diachronic scenario is discussed further in Nevins and Vaux 2003 and Hansson 2007b.)

In Karaim, all consonants (except glides) participate in harmony, because they are contrastive for [±back], and all noninitial vowels do not participate, because they are not contrastive for [±back]. This leads to the interesting phenomenon of "consonant harmony." Karaim suffixal consonants seeking a harmonic value for [±back] can skip right over vowels and copy their value from another consonant.

The transparency of Karaim vowels to [±back] harmony in noninitial syllables may be understood as another instantiation of search domains that exclude noncontrastive segments. For Karaim, this transparency must be relativized to positional contrast, since it is not the case that the feature [±back] is absolutely noncontrastive in its feature-set on certain vowels; rather, it is only noncontrastive on those vowels *in certain positions*. Like Turkish, Karaim has the inventory of eight surface vowels shown in (24).

(24) *Karaim vowel inventory*

[−back, −rd]	[−back, +rd]	[+back, −rd]	[+back, +rd]	
i	⟨ü⟩	⟨ɯ⟩	u	[+high]
⟨e⟩	⟨ö⟩	a	o	[−high]

Unlike what we find with Turkish vowels, however, the bracketed vowels in (24) are distributionally restricted. In noninitial syllables, there are no contrasts between the [−high, −round] vowels /a,e/ or between the [+round] vowels /ü,u/ and /ö,o/, and there is a limited contrast between the [+high, −round] vowels /i,ɯ/. Let us turn to the details of these positional restrictions on contrast.

The vowel /e/ is found only in initial syllables; in noninitial syllables, only /a/ occurs (and /a/ can also occur in initial syllables). The contrast in initial syllables is observed in [k^{hj}el^j] 'to come' versus [k^{h}al$^\gamma$] 'to remain'. Lack of the contrast in noninitial syllables can be seen in forms such as [el^j-d^{j}an^j] 'hand-ABL' (cf. Turkish [el-den]); only [a] is found in the suffix, despite the [−back] harmonic value of the root.

The contrasts among the [+round] vowels are confined to absolute word-initial position (i.e., to vowel-initial words): one finds [öz^j] 'self' versus [on] 'ten', as well as [üsʲtʲ] 'top, upper' versus [us] 'reason, intellect' (cf. Turkish [üst], [us]). Neutralization of the contrast to [+back] /u,o/ is observed in all other environments: for example, [tʰʲuzʲ] 'smooth' and [tʰuz] 'salt' (cf. Turkish [düz], [tuz]).

In Karaim, therefore, vowels with [±back] contrasts among [−high] vowels and [+round] vowels occur *only in initial syllables*. The [+high, −round] pair /i,ɯ/, as shown in (25) for the genitive [-nɯn]/[-nʲinʲ], does contrast in noninitial syllables (though only /i/ is allowed in absolute-initial position: for example, [inʲa] 'needle' and [irlˠa-] 'to sing' (cf. Turkish [iːne], [irla])).

In suffixes such as [-nɯn]/[-nʲinʲ], the initial consonant [n]/[nʲ] of the suffix copies the closest leftward [±back] value, and subsequent segments in turn copy the value of [±back] from it.

(25) *Complete harmony for [±back] genitive suffixes in Karaim*
    a. tʰav   tʰav-nɯn   'mountain / mountain-GEN'   (cf. Tk. [dağ-in])
    b. elʲ   elʲ-nʲinʲ   'hand / hand-GEN'   (cf. Tk. [el-nin])

Whereas Karaim shares with other Turkic languages the property of [±back] harmony in suffixes that contain [−high] or [+round] vowels, it differs insofar as the harmonic feature surfaces on consonants rather than vowels. Representative alternations for the plural [-lʲarʲ]/[-lar] and the ablative [-tʰʲanʲ]/[-tan] are shown in (26) and (27).

(26) *Consonant [±back] harmony for plural and ablative suffixes in Karaim*
    a. suv   suv-dan   'water / water-ABL'   (cf. Tk. [su-dan])
    b. tʰaʃ   tʰaʃ-tʰan   'stone / stone-ABL'   (cf. Tk. [taş-tan])
    c. mʲenʲ   mʲenʲ-dʲanʲ   'I / I-ABL'   (cf. Tk. [ben-den])
    d. kʰʲunʲ   kʰʲunʲ-dʲanʲ   'day / day-ABL'   (cf. Tk. [gün-den])
    e. kʰʲunʲ   kʰʲunʲ-lʲarʲ-dʲanʲ   'day / day-PL-ABL'   (cf. Tk. [gün-ler-den])
    f. kʰun   kʰun-lar-dan   'servant / servant-PL-ABL'   (cf. Tk. [kul-lar-dan])

In addition, Karaim exhibits forms that demonstrate multiple copying of [±back] by one suffix from another, such as that in (27) (Kowalski 1929, 69).

(27) *Iteration of back harmony through multiple suffixes in Karaim*
    tʰorʲa-sʲizʲ-lʲigʲ-imʲ-dʲanʲ   'from my injustice'

Notably, the palatal glide /j/ does not group with the palatalized consonants; it can occur in palatalized and nonpalatalized contexts alike, as the examples in (28) illustrate.

(28) *Nonparticipation of [−back] glide in Karaim consonant [+back] harmony*
    a. jol-daʃ-ɯm   'my fellow traveler'   (cf. Tk. [jol-daʃ-im])
    b. koj-maχ   'placing, putting'   (cf. Tk. [koj-mak])

Since glides are not contrastive for [±back] (as there is no [−consonantal, −vocalic, +high, +**back**, −round] segment in the Karaim inventory), the fact that the glide does not participate in harmony does not have to be stipulated: glides are noncontrastive in the inventory and are thereby excluded from the search domain.

In the examples above, noninitial [+back] vowels /a,o,u/ are transparent to consonant harmony even though they have [−back] counterparts that are allowed to surface in initial syllables. Supporting evidence for the phonetic transparency of these noninitial vowels is provided in Nevins and Vaux 2003, where spectrographic analysis reveals that F2 (the primary acoustic correlate of backness) is high for the palatalized consonants and dips low for the intervening back vowels. In other words, the intervening noncontrastive [+back] vowels phonetically "interrupt" the [−back] harmony across them, but phonologically are irrelevant for harmony.

In summary, Karaim exhibits the following positional restrictions:

(29) a. In Karaim, [−back] is banned from cooccurring with [+round] outside of absolute-initial position (i.e., onsetless initial syllables).
    b. [−back] is banned from cooccurring with [−high] outside of initial syllables (e.g., initial syllables, onsetless or not).
    c. [+back] is banned from cooccurring with [+high, −round] in absolute-initial position (i.e., onsetless initial syllables).

There are many languages that exhibit restrictions on the distribution of segments or features in noninitial positions. Karaim is thus not unique in this respect; compare for example Tamil, which systematically bans mid vowels from noninitial syllables (Christdas 1988). Given the positionally restricted distribution of the above-mentioned vowels in Karaim's harmony system, the relativization to contrastive status for [±back] is not only a function of the inventory, but also a function of position within a word.

(30) *Positional contrastiveness*
    A segment S in position P is *contrastive* for the feature [F] iff there is a segment S′ in the inventory that is featurally identical to S for all values except [F], *and* S′ can occur in position P as well.

Contrastiveness, Markedness, and Feature-Based Locality

The inclusion of positional contrastiveness within the harmony specification for a morpheme is exemplified in (31).

(31) *Karaim genitive, ablative, plural suffixes must:*
   Back-Harmonize: δ = left, F = [positionally contrastive: ±back]

The effect of positional contrastiveness is illustrated for [k^{hj}un^j-l^{j}ar^j] 'day-PL' in (32)–(35). The initial consonant of the plural suffix finds the closest positionally contrastive value ([−back] in this case), and the final consonant of the plural suffix subsequently copies [−back] from it, across the noncontrastive [+back] vowel.

(32) *Plural suffix begins positionally contrastive Back-Harmonize in [k^{hj}un^j-l^{j}ar^j]*

$$\begin{array}{cccccc} x_1 & x_2 & x_3 & \leftarrow \quad x_4 & x_5 & x_6 \\ \begin{bmatrix} -\text{voc} \\ \text{dors} \\ -\text{cont} \\ -\text{voi} \\ -\text{back} \end{bmatrix} & \begin{bmatrix} +\text{voc} \\ +\text{high} \\ +\text{rd} \\ +\text{back} \end{bmatrix} & \begin{bmatrix} -\text{voc} \\ \text{cor} \\ +\text{nas} \\ -\text{back} \end{bmatrix} & \begin{bmatrix} -\text{voc} \\ \text{cor} \\ +\text{lat} \\ +\text{son} \\ -\text{nas} \end{bmatrix} & \begin{bmatrix} +\text{voc} \\ -\text{high} \\ -\text{rd} \\ +\text{back} \end{bmatrix} & \begin{bmatrix} -\text{voc} \\ \text{cor} \\ +\text{lat} \\ -\text{liq} \end{bmatrix} \end{array}$$

(33) *Initial consonant of plural suffix copies [−back] in [k^{hj}un^j-l^{j}ar^j]*

$$\begin{array}{cccccc} x_1 & x_2 & x_3 & \text{↱} \quad x_4 & x_5 & x_6 \\ \begin{bmatrix} -\text{voc} \\ \text{dors} \\ -\text{cont} \\ -\text{voi} \\ -\text{back} \end{bmatrix} & \begin{bmatrix} +\text{voc} \\ +\text{high} \\ +\text{rd} \\ +\text{back} \end{bmatrix} & \begin{bmatrix} -\text{voc} \\ \text{cor} \\ +\text{nas} \\ \mathbf{-back} \end{bmatrix} & \begin{bmatrix} -\text{voc} \\ \text{cor} \\ +\text{lat} \\ +\text{son} \\ -\text{nas} \\ \mathbf{-back} \end{bmatrix} & \begin{bmatrix} +\text{voc} \\ -\text{high} \\ -\text{rd} \\ +\text{back} \end{bmatrix} & \begin{bmatrix} -\text{voc} \\ \text{cor} \\ +\text{lat} \\ -\text{liq} \end{bmatrix} \end{array}$$

(34) *Final consonant of plural suffix begins positionally contrastive Back-Harmonize in [k^{hj}un^j-l^{j}ar^j]*

$$\begin{array}{cccccc} x_1 & x_2 & x_3 & x_4 & x_5 & \leftarrow \quad x_6 \\ \begin{bmatrix} -\text{voc} \\ \text{dors} \\ -\text{cont} \\ -\text{voi} \\ -\text{back} \end{bmatrix} & \begin{bmatrix} +\text{voc} \\ +\text{high} \\ +\text{rd} \\ +\text{back} \end{bmatrix} & \begin{bmatrix} -\text{voc} \\ \text{cor} \\ +\text{nas} \\ -\text{back} \end{bmatrix} & \begin{bmatrix} -\text{voc} \\ \text{cor} \\ +\text{lat} \\ +\text{son} \\ -\text{nas} \\ -\text{back} \end{bmatrix} & \begin{bmatrix} +\text{voc} \\ -\text{high} \\ -\text{rd} \\ +\text{back} \end{bmatrix} & \begin{bmatrix} -\text{voc} \\ \text{cor} \\ +\text{lat} \\ -\text{liq} \end{bmatrix} \end{array}$$

(35) *Final consonant of plural suffix copies [−back]*

x_1	x_2	x_3	x_4	x_5	x_6
$\begin{bmatrix} -\text{voc} \\ \text{dors} \\ -\text{cont} \\ -\text{voi} \\ -\text{back} \end{bmatrix}$	$\begin{bmatrix} +\text{voc} \\ +\text{high} \\ +\text{rd} \\ +\text{back} \end{bmatrix}$	$\begin{bmatrix} -\text{voc} \\ \text{cor} \\ +\text{nas} \\ -\text{back} \end{bmatrix}$	$\begin{bmatrix} -\text{voc} \\ \text{cor} \\ +\text{lat} \\ +\text{son} \\ -\text{nas} \\ -\textbf{back} \end{bmatrix}$	$\begin{bmatrix} +\text{voc} \\ -\text{high} \\ -\text{rd} \\ +\text{back} \end{bmatrix}$	$\begin{bmatrix} -\text{voc} \\ \text{cor} \\ +\text{lat} \\ -\text{liq} \\ -\textbf{back} \end{bmatrix}$
k^{hj}	u	n^j	l^j	a	r^j

Karaim's unusual system of [±back] harmony that skips noncontrastive vowels and includes contrastive consonants enables us to draw an important conclusion. Karaim constitutes a system with a harmony rule identical to that of Finnish (and indeed, Turkish as well), in which [±back] harmony is relativized to copy only from contrastively [±back] donors. However, because of the radically different segmental inventory of Karaim, this single principled Search procedure yields surprising effects. As the paradigmatic component of language (in this case, the basic "lexicon" of consonants and vowels) is the locus of idiosyncratic patterning due to arbitrary historical effects (in the case of Karaim, these historical effects included intense language contact between Turkic and Balto-Slavic), this is the component of linguistic structure that we expect to yield variation in syntagmatic patterning in turn. Importantly, however, all three languages, Finnish, Turkish, and Karaim, can be argued to follow exactly the same algorithm: suffixal segments in need of a value for [±back] copy it from the closest source that is positionally contrastive for that value.[7]

Thus far, we have considered how the Search algorithm for harmony may exhibit crosslinguistic variation as the result of the search domain itself being pruned of certain segments, specifically the noncontrastive ones. Besides contrastiveness, the second important inventory-based property of segments bearing a feature [±F] is whether [αF] is the marked or unmarked value of the feature. Finnish and Karaim have been demonstrated to show "transparency" effects for segments that are not contrastive for [±F]; we now turn to cases where segments act transparent because they do not have the marked value for [±F].

3.6 Markedness in Binary Feature Systems

Trubetzkoy (1931) was one of the first to propose that in certain binary oppositions, grammatical processes treat one member of the opposition differently from the other. In the binary opposition encoded featurally by [±voice], grammar does not treat both values equally, instead seeming to "prefer" [−voice] over [+voice], in the sense that inventories are more often built out of [−voice] segments than out of [+voice] segments. In addition, positionally restricted contrasts neutralize the opposition to [−voice], as in the widespread process of coda devoicing found in German, Turkish, Russian, and many other languages. The value of a binary feature that is asymmetrically dispreferred in paradigmatic arrangements and in syntagmatic neutralization rules is referred to as the *marked* value of the feature, notated here as [mF], as opposed to [uF], the unmarked value.

Jakobson (1941) developed psycholinguistic correlates of the theory of markedness, focusing on the asymmetric treatment of marked features in language acquisition and aphasia, in both of which marked features are produced less frequently than their unmarked counterparts. Greenberg (1963) advanced the notion of markedness in his crosslinguistic work on universals of language inventories, proposing that an implicational relation holds between the marked and unmarked values of a feature: if a language allows [mF] in a feature bundle B, it will also allow [uF] in B. For example, languages that possess voiced fricatives will also possess voiceless fricatives. Both Jakobson's and Greenberg's strands of research converged on the conclusion that language change favors loss of the marked member of a binary featural opposition rather than the converse.

Following the implicational treatment of markedness by Greenberg and the neutralizational treatment of markedness of Trubetzkoy, markedness enjoyed continued interest in the generative tradition, launched by Chomsky and Halle (1968, chap. 9).[8] In the last twenty years, phonological research has continued to focus on markedness values of particular features in predicting implicational relations among vowel inventories (e.g., Calabrese 1988; Archangeli and Pulleyblank 1994), and in predicting patterns of contrast-neutralization to the unmarked feature. De Lacy (2006), in a thorough study of syntagmatic processes of neutralization and assimilation, concludes that phonological processes (encoded as constraints in his formulation) may refer to [±F] or to [mF], but never solely to [uF]. In other words, a phonological process banning the occurrence of a feature in a certain position may refer to both values of a given feature, or to only the marked value of a feature, but never to the unmarked feature alone.

The treatment of segments included in the search domain of a vowel harmony process follows the same logic. A vowel harmony rule may be formulated so as to allow copying from either value of the harmonic feature (e.g., either value of [±low] in a two-height system) or from the marked value alone (e.g., [+low] alone), but never from the unmarked value alone (e.g., [−low] alone).

3.7 Sibe Harmony and the Context-Free Markedness Value [+low]

Sibe (pronounced [ʃi-be]) is a Tungusic language of western China, described by Li (1996), which demonstrates context-free markedness in long-distance harmony. The vowel inventory of Sibe is composed of three binary distinctions, [±back], [±round], and [±low], resulting in eight vowels.

(36) *Sibe vowel inventory*

[−back, +rd]	[−back, −rd]	[+back, −rd]	[+back, +rd]	
ü	i	ɨ	u	[−low]
ö	ɛ	a	ɔ	[+low]

Long-distance harmony in Sibe occurs in a feature-copying process whereby a suffixal consonant seeks a value for [±low] from a leftward vowel. The search for a value-donor can potentially skip intervening vowels, even ones contrastive for this feature. The transparency of all vowels except those that bear the marked feature value for [±low] yields a long-distance harmonic copying between a suffixal velar consonant and a preceding low vowel. Before illustrating this process, I discuss the markedness of this feature-value in Sibe.

3.7.1 The Markedness of [+low] in Sibe

I assume that certain feature-values may be subject to language-specific markedness statements, and that while [+low] may be naturally unmarked, as Jakobson (1941) proposes, it is *logically* marked in Sibe, as determined by the observation and analysis of language-specific phonotactics.[9] We can see that [+low] is the marked value in Sibe by looking at three sources of distributional evidence, all of which point to the asymmetric grammatical treatment of this feature value as opposed to its unmarked counterpart. The first source of evidence is cooccurrence restrictions: on the basis of observations over the Sibe lexicon, Li (1996, 203) concludes that "Sibe has a restriction on low vowel co-occurrence within the domain of a phonological word." Li notes that, by and large, the appearance of multiple low vowels in a word is disfavored. The observation that a marked feature-value may occur in a word, but to a limited extent, is found also in cooccurrence biases in the lexicon of Japanese, where more than one instance of marked [+voice] in a word is dispreferred (Ito and Mester 2003). This often-used diagnostic for markedness points toward a cooccurrence bias in Sibe against multiple instances of the marked value [+low].

A second source of evidence is the distribution of vowels in suffixes. Most suffixes in Sibe contain a single high vowel (Li 1996, 199–203). The relative distributional bias toward [−low] vowels in suffixes suggests that this is the unmarked value for [±low] in Sibe, especially in light of research suggesting that affixes tend to draw from the unmarked pool of segments within a given language. For example, English inflectional affixes draw only from the coronal consonants, Lushootseed has glottalized consonants only in roots and lexical suffixes (Urbanczyk 1995), and Cuzco Quechua does not have aspirated stops in suffixes (Beckman 1998). These cases illustrate that affixal inventories are very often reduced in favor of the unmarked values of segmental contrasts, and they support the view that the relative dearth of [+low] vowels in Sibe suffixes is due to their marked status.

In addition, vocalic epenthesis in Sibe always inserts a [−low] vowel (either high back round [u] or high back unround [ɨ], owing to [±round] harmony with the immediately preceding vowel). Examples are shown in (37) and (38).

(37) *Sibe epenthesis with accusative ending /-v/*
    a. εχ-i-v   'large.bead-ACC'
    b. tasχ-i-v   'tiger-ACC'
    c. döv-u-v   'fox-ACC'
    d. mul-u-v   'beam-ACC'

(38) *Sibe epenthesis between causative /-v/ and present-future tense /-m/*
    a. ömi-v-i-m   'drink-CAUS-PRES.FUT'
    b. va-v-i-m   'kill-CAUS-PRES.FUT'
    c. çöndʐü-v-u-m   'elect-CAUS-PRES.FUT'
    d. bu-v-u-m   'give-CAUS-PRES.FUT'

Finally, diachronic evidence also points to the conclusion that low vowels are marked in Sibe. Zhang (1996) compares Sibe with its predecessor, Classical Manchu. Classical Manchu had stress on the final syllable, while Sibe has moved stress to the initial syllable, likely under the influence of Mandarin Chinese (Zhang 1996, 151). Importantly, Sibe has raised Classical Manchu /a/ and /o/ to /ɨ/ and /u/, respectively. The raising of [+low] vowels under loss of stress can be directly attributed to the markedness of [+low] in vowels. Stem vowels no longer protected by positional prominence lost their marked [+low] feature in Sibe.[10] The diachronic loss of [+low] on what became unstressed vowels therefore supports the claim that [+low] is marked in Sibe.

The totality of evidence to the language learner from distributional asymmetries and from the quality of suffixes and epenthetic vowels that [+low] is the marked value of the feature—coupled with the hypothesis that one way for vowel harmony to narrow the search domain is to look only at marked values of the feature—leads us to expect that in such a language, unmarked values of [±low] may be treated as "transparent." As a result, search will continue until a marked value-source is found. This may yield the surface appearance of a long-distance harmony process: just like Finnish, where in a case like [koti-na] the suffix copies from a vowel as many as two syllables away because it is the closest contrastive-value source, Sibe has a process whereby a suffixal segment may copy from two syllables away because that will be the closest marked-value source.

3.7.2 Velar/Uvular Alternations as [+low] Harmony

The [+low] harmony process in Sibe takes place in a consonant-vowel interaction in which dorsal consonants (i.e., velar/uvular obstruents) engage in a harmonic search for a value of [±low] to their left and copy this value from a vowel.

Sibe opposes four pairs of velar and uvular consonants: /k/ and /q/, /g/ and /ɢ/, /x/ and /χ/, and /ɣ/ and /ʁ/. These segments are all dorsal consonants, articulated with the tongue body, but the pairs differ in their specification for [±low]. The [−low] segments /k,g,x,ɣ/ are velar, while the [+low] segments /q,ɢ,χ,ʁ/ are uvular.

Languages that oppose velar and uvular consonants may do so featurally with different means, depending on whether the particular language independently activates the features [±ATR], [±high], and/or [±low] (see Trigo 1991 for a thorough discussion). Chomsky and Halle (1968) suggested that uvulars are [−high, +back]. Trigo (1991) provides arguments that Turkana and Akha uvularization requires [−high] and demonstrates that in these languages, both [+ATR] /o/ and [−ATR] /ɔ/ can yield uvularization. Thus, in some languages, vowel height alone is sufficient for uvularization. In addition, it can be shown that the feature [+back] is not always necessary to induce uvularization. Yakut (Krueger 1962) illustrates such a case.

Yakut has an eight-vowel system, as shown in (39), with [±back] and [±round] harmony. [±round] harmony distinguishes two heights, [±high], where [−high] suffixal vowels alternate between [o] and [a].

(39) *Yakut vowel inventory*

[−back, +rd]	[−back, −rd]	[+back, −rd]	[+back, +rd]	
ü	i	ɨ	u	[+high]
ö	e	a	o	[−high]

Yakut dorsal consonants require [−high] for uvularization. Importantly, both /ö/ and /o/ can trigger uvularization, and therefore [+back] is not necessary for uvularization in this language. Consonantal alternations of this sort in suffixes can be illustrated with 2nd person plural /-gɨt/ (Krueger 1962, 89). Both [+back] (40c–d) and [−back] (40e–f) harmonic vowels may trigger uvularization, as long as they are [−high].

(40) *Yakut velar/uvular alternations*
    a. tiː-git   'boat-your.PL'
    b. kel-li-git   'came-2PL'
    c. saː-ʁit   'gun-your.PL'
    d. oʁo-ʁut   'child-your.PL'
    e. kinige-ʁit   'book-your.PL'
    f. öŋö-ʁüt   'service-your.PL'

We may conclude that velar/uvular alternations induced by vowels may be conditioned by [±low], [±high], or [±ATR], depending on the vowel features already present in the language. Returning to Sibe, let us adopt the following featural specifications for its dorsal consonants, given that Sibe does not have [±ATR] or [±high] contrasts among the vowels.

(41) *Sibe dorsal consonant inventory*

[−voi, −cont]	[+voi, −cont]	[−voi, +cont]	[+voi, +cont]	
k	g	x	ɣ	[−low]
q	ɢ	χ	ʁ	[+low]

The diminutive suffix for adjectives has four variants in Sibe (Li 1996, 201).[11] The alternation between a velar ([−low]) and uvular ([+low]) consonant in the suffix is determined by whether or not there is a preceding [+low] vowel anywhere in the word.[12]

(42) *Sibe diminutive suffix shows marked [+low] harmony*
    a. ildɨ(n)-kin   'bright-DIM'
    b. ɕümi(n)-kin   'deep-DIM'
    c. muxuli(n)-kin   'round-DIM'

d. udʐi(n)-kɨn 'heavy-DIM'
e. ça(n)-qɨn 'good-DIM'
f. sula-qɨn 'loose-DIM'
g. ɢɔlmi(n)-qɨn 'long-DIM'
h. adʐi(g)-qɨn 'small-DIM'
i. untuxu(n)-kun 'empty-DIM'
j. ulu-kun 'soft-DIM'
k. gɨltu(xun)-kun 'severe-DIM'
l. ɨrsu(n)-kun 'ugly-DIM'
m. tɔndɔ-qun 'honest-DIM'
n. χɔdu(n)-qun 'quick-DIM'
o. dzạlu-qun 'full-DIM'
p. farχu(n)-qun 'dark-DIM'

In (42a–d) and (42i–l), no [+low] vowel precedes the suffix, and as a result, the initial consonant of the suffix is supplied with default [−low] [k]. In (42e–f) and (42m), where the stem vowel that is closest to the suffix is [+low], the suffix surfaces with [q]. The most surprising cases are (42g–h) and (42n–p), in which the suffix surfaces with [q], even though the determining [+low] vowel is two syllables away and a [−low] vowel intervenes.

This velar/uvular alternation may demonstrate long-distance effects even across intervening suffixes. Hence, when the reciprocal suffix /-ndu/ precedes the past tense suffix, the uvular variant of the past tense suffix can be copied from a [+low] vowel three syllables away (43a). When there are no preceding [+low] vowels in the word, the suffix is realized as a velar (43b).

(43) *Sibe [+low] harmony separated by three syllables*
    a. qarɨ-ndu-χu 'protect-RECIP-PAST'
    b. nikɨ-ndu-xu 'rely.on-RECIP-PAST'

Velar/uvular alternations are not limited to the [−continuant] series of dorsal consonants. The suffix of the non-self-perceived immediate past tense shows an alternation between the voiceless velar fricative [x] and the voiceless uvular fricative [χ] (Li 1996, 202).

(44) *Long-distance uvularization harmony in Sibe past tense suffix*
    a. dzi̦-xɨ 'come-PAST'
    b. ti-xɨ 'sit-PAST'
    c. içi-xɨ 'be.enough-PAST'
    d. gɨnɨ-xɨ 'go-PAST'
    e. tɨsu-xu 'satisfy-PAST'

f. türü-xu   'rent-PAST'
g. utu-xu   'dress-PAST'
h. xinu-xu   'hate-PAST'
i. tükɛ-χi̵   'watch-PAST'
j. sav-χi̵   'see-PAST'
k. fɔndz̪i-χi̵ 'ask-PAST'
l. ömi-χi̵   'drink-PAST'
m. tɔ-χu   'curse-PAST'
n. gö-χu   'hit (the target)-PAST'
o. bɔdu-χu   'consider-PAST'
p. lavdu-χu   'become.more-PAST'

The Sibe data involving velar/uvular suffixes copying [+low] at long distance are of special interest to theories of the locality of phonological processes. In particular, a [+low] consonant copying across an intervening [−low] vowel exemplifies a case in which even *contrastive* segments are transparent to a harmony process.

The theory of locality that best explains the Sibe data is one that emphasizes the exclusion of certain intervening segments from the search domain. In an intervener-based theory of locality, a featural relation (such as harmony) may take place between any two segments within the word domain, as long as no segment *of the relevant type* intervenes. The notion of intervention in this approach depends not only on the presence of a feature but also on its values. Recall the main concept of this chapter, that each harmony process may vary parametrically *in its sensitivity to the values* of intervening segments.

Feature-sensitive relativization permits us to formulate the locality condition for Sibe uvularization: the suffixes in question seek the marked value [+low] anywhere in the word.[13] This process is illustrated in (45)–(46) for long-distance harmony of the initial consonant of the suffix in [χɔdu-qun] 'quick-DIM'.

(45) *Diminutive suffix begins marked [+low]-Harmonize in [χɔdu-qun]*

$$\begin{array}{cccccc} x_1 & x_2 & x_3 & \leftarrow \quad x_4 & x_5 & x_6 \\ \begin{bmatrix} +\text{voc} \\ +\text{rd} \\ +\text{back} \\ +\text{low} \end{bmatrix} & \begin{bmatrix} -\text{voc} \\ \text{cor} \\ -\text{cont} \\ +\text{voi} \end{bmatrix} & \begin{bmatrix} +\text{voc} \\ +\text{rd} \\ +\text{back} \\ -\text{low} \end{bmatrix} & \begin{bmatrix} -\text{voc} \\ \text{dors} \\ -\text{cont} \\ -\text{voi} \end{bmatrix} & \begin{bmatrix} +\text{voc} \\ +\text{back} \\ -\text{low} \end{bmatrix} & \begin{bmatrix} -\text{voc} \\ \text{cor} \\ +\text{nas} \end{bmatrix} \end{array}$$

(46) *Diminutive suffix finds and copies marked [+low]*

	x_1	⤺	x_2	x_3	x_4	x_5	x_6
	$\begin{bmatrix} +\text{voc} \\ +\text{rd} \\ +\text{back} \\ +\textbf{low} \end{bmatrix}$		$\begin{bmatrix} -\text{voc} \\ \text{cor} \\ -\text{cont} \\ +\text{voi} \end{bmatrix}$	$\begin{bmatrix} +\text{voc} \\ +\text{rd} \\ +\text{back} \\ -\text{low} \end{bmatrix}$	$\begin{bmatrix} -\text{voc} \\ \text{dors} \\ -\text{cont} \\ -\text{voi} \\ +\textbf{low} \end{bmatrix}$	$\begin{bmatrix} +\text{voc} \\ +\text{back} \\ -\text{low} \end{bmatrix}$	$\begin{bmatrix} -\text{voc} \\ \text{cor} \\ +\text{nas} \end{bmatrix}$
	ɔ		d	u	q	u	n

When there is no marked value [+low] anywhere leftward in the word, the search fails to find a copy-source and must as a last resort insert the default value [−low] on the dorsal consonant, as illustrated in (47)–(48) for [ulu-kun] 'soft-DIM'.

(47) *Diminutive suffix searches for marked [+low] in [ulu-kun]*

	x_1	x_2	x_3	←	x_4	x_5	x_6
	$\begin{bmatrix} +\text{voc} \\ +\text{rd} \\ +\text{back} \\ -\text{low} \end{bmatrix}$	$\begin{bmatrix} -\text{voc} \\ \text{cor} \\ +\text{lat} \end{bmatrix}$	$\begin{bmatrix} +\text{voc} \\ +\text{rd} \\ +\text{back} \\ -\text{low} \end{bmatrix}$		$\begin{bmatrix} -\text{voc} \\ \text{dors} \\ -\text{cont} \\ -\text{voi} \end{bmatrix}$	$\begin{bmatrix} +\text{voc} \\ +\text{back} \\ -\text{low} \end{bmatrix}$	$\begin{bmatrix} -\text{voc} \\ \text{cor} \\ +\text{nas} \end{bmatrix}$

(48) *Diminutive suffix fails to find marked [+low]; last-resort insertion takes place*

↔	x_1	x_2	x_3	x_4	x_5	x_6
	$\begin{bmatrix} +\text{voc} \\ +\text{rd} \\ +\text{back} \\ -\text{low} \end{bmatrix}$	$\begin{bmatrix} -\text{voc} \\ \text{cor} \\ +\text{lat} \end{bmatrix}$	$\begin{bmatrix} +\text{voc} \\ +\text{rd} \\ +\text{back} \\ -\text{low} \end{bmatrix}$	$\begin{bmatrix} -\text{voc} \\ \text{dors} \\ -\text{cont} \\ -\text{voi} \\ -low \end{bmatrix}$	$\begin{bmatrix} +\text{voc} \\ +\text{back} \\ -\text{low} \end{bmatrix}$	$\begin{bmatrix} -\text{voc} \\ \text{cor} \\ +\text{nas} \end{bmatrix}$
	u	l	u	k	u	n

As soon as the Sibe learner has determined that velar/uvular alternations are based on relativization to the marked value of [±low], the locality properties of the harmony process will follow: the search domain excludes all instances of unmarked values of [±low], even if they are contrastive, and proceeds leftward, potentially unboundedly. Like Finnish and Uyghur roots that contain no instances of contrastive vowels and thus require last-resort insertion in their suffixes, Sibe roots that contain no instances of marked vowels require last-resort insertion in their suffixes.

It is worth emphasizing again that crosslinguistic variation in "transparency"—the invisibility of intervening segments to the syntagmatic process of harmony—is not the result of a fundamentally different Search procedure, but the result of one small tweak in the feature-values included or excluded in the relativization of the search domain. These "tweaks" form a parametric space in which the Search procedure may be relativized to *all* values [±F], contrastive-only values [cF], or marked-only values [mF]. In all of the case studies considered here, the only ways in which the search procedure itself may vary (besides varying in the inventory of segments in the language and the inventory of affixes that require harmony) is (1) in the direction of search δ and (2) in the delimitation of the search domain by value-type τ: [±F, cF, mF].

Under this type of principles-and-parameters approach to crosslinguistic variation in harmony systems, in which the fundamental *copy-from-closest* principle of Search is invariant and a small number of parameters restrict the variation in the search domain itself, we may well expect to find "microvariation" between closely related languages showing identical harmony processes save for the setting of one of these parameters. A good example is the uvularization process of Sanjiazi Manchu, a sister language of Sibe, in which search is relativized is to [cF] and not to [mF], with ensuing differences in the resulting pattern of harmony.

3.7.3 Contrastive-Value Harmony in Sanjiazi Manchu

This emerging system of parametric differences in value-relativization predicts the possibility of a related language, completely analogous to Sibe, but in which access to contrastive values of [±low] determines the locality conditions of vowel-consonant uvularization. As another descendent of Classical Manchu, Sanjiazi Manchu is one of the languages most closely related to Sibe. Li (1996) examines the dialect spoken in Sanjiazi, in the western part of Heilongjiang province. Sanjiazi Manchu and Sibe have identical consonant inventories and almost identical vowel inventories.

(49) *Sanjiazi Manchu vowel inventory*

[−back, −rd]	[−back, +rd]	[+back, −rd]	[+back, +rd]	
i	ü	ɨ	u	[−low]
æ		a	ɔ	[+low]

Like Sibe, Sanjiazi Manchu shows velar/uvular alternations in the dorsal consonants of the past tense suffix, [-xa]/[-xɨ]/[-xu]/[-xɔ], with rounding harmony determining the quality of the suffix vowel. However, unlike in Sibe, the visibility of intervening feature-values in Sanjiazi Manchu is sensitive to all *contrastive* values for [±low].

(50) *Sanjiazi Manchu alternations in the past tense (Li 1996, 182)*
    a. qa-χa   'obstruct-PAST'
    b. mɨla-χa   'roar-PAST'
    c. ṣudẓa-χa   'rely on-PAST'
    d. sæ-χa   'bite-PAST'
    e. ɔm-χɔ   'drink-PAST'
    f. davɨ-xɨ   'stride-PAST'
    g. ildɨ-xɨ   'shine-PAST'
    h. dazɨ-xɨ   'repair-PAST'
    i. tæri-xɨ   'plant-PAST'
    j. sü-xu   'mix-PAST'
    k. dɔndẓi̯-xɨ   'listen-PAST'
    l. matʃu-xu   'grow.thinner-PAST'

As (50a–e) show, when the contrastive value for [±low] nearest to the dorsal consonant of the suffix is borne by a [+low] vowel, the suffix surfaces with [+low] uvular [χ]. On the other hand, as (50f–l) show, when the closest contrastive value is [−low], the suffix surfaces with [−low] velar [x]. Thus, no long-distance copying of [+low] across an intervening [−low] segment can occur in Sanjiazi Manchu, because the intervening values of [−low] are contrastive.[14]

The distinct parameterization of intervener visibility between Sanjiazi Manchu and Sibe is apparent when we compare Sanjiazi Manchu [dɔndẓi̯-xɨ], in which contrastive [−low] is visible and yields a velar alternant in the suffix, with its near-minimal-pair Sibe counterpart [fɔndẓi̯-χi] 'ask-PAST', where only marked [+low] is visible, yielding a uvular alternant. Sanjiazi Manchu uvularization is thus formally identical to uvularization in Sibe, with the difference in parametric visibility of the specified features resulting in different harmony behavior.

One might ask whether the differing parametric setting of Sanjiazi Manchu—namely, contrastive-only rather than marked-only harmony for [±low]—correlates with any other aspect of the language. It is suggestive to notice that unlike Sibe, Sanjiazi Manchu has a process of contrastive [±low] harmony affecting suffixal vowels as well as the suffix-initial dorsal consonant: compare Sibe past tense [-xi]/[-χi] with Sanjiazi Manchu [-xi]/[-xu]/[-xa]/[-xɔ]/[-χi]/[-χu]/[-χa]/[-χɔ]. In Sanjiazi Manchu, the suffixal vowel alternates according to [±low] harmony (as well as [±round] harmony). While there is no formal mechanism within the present theory to link the presence of featural harmony for [±F] on the nucleus of an affix to the pattern of featural harmony for [±F] on a separate consonant of that affix (and indeed, the theory should be flexible enough to allow independent harmonic needs on distinct segments of a suffix, as discussed for Turkish progressive /-ijor/ in section 2.6), the existence of [cF] harmony among Sanjiazi Manchu suffixal vowels may bias the learner to adopt a uniform parametric setting for the suffixal consonants.

To conclude, the [±low] harmony values sought by dorsal consonants in two closely related languages, Sanjiazi Manchu and Sibe, differ only in which paradigmatic property they are sensitive to: contrastiveness or markedness. In the following section, we examine other harmony systems that relativize their search domain to marked values.

3.8 Context-Sensitive Markedness and Sources of [+round]

The distributional evidence for the marked status of [+low] in Sibe in section 3.7.1 pointed to the conclusion that, along the binary opposition [±low], one value of the feature is clearly dispreferentially treated by grammatical processes. However, it is not always the case that the marked value of a binary feature can be identified in purely context-free terms. In particular, for many binary features, their marked value is really only marked within the context of other features. For example, even [+voice], one of the most canonically discussed cases of a marked feature-value, is only marked in obstruents—for example, in the context of [−sonorant]. In languages where [±voice] is neutralized to [−voice] in coda positions (e.g., Turkish, Russian, German), this neutralization only affects [−sonorant] segments; and indeed, [+sonorant] segments are all [+voice]. Thus, even some of the most well-known examples of marked feature-values carry an implicit contextual restriction imposed by other features with which the opposition occurs.

When it comes to features such as [±round], there is no obvious context-free value that is the marked one crosslinguistically or psycholinguistically. However, when [+round] is paired with certain other feature-values (e.g., [−back]), it is marked, and when [−round] is paired with certain other feature-values (e.g., [+back]), *it* is marked. It becomes apparent that while [+round] is not inherently marked, once it is in the context of a feature bundle that includes [−back], [+round] is the marked value of the opposition. In other words, [+round] is context-sensitively marked when in the presence of [−back], most likely because of the antagonistic effects that these two features have on the length of the vocal tract "tube" corresponding to F2. Similarly, [+round] is marked when in the context of [−high] (the vowel /o/ being more marked than /u/), arguably because of the interaction between lip rounding and lower jaw position. In sections 3.8.1 and 3.8.2, we examine the patterning of [±round] harmony in several languages, as harmony for this feature exhibits a number of instructive interactions with context-sensitive markedness.

3.8.1 Context-Sensitive Markedness of [+round]

As discussed above, neither [+round] nor [−back] is marked by itself in vowel systems, but their combination is marked. The context-sensitive markedness of [+round] in [−back] and [−high] vowels is proposed in Chomsky and Halle 1968, 405; Calabrese 1988, 22; and Archangeli and Pulleyblank 1994, 78.

(51) *Context-sensitive markedness statements*
 a. [+round] is marked in the context of [−back].
 b. [+round] is marked in the context of [−high].

In addition to the implicational relationships between marked and unmarked supporting (51) (e.g., a language with [−back, +round] will also have [−back, −round], and a language with [−high, +round] will also have [−high, −round]), there is articulatory, acoustic, and perceptual evidence for these context-sensitive markedness values. Using photographic evidence, Linker (1982) shows that lip-rounding activity for [+round] is greater in high vowels than in their nonhigh counterparts and that back vowels are more rounded than their nonback counterparts. In the realm of acoustic phonetics, Stevens (1998, 293–294) concludes that the acoustic consequences of adding lip rounding to back vowels are greater than would be achieved by adding lip rounding to front vowels; similarly, lip rounding has more dramatic acoustic consequences for high vowels than for nonhigh vowels. Finally, Kaun (1995, 121) interprets the results reported by Terbeek (1977) as demonstrating that rounding is perceptually more robust in [u] than in [o,ü,ö].

The typology of rounding harmony in the Altaic (e.g., Turkic, Tungusic, and Mongolian) languages is quite well-studied; see Korn 1969, Vaux 1993, and Kaun 1995 for extensive surveys of various types. Here, we will examine the effects of relativizing the search domain to marked values of [±round] as delimited in (51), thereby focusing on two of the widespread sources of parametric variation.[15]

Altai and Shor (two Turkic languages) have low-vowel suffixes that may only copy [+round] from marked sources—namely, vowels that are [−high] or [−back] (Korn 1969, 101). As a somewhat surprising result, these languages do not copy [+round] from /u/, even though this vowel clearly bears the feature [+round].

(52) *Altai rounding harmony: Limited to marked [+round] sources*
    a. kol   kol-do   'arm / arm-LOC'
    b. kös   kös-tör   'eye / eye-PL'
    c. kün   kün-dö   'day / day-LOC'
    d. už   už-ar   'fly / fly-AOR'

(53) *Shor rounding harmony: Limited to marked [+round] sources*
    a. kol   kol-don   'arm / arm-ABL'
    b. sös   sös-ton   'word / word-ABL'
    c. külük   külük-tö   'brave / brave-LOC'
    d. ug   ug-ar   'grasp / grasp-AOR'

Like Sibe marked [+low] harmony, illustrated earlier, Shor (and Altai) marked [+round] harmony involves relativizing the search domain so as to include only marked values of [±round]. For example, in [sös-ton], the affix finds a marked [+round] value (context-sensitively marked in the presence of [−back]).

(54) *Shor ablative suffix searches for marked [+round] source in [sös-ton]*

x_1	x_2	x_3	←	x_4	x_5	x_6
−voc cor +cont −voi	+voc −back −high +rd	−voc cor +cont −voi		−voc cor −cont −voi	+voc −back −high	−voc cor +nas

(55) *Ablative suffix finds and copies from marked [+round] source*

x_1	x_2	↰	x_3	x_4	x_5	x_6
−voc cor +cont −voi	+voc −back −high **+rd**		−voc cor +cont −voi	−voc cor −cont −voi	+voc −back −high **+rd**	−voc cor +nas
s	ö		s	t	o	n

When a root contains no marked values of [±round], the Search procedure will come back empty-handed. For example, in [ug-ar], the affix's search proceeds leftward, never finding a marked value of [±round] and thereby requiring last-resort insertion of the default value.

(56) *Shor aorist suffix searches for marked [+round] source in [ug-ar]*

$$x_1 \quad x_2 \quad \leftarrow \quad x_3 \quad x_4$$

$$\begin{bmatrix} +\text{voc} \\ +\text{back} \\ +\text{high} \\ +\text{rd} \end{bmatrix} \begin{bmatrix} -\text{voc} \\ \text{dors} \\ -\text{cont} \\ +\text{voi} \end{bmatrix} \begin{bmatrix} +\text{voc} \\ -\text{high} \\ +\text{back} \end{bmatrix} \begin{bmatrix} -\text{voc} \\ \text{cor} \\ +\text{son} \\ -\text{nas} \\ -\text{lat} \end{bmatrix}$$

(57) *Aorist suffix fails to find marked [+round] source; Last-resort insertion of [−round] takes place*

$$\leftarrow \quad x_1 \quad x_2 \quad x_3 \quad x_4$$

$$\begin{bmatrix} +\text{voc} \\ +\text{back} \\ +\text{high} \\ +\text{rd} \end{bmatrix} \begin{bmatrix} -\text{voc} \\ \text{dors} \\ -\text{cont} \\ +\text{voi} \end{bmatrix} \begin{bmatrix} +\text{voc} \\ -\text{high} \\ +\text{back} \\ -rd \end{bmatrix} \begin{bmatrix} -\text{voc} \\ \text{cor} \\ +\text{son} \\ -\text{nas} \\ -\text{lat} \end{bmatrix}$$

u　　　　g　　　　a　　　　r

The fact that Shor and Altai low vowels copy [+round] from /ü,ö,o/ but not /u/ and that no round harmony system has the opposite pattern (i.e., low vowels copy [+round] from /u/ but not from /ü,ö,o/) confirms that the Search algorithm can be relativized to include both values of [±round] or only the marked value of [±round], but can never be relativized to only include only the unmarked value of [±round].[16]

3.8.2 Microvariation in Kirghiz Dialects

In the earlier discussion of context-free markedness in harmony systems, we compared two closely related languages, Sibe and Sanjiazi Manchu, and we saw that they differ in a minimal parametric way: one is set to [search: cF] while the other is set to [search: mF]. In a parallel vein, minimal parametric variation based on value-relativization can be demonstrated with context-sensitive harmony systems, in this case from two different descriptions (arguably two distinct dialects or idiolects) of the same language: Kirghiz. I will refer to these two dialects as Kirghiz A and Kirghiz B.

Kirghiz A, as described by Comrie (1981), copies [+round] from /u/, thereby instantiating a system of copying from any contrastive [±round] source.

(58) *Kirghiz A rounding harmony (Comrie 1981, 61)*
　　a. köl　　köl-dön　　'lake / lake-ABL'
　　b. üy　　üy-dön　　'house / house-ABL'

c. tokoy   tokoy-don   'forest / forest-ABL'
d. tuz   tuz-don   'salt / salt-ABL'

However, Kirghiz B, as described by Hebert and Poppe (1963) (see also Johnson 1980), copies [±round] only from marked sources (like Altai and Shor), thereby failing to copy from /u/.

(59) *Kirghiz B rounding harmony (Hebert and Poppe 1963, 8)*
    a. köl   köl-dön   'lake / lake-ABL'
    b. üy   üy-dön   'house / house-ABL'
    c. tokoy   tokoy-don   'forest / forest-ABL'
    d. turmuš   turmus-tan   'life / life-ABL'

I assume that the differences in vowel harmony patterns described by Hebert and Poppe (1963) and Comrie (1981) represent coherent dialectal/idiolectal differences, of exactly the type we would expect in a model of harmony where the choice between [search: cF] and [search: mF] represents a restricted means for permitting individual grammars to vary while maintaining the same inventories and Search procedure.

(60) *Kirghiz A*
Ablative suffix must search leftward for closest contrastive value of [±round].
Kirghiz B
Ablative suffix must search leftward for closest marked value of [±round].

The more general conclusion to be drawn is that a system of restricted parametric options for what the domain of harmonic search is relativized to contain can capture the attested pattern of microvariation—without generating unattested patterns—by the mere "flipping of a switch": whether unmarked values of [±F] are excluded from search or not.

3.9 Microvariation in Yoruba Dialects

A further example of how dialectal variation can arise from one difference in setting the value-relativization parameter comes from comparing the Ifẹ dialect of Yoruba with the Standard dialect. As briefly introduced in chapter 1, in Yoruba vowel harmony all [−high, −low] vowels that are not the final vowel of the word must search for and copy a value of [±ATR] from their right. In other words, within a disyllabic root, the initial vowel depends on the value of [±ATR] from the final vowel.

(61) *Yoruba [±ATR] harmony in disyllabic roots*
    a. èwé   'lip'
    b. olè   'thief'
    c. èrò   'crowd'
    d. òd͡ʒò   'rain'
    e. ègɛ́   'cassava'
    f. ɔsɛ   'soap'
    g. ɛ̀fɔ́   'vegetable'
    h. ɔwɔ́   'hand'

Only the mid vowels are contrastive for [±ATR]. If vowel harmony is relativized to pay attention only to contrastive values of the harmonic feature, the high [+ATR] vowels—which have no contrastive counterpart—will be skipped in harmony, as is the case in Ifẹ Yoruba (Ola Orie 2001).

(62) *Ifẹ Yoruba contrastive [±ATR] harmony skips the irrelevant high vowel*
    a. ɔrúkɔ   'name'
    b. èlùbɔ́   'yam flour'
    c. ɛúrɛ́   'goat'
    d. ɔdídɛ   'parrot'
    e. ɔ̀títɔ́   'truth'

The formalization of Ifẹ Yoruba [±ATR] harmony in terms of the Search procedure and its parameters is provided in (63).

(63) *Ifẹ Yoruba nonfinal mid vowels must:*
    ATR-Harmonize: δ = right, F = [contrastive: ATR]

As a result of the setting in Ifẹ to contrastive values of [±ATR], medial high vowels in (62) exhibit "transparency," being skipped over for [−ATR] copying across them, even though they themselves are [+ATR]. Even more interestingly, the harmony pattern of Ifẹ Yoruba differs from that of Standard Yoruba, in which all of the words in (62) copy [+ATR] from the adjacent high vowel.

(64) *Standard Yoruba copies [+ATR] from the adjacent high vowel*
    a. orúkɔ   'name'
    b. èlùbɔ́   'yam flour'
    c. ewúrɛ́   'goat'
    d. odídɛ   'parrot'
    e. òtítɔ́   'truth'

The characterization of [±ATR] harmony in Standard Yoruba, then, is that it is sensitive to *all* values of [±ATR], whether contrastive or not.

(65) *Standard Yoruba nonfinal mid vowels must:*
ATR-Harmonize: δ = right, F = [all: ATR]

Parameterization in (65) does not permit skipping of noncontrastive high vowels in (64); everything is included in the search. (In chapter 5, I complete the analysis of Yoruba [±ATR] harmony with a discussion of the [+low] vowel /a/ in harmony.) Ifẹ and Standard Yoruba are two closely related dialects, with identical inventories and directionality of harmony, but they differ in what values of [±ATR] the Search algorithm "counts as relevant."

3.10 Variation in Obstruent Transparency in [±nasal] Harmony

Nasal harmony systems (e.g., as found throughout Colombia, Venezuela, and Brazil), in which the feature [±nasal] is copied by a variety of segments throughout a word, exhibit two distinct patterns of relativization (Piggott 1992). In the first pattern, inherently [−nasal] consonants such as /p,t,k/ are copied from. In the second, [−nasal] consonants such as /p,t,k/ are skipped over, and [+nasal] is copied across them (see Walker 1999 for phonetic evidence of transparency in such cases).

The difference between these two patterns lies in the relativization of the search: if all values of [±nasal] are included in the search, then clearly the [−nasal] voiceless obstruents will be copied from as well. If, on the other hand, only contrastive values of [±nasal] are included, then /p,t,k/ will be excluded from the search, as they are not contrastive for [±nasal], there being no other segments in the inventory that are [−continuant, −voice] but [+nasal].

In the first type of relativization, instantiated by Warao (Osborn 1966), voiceless obstruents "interrupt" [±nasal] harmony, as illustrated in (66) and (67). I assume that all noninitial vowels, glides, and /h/ (i.e., the [−consonantal] elements) are needy for the feature [±nasal] and must copy it from the closest source to their left. Like the pattern of [±back] harmony in the Turkic languages, in Warao [+nasal] harmony the initial vowel in the root is the only nonneedy segment. All [+consonantal] segments are inherently [+nasal] or [−nasal].

(66) *Warao segments copy [±nasal] from closest leftward source (Osborn 1966, 111–112)*
    a. ĩõ   'turtle'
    b. ũĩ   'angoleta bird'
    c. mõỹõ   'cormorant'
    d. mẽh̃õkohi 'shadow'
    e. nãõte   'he will come'
    f. mõãũpu 'give them to him'

(67) *Warao [−cons] segments must:*
Nasal-Harmonize: δ = left, F = [all: ±nasal]

The derivation for *nãõte* is shown in (68)–(71). There are two noninitial [−consonantal] segments; the first copies [+nasal] from the closest element to its left, and the second copies [−nasal] from the closest element to its left.

(68) *First noninitial [−consonantal] segment searches for [±nasal] in [nãõte]*

$$x_1 \quad x_2 \quad \leftarrow \quad x_3 \quad x_4 \quad x_5$$

$$\begin{bmatrix} +\text{cons} \\ +\text{son} \\ \text{cor} \\ -\text{cont} \\ +\text{nas} \end{bmatrix} \begin{bmatrix} -\text{cons} \\ +\text{son} \\ -\text{high} \\ +\text{low} \\ -\text{rd} \\ +\text{back} \\ +\text{nas} \end{bmatrix} \begin{bmatrix} -\text{cons} \\ +\text{son} \\ -\text{high} \\ -\text{low} \\ +\text{rd} \\ +\text{back} \end{bmatrix} \begin{bmatrix} +\text{cons} \\ -\text{son} \\ \text{cor} \\ -\text{cont} \\ -\text{nas} \end{bmatrix} \begin{bmatrix} -\text{cons} \\ +\text{son} \\ -\text{high} \\ -\text{low} \\ -\text{rd} \\ -\text{back} \end{bmatrix}$$

(69) *First noninitial [−consonantal] segment finds [+nasal]*

$$x_1 \quad x_2 \quad \uparrow \quad x_3 \quad x_4 \quad x_5$$

$$\begin{bmatrix} +\text{cons} \\ +\text{son} \\ \text{cor} \\ -\text{cont} \\ +\text{nas} \end{bmatrix} \begin{bmatrix} -\text{cons} \\ +\text{son} \\ -\text{high} \\ +\text{low} \\ -\text{rd} \\ +\text{back} \\ +\textbf{nas} \end{bmatrix} \begin{bmatrix} -\text{cons} \\ +\text{son} \\ -\text{high} \\ -\text{low} \\ +\text{rd} \\ +\text{back} \\ +\textbf{nas} \end{bmatrix} \begin{bmatrix} +\text{cons} \\ -\text{son} \\ \text{cor} \\ -\text{cont} \\ -\text{nas} \end{bmatrix} \begin{bmatrix} -\text{cons} \\ +\text{son} \\ -\text{high} \\ -\text{low} \\ -\text{rd} \\ -\text{back} \end{bmatrix}$$

(70) *Final Noninitial [−consonantal] segment searches for [±nasal]*

x_1	x_2	x_3	x_4	←	x_5
$\begin{bmatrix} +\text{cons} \\ +\text{son} \\ \text{cor} \\ -\text{cont} \\ +\text{nas} \end{bmatrix}$	$\begin{bmatrix} -\text{cons} \\ +\text{son} \\ -\text{high} \\ +\text{low} \\ -\text{rd} \\ +\text{back} \\ +\text{nas} \end{bmatrix}$	$\begin{bmatrix} -\text{cons} \\ +\text{son} \\ -\text{high} \\ -\text{low} \\ +\text{rd} \\ +\text{back} \\ +\text{nas} \end{bmatrix}$	$\begin{bmatrix} +\text{cons} \\ -\text{son} \\ \text{cor} \\ -\text{cont} \\ -\text{nas} \end{bmatrix}$		$\begin{bmatrix} -\text{cons} \\ +\text{son} \\ -\text{high} \\ -\text{low} \\ -\text{rd} \\ -\text{back} \end{bmatrix}$

(71) *Final noninitial [−consonantal] segment finds [−nasal]*

x_1	x_2	x_3	x_4	↰	x_5
$\begin{bmatrix} +\text{cons} \\ +\text{son} \\ \text{cor} \\ -\text{cont} \\ +\text{nas} \end{bmatrix}$	$\begin{bmatrix} -\text{cons} \\ +\text{son} \\ -\text{high} \\ +\text{low} \\ -\text{rd} \\ +\text{back} \\ +\text{nas} \end{bmatrix}$	$\begin{bmatrix} -\text{cons} \\ +\text{son} \\ -\text{high} \\ -\text{low} \\ +\text{rd} \\ +\text{back} \\ +\text{nas} \end{bmatrix}$	$\begin{bmatrix} +\text{cons} \\ -\text{son} \\ \text{cor} \\ -\text{cont} \\ \mathbf{-nas} \end{bmatrix}$		$\begin{bmatrix} -\text{cons} \\ +\text{son} \\ -\text{high} \\ -\text{low} \\ -\text{rd} \\ -\text{back} \\ \mathbf{-nas} \end{bmatrix}$
n	ã	õ	t		e

In the second type of relativization, only contrastive values of [±nasal] are visible to the search. This is illustrated below for Southern Barasano; a similar pattern is found in Desano (Kaye 1971) and Guaraní (Walker 1999). In Barasano, all [±sonorant] segments are contrastive for [±nasal], but the voiceless stops and voiceless fricatives are not.

Interestingly, Barasano has voiced stops that are occasionally realized as prenasalized stops (although even when they are prenasalized, they do not induce nasal harmony). I follow Piggott's proposal that nasals are [−continuant] (Anderson 1976) and that all voiced segments, including the prenasalized stops, are in fact sonorants (Piggott 1992, 49). Rice (1993) provides evidence from Rotokas, Slavey, and other languages that certain "obstruents" may in fact be [−continuant, +sonorant]. Thus, the voiced stops of Barasano/Tucanoan are [+voice, −continuant, +sonorant, −nasal] while the nasal stops are [+voice, −continuant, +sonorant, +nasal]. As a result, the voiced stops and the nasal stops are contrastive for [±nasal] and are included in the search domain for harmony.

(72) *Southern Barasano affixes copy contrastive [±nasal] from closest leftward source (Piggott 1992, 47; 2003, 379)*
   a. mãhã-mã   'go up!'
   b. wa-ᵐba   'come!'
   c. ĩã-mĩ   'I saw'
   d. wa-ᵐbɪ   'I went'
   e. mãã-r̃e   'to seize by the handful'
   f. baa-re   'to swim'
   g. mĩnĩ-ãkã   'small bird'
   h. coti-aka   'small pot'

(73) *Barasano [+son] segments must:*
   Nasal-Harmonize: δ = left, F = [all: ±nasal]

The derivation for words such as [mĩnĩ-ãkã], in which the voiceless obstruent is transparent to harmony across it, is shown in (74)–(77) for the two affixal vowels.

(74) *First affixal [+sonorant] segment searches for [±nasal] in [mĩnĩ-ãkã]*

$x_1 \leftarrow x_2 \quad x_3 \quad x_4$

$$\begin{bmatrix} -\text{cons} \\ +\text{son} \\ +\text{high} \\ -\text{low} \\ -\text{rd} \\ -\text{back} \\ +\text{nas} \end{bmatrix} \begin{bmatrix} -\text{cons} \\ +\text{son} \\ -\text{high} \\ +\text{low} \\ -\text{rd} \\ +\text{back} \end{bmatrix} \begin{bmatrix} +\text{cons} \\ -\text{son} \\ \text{dors} \\ -\text{cont} \\ -\text{nas} \end{bmatrix} \begin{bmatrix} -\text{cons} \\ +\text{son} \\ -\text{high} \\ +\text{low} \\ -\text{rd} \\ +\text{back} \end{bmatrix}$$

(75) *First affixal [+sonorant] segment finds [+nasal]*

$x_1 \quad x_2 \quad x_3 \quad x_4$

$$\begin{bmatrix} -\text{cons} \\ +\text{son} \\ +\text{high} \\ -\text{low} \\ -\text{rd} \\ -\text{back} \\ \mathbf{+nas} \end{bmatrix} \begin{bmatrix} -\text{cons} \\ +\text{son} \\ -\text{high} \\ +\text{low} \\ -\text{rd} \\ +\text{back} \\ \mathbf{+nas} \end{bmatrix} \begin{bmatrix} +\text{cons} \\ -\text{son} \\ \text{dors} \\ -\text{cont} \\ -\text{nas} \end{bmatrix} \begin{bmatrix} -\text{cons} \\ +\text{son} \\ -\text{high} \\ +\text{low} \\ -\text{rd} \\ +\text{back} \end{bmatrix}$$

(76) Second affixal [+sonorant] segment searches for [±nasal]

$$
\begin{array}{cccc}
x_1 & x_2 & x_3 & \leftarrow & x_4 \\
\begin{bmatrix} -\text{cons} \\ +\text{son} \\ +\text{high} \\ -\text{low} \\ -\text{rd} \\ -\text{back} \\ +\text{nas} \end{bmatrix} &
\begin{bmatrix} -\text{cons} \\ +\text{son} \\ -\text{high} \\ +\text{low} \\ -\text{rd} \\ +\text{back} \\ +\text{nas} \end{bmatrix} &
\begin{bmatrix} +\text{cons} \\ -\text{son} \\ \text{dors} \\ -\text{cont} \\ -\text{nas} \end{bmatrix} & &
\begin{bmatrix} -\text{cons} \\ +\text{son} \\ -\text{high} \\ +\text{low} \\ -\text{rd} \\ +\text{back} \end{bmatrix}
\end{array}
$$

(77) Second affixal [+sonorant] segment finds [+nasal]

$$
\begin{array}{cccc}
x_1 & x_2 & x_3 & \leftarrow & x_4 \\
\begin{bmatrix} -\text{cons} \\ +\text{son} \\ +\text{high} \\ -\text{low} \\ -\text{rd} \\ -\text{back} \\ +\text{nas} \end{bmatrix} &
\begin{bmatrix} -\text{cons} \\ +\text{son} \\ -\text{high} \\ +\text{low} \\ -\text{rd} \\ +\text{back} \\ \mathbf{+nas} \end{bmatrix} &
\begin{bmatrix} +\text{cons} \\ -\text{son} \\ \text{dors} \\ -\text{cont} \\ -\text{nas} \end{bmatrix} & &
\begin{bmatrix} -\text{cons} \\ +\text{son} \\ -\text{high} \\ +\text{low} \\ -\text{rd} \\ +\text{back} \\ \mathbf{+nas} \end{bmatrix} \\
\tilde{\imath} & \tilde{a} & k & & \tilde{a}
\end{array}
$$

In sum, the variation between Warao and Barasano with respect to whether voiceless stops are visible for [±nasal] is yet another case of parametric variation, in which search may be relativized to a certain (sub)set of the values of the harmonic feature.

3.11 Microvariation in Finnish Loanwords

The differences between Kirghiz A and Kirghiz B reduced to whether the value-relativization parameter was set to *contrastive values* or *marked values*; and the differences between Ifẹ Yoruba and Standard Yoruba varied as a function of whether the parameter was set to *contrastive values* or *all values* (as did the differences in patterns of nasal harmony between Warao and Barasano). In this section, I analyze microvariation among speakers of Finnish for a particular class of loanwords that stray from the basic phonotactics of Finnish roots, and for which speakers may set the visibility parameter differently as well. Recall the Finnish vowel system:

(78) *Finnish vowel inventory*

[−back, −rd]	[−back, +rd]	[+back, +rd]	[+back, −rd]	
i	ü	u		[+high, −low]
e	ö	o		[−high, −low]
ä			a	[−high, +low]

As discussed by Campbell (1980) and Kiparsky (1981), while the Finnish vowel harmony pattern is straightforward for roots that contain all [+back] vowels, all contrastive [−back] vowels, or all noncontrastive [−back] vowels, the vowel harmony pattern for suffixes concatenated to loanwords that mix contrastive [+back] and contrastive [−back] exhibits idiolectal variability. The words [marttüüri] and [türanni], for example, contain a [+back] /a/ and a [−back] /ü/. Interestingly, while the vowel harmony pattern varies among speakers for words like [marttüüri],[17] it does not vary for [türanni]. This difference results in two dialects, which we may call *Finnish A* and *Finnish B*.

(79) *Finnish A*
    a. marttüüri-ä   'martyr-PARTIT.SG'
    b. türanni-a   'tyrant-PARTIT.SG'

(80) *Finnish B*
    a. marttüüri-a   'martyr-PARTIT.SG'
    b. türanni-a   'tyrant-PARTIT.SG'

Putting it differently, these two dialects do not differ in their treatment of contrastively [−back] words followed by [+back] vowels (79b) vs. (80b), but they do differ in their treatment of [+back] vowels followed by contrastively [−back] vowels (79a) vs. (80a)): for Finnish A, the contrastively [−back] vowels are part of the harmonic search; for Finnish B, they are not.

By now, the explanation for the difference between the dialects should be familiar: Finnish A's harmonic search is parameterized to include contrastively [−back] vowels, and Finnish B's harmonic search is parameterized to include only [+back] vowels, the marked value of the feature in Finnish (Kiparsky 1981). In Finnish B, if a word contains all [−back] vowels (i.e., contains no marked values of [+back]), then last-resort insertion will insert the default value. This microparametric difference is captured in (81).[18]

(81) *Finnish A*
Ablative suffix must search leftward for closest contrastive value of [±back].
Finnish B
Ablative suffix must search leftward for closest marked value of [±back].

One of the interesting results of the formulation of Finnish A versus Finnish B in (81) is that the two dialects will produce identical outputs for words analyzed earlier in this chapter such as [pouta], [pöütä], [tie], [koti]: in all-[+back] words, both dialects will copy [+back]; in all-[−back] words, both dialects will end up with a [−back] suffix (though through different means); and in words with [+back] followed by noncontrastive [−back], both dialects will copy [+back]. In fact, since the native vocabulary is predominantly composed of these three classes of words, all of which are compatible with both Finnish A and Finnish B, a clear conclusion to be drawn is that all of these words are *parametrically ambiguous* between [search: cF] and [search: mF], and that the variation emerges as the result of which option is chosen in the face of ambiguous input. Which option was actually chosen will only reveal itself on inputs for which these two parametric settings diverge, namely, loanwords of the [marttüüri] type. In the words of Andersen (1973, 774), "Innovation in the phonological structure of a language can only be explained on the basis of ambiguities in the corpus of utterances from which the new grammar is inferred." While this statement may not be universally true for all phonological innovations (e.g., epenthesis or syncope may not necessarily involve reanalysis of parametrically ambiguous input), I would argue that where microvariation in locality computation for vowel harmony is concerned, ambiguity is the wellspring of innovative analyses of value-relativization that lead to divergent results when loanwords introduce new structures into the language.

3.12 Set Union of Marked and Contrastive Values in Oroch

We have considered a number of cases in which search includes only the marked values or the contrastive values of the harmonic feature. In this section, we will consider a fusion of these two visibility parameters.

Before we proceed, I should note that the set of marked values and the set of contrastive values in an inventory are not always in a subset/superset relation. Whenever a language has at least three vowels, {A,B,C}, with marked [+F] on {B,C}, where {A,B} are contrastive for [±F] and C is not, then the set of marked values will include {B,C} and the set of contrastive values will include {A,B}. If the language has a fourth vowel, D, which is noncontrastive and unmarked for [±F], then the set of all vowels = {A,B,C,D}, the set of contrastive vowels = {B,C}, and the set of marked vowels = {A,B}. I claim that search-parameterization can include the set union operator and hence can select the set of vowels that are either contrastive or marked, namely, {A,B,C}. Such an operation becomes empirically necessary for analyzing the [±ATR] harmony of Oroch, a Tungusic language described by Tolskaya (2008).

(82) *Oroch vowel inventory*

[−back, −rd]	[+back, −rd]	[+rd]	
i		u	[+high, +ATR]
		ʊ	[+high, −ATR]
æ	ə		[−high, +ATR]
	a	ɔ	[−high, −ATR]

I assume that /æ/ is [+ATR] and that [−ATR] is the marked value of the feature, as Tolskaya (2008) notes that [æ] is in free variation with [iə], [i], or [ia] in some lexical items and that it is slightly diphthongal, starting with an ultrashort [i]. Observations from the Tungusic family suggest that /æ/ is related to the [+ATR] /e/ of Evenki: "ATR harmony is characteristic of the whole Tungusic family and Evenki is no exception in this regard; the alternation primarily consists of $a \sim e/ə$" (Anderson 2004, 39). In Oroch, however, the alternation is between [a] and [ə], and /æ/ is [+ATR] but unpaired. Most revealingly, Avrorin and Boldyrev (2001, 30) state that the velars /k,g/ have an allophonic realization as uvular [q,ɣ] when following the vowels /a,ɔ,ʊ/, but not when following /æ,ə,u/, which can be taken as evidence that only the [−ATR] vowels induce uvularization (e.g., [baqi] 'lazy' vs. [gæki] 'hawk').

Oroch has two distinct patterns of vowel harmony: [±ATR] harmony and [±round] harmony. Interestingly, while /i,æ/ are invisible for [±ATR] harmony, they participate in [±round] harmony (e.g., [ɔtɔŋgoɲi-də] 'kayak-3SG-FOC', analyzed in section 4.6).

As /u,ʊ/ and /ə,a/ are contrastive for [±ATR], and /ʊ,a,ɔ/ are marked for [±ATR], set union for the properties of marked and contrastive [±ATR] will include all vowels in the inventory except /i,æ/. The value-relativized sensitivity to contrastiveness or markedness will exclude these vowels from the search and render them invisible for [±ATR] harmony, as shown in (83).

(83) *Invisibility of /i,æ/ in Oroch [±ATR] harmony*
    a. ugda-va-da   'boat-ACC-FOC'
    b. xuŋkə-və-də   'canoe-ACC-FOC'
    c. ugda-ɲi-da   'boat-3SG-FOC'
    d. xuŋkə-ɲi-də   'canoe-3SG-FOC'
    e. əʒæ lənidə   'just below'
    f. ʒaŋgæ-ra   'judge-DENOM'
    g. sɔrɔdæ-da   'greet-FOC'

As shown in (83c–d), /i/ is invisible to [±ATR] harmony across itself, and as shown in (83e–g), /æ/ is invisible to [±ATR] harmony across itself. At this point, it is instructive to compare the theory of value-relativization developed in this chapter with one of the other widespread attempts within phonological theory to render certain vowels invisible for harmony, namely, underspecification theory. The rationale behind underspecification theory is that there is no need to specify in the featural representation of vowels the values that are predictable on independent grounds. For example, in a language such as Finnish with no [+high, +back, +round] vowel, the [±back] value of a [+high, −round] vowel is predictable and hence would not be included in its representation.

In underspecification theory, vowels that are invisible for harmony literally lack the harmonic feature, not acquiring it until a very late stage of the derivation, if at all. In Dresher's (2005) theory, for example, an algorithm for successive contrast-based division of the inventory (the Successive Division Algorithm) assigns feature-values to all vowels in the inventory in a certain order, and certain vowels are never assigned certain features. The assignment of features depends on a set of hierarchical orderings among features that determine the relative scope of a feature over the inventory.

For example, in an inventory consisting of /i,u,a/, and the features [±high, ±back, ±round], the algorithm has four possible outcomes, depending on the scope of the features.

(84) *Possible outcomes of the Successive Division Algorithm for /i,u,a/*
    a. Choose [±back]: /i/ [−back], /u/ [−back], /a/ [+back]
       Choose [±high] next: /i/ [−back], /u/ [+high, +back], /a/ [−high, +back]
    b. Choose [±round]: /i/ [−round], /u/ [+round], /a/ [−round]
       Choose [±high] next: /i/ [−round], /u/ [+high, +round], /a/ [−high, −round]
    c. Choose [±high]: /i/ [+high], /u/ [+high], /a/ [−high]
       Choose [±back] next: /i/ [+high, −back], /u/ [+high, +back], /a/ [−high]
    d. Choose [±high]: /i/ [+high], /u/ [+high], /a/ [−high]
       Choose [±round] next: /i/ [+high, −round], /u/ [+high, +round], /a/ [−high]

The Successive Division Algorithm claims that crosslinguistic variation in which vowels are active for which processes arises from the features' scope. For example, given (84a), /i/ cannot participate in [±high] harmony; given (84b), /i/ cannot participate in [±round] harmony; given (84c), /a/ cannot participate in [±back] harmony; and given (84d), /a/ cannot participate in [±round] harmony.

The Successive Division Algorithm represents a principled way to exhaustively assign just enough feature specifications to make every vowel contrastive. Dresher (2003) demonstrates a number of empirical advantages of the Successive Division Algorithm over earlier algorithms for assigning feature specifications that use predictability of features to determine which vowels should be underspecified (e.g., Archangeli's (1988) Radical Underspecification Algorithm). One of the celebrated advantages of the Successive Division Algorithm is that it can accommodate cross-linguistic variation simply by rearranging the scope of features within the hierarchy.

This stands in stark contrast to the framework adopted here, in which all vowels are fully specified for all features and it is the harmony processes themselves that are relativized to ignore or include certain features. In what follows, I will demonstrate that given the Oroch inventory and the four features [±high, ±back, ±round, ±ATR], any possible scope ordering of the features fails to generate the right specifications. Recall that in Oroch, /i,æ/ are invisible to [±ATR] harmony and therefore must lack a specification for [±ATR] given underspecification theory, while they are visible to [±round] harmony (as shown in section 4.6), and therefore must have a specification for [±round].

(85) *Desired outcomes of underspecification in Oroch, given an underspecification approach to harmonic participation*
   a. Desideratum 1 (D1): /i,æ/ must lack specification for [±ATR], all other vowels must have it
   b. Desideratum 2 (D2): /i,æ/ must bear specifications for [±round]

(86) *Possible outcomes of the Successive Division Algorithm for Oroch given [±high, ±back, ±round, ±ATR]*
   a. Choose [±ATR] first: FAILS, since it will assign [±ATR] to /i,æ/, contra D1
   b. Choose [±back] first: FAILS, since /i/ will not be later assigned [−round], contra D2
   c. Choose [±high] first: assigns [+high] to /i,u,ʊ/, [−high] to /æ,ə,a,ɔ/
      i. If [±ATR] chosen next: FAILS, since it will assign [±ATR] to /i,æ/, contra D1
      ii. If [±back] chosen next: FAILS, since /i/ will not be later assigned [−round], contra D2
      iii. If [±round] chosen next: only /ɔ/ will have [−high, +round], and as /ɔ/ will not be later assigned [±ATR], contra D1, FAILS

d. Choose [±round] first: assigns [+round] to /u,ʊ,ɔ/ and [−round] to /i,æ,ə,a/
  i. If [±ATR] chosen next: FAILS, since it will assign [±ATR] to /i,æ/, contra D1
  ii. If [±high] chosen next: only /ɔ/ will have [−high, +round], and as /ɔ/ will not be later assigned [±ATR], contra D1, FAILS
  iii. If [±back] chosen next: assigns [+back] to /u,ʊ,ɔ,ə,a/ and [−back] to /i,æ/
  If [±high] chosen next: only /ɔ/ will have [−high, +back, +round], and as /ɔ/ will not be later assigned [±ATR], contra D1, FAILS
  If [±ATR] chosen next: FAILS, since it will assign [±ATR] to /i,æ/, contra D1

As shown in (86), the most successful underspecification algorithm developed to date cannot yield the right pattern of feature specification to guarantee nonparticipation of Oroch /i,æ/ in [±ATR] harmony and their concomitant participation in [±round] harmony. Rather, all vowels must be specified for all values of these features, regardless of whether one might be predictable from the other.[19] I conclude that the right place to situate feature-visibility is in the harmony processes themselves, rather than in the inventory.

3.13 Conclusion: Transparent Items Are Pruned Away Because of Irrelevancy

Before concluding this chapter, I would like to reflect on how the present model may be viewed as an outgrowth of the steps toward constraints on possible long-distance assimilation rules, from the formal constraints on rules proposed by Howard (1972), Jensen (1974), Battistella (1982), and Yamada (1983) to the representationally based constraints on rules proposed by Clements (1985), Sagey (1986), Steriade (1987), Calabrese (1988), McCarthy (1988), Archangeli and Pulleyblank (1994), and Odden (1994). Importantly, as argued in chapter 2, the current formulation of locality is *target-centric* (locality being defined from the point of view of the needy suffix), and therefore the question of what may "intervene" transparently in a rule is defined in terms of segments that the suffix ignores during its leftward search. I have argued that there are three ways that segments can be ignored in the search: (1) they can fail to bear the harmonic feature at all, (2) they can fail to bear a contrastive value of the harmonic feature, or (3) they can fail to bear a marked value of the harmonic feature. These relativizations serve to prune the search domain of segments that do not bear the relativized values. Once the search domain is set, copying takes place from the closest element, period.

An inspiration for this formulation of locality is the model of relativized minimality developed within syntactic theory, particularly by Rizzi (1990, 2001). Rizzi argues that the *most local* syntactic phrase for movement or government relations is not to be measured "as the crow flies," but only once the domain is pruned of irrelevant elements; thus, A-bar elements are not relevant for the computation of A-locality, and vice versa. In fact, the notion of relativization is implicit in all models of syntactic agreement that take elements such as prepositional phrases to be "transparent" for agreement across them. For example:

(87) There lay(*s) in the grass two frogs.

The implicit consensus in syntactic theory is that prepositional phrases do not enter into the search for agreement because they do not bear ϕ-features to begin with; there is an implicit relativization of the search for an agreement controller to only those phrases that bear agreement features.

One of the closest precursors to the current theory of what is excluded from the search domain within phonological theory can be found in the work of Yamada (1983). Yamada posits the *Class Complement Constraint*, stating that what may benignly intervene between the source of assimilatory copying and the target of copying is anything that bears the set of features complementary to those of the source.[20] The current set of relativizations can be stated very naturally in these terms.

(88) a. When [search: ±F], the complement class consists of those segments that do not bear [±F] at all (e.g., labial consonants do not bear [±back] in Turkish).
  b. When [search: cF], the complement class consists of those segments that do not bear a contrastive value of the feature (e.g., /i/ does not bear a contrastive value of [±back] in Finnish).
  c. When [search: mF], the complement class consists of those segments that do not bear a marked value of the feature (e.g., /u/ does not bear a marked feature of [±low] in Sibe).

Let us suppose that the notion of complement class can only be defined on the basis of (88a–c) (i.e., the harmonic feature and certain values of it), and not on the basis of other features orthogonal to the one for which harmony is occurring. If so, then the spirit of Yamada's proposal may be upheld here: elements in the complement of the feature-values for which the search is relativized are allowed to be "transparently" ignored in search.[21]

As far as visibility of interveners is concerned, the three value-relativization parameters characterize possible and impossible harmony rules in terms of specification of the search domain of the rules themselves.[22] Importantly, this parametric space prohibits the harmonic pattern in which both contrastive values of a feature are invisible. This is a strong and falsifiable prediction, not shared by a wide class of alternative theories of possible harmony systems.

This specific case, prohibited by the parameters, would be a harmony pattern in which, say, [±back] harmony copied from {o,ö,a,ä} but skipped {u,ü}—in other words, a system in which *both* members of a contrastive pair were invisible to harmony, neither valuing nor undergoing the process. Such a system would clearly be prohibited under *all-value* visibility, since all values, including those in {u,ü}, would be visible. Such a system would also be prohibited under *marked-value* visibility, since if only [+back] values were visible, then /u/ would still remain the visible member of this pair. Finally, such a system would be prohibited under *contrastive-value* visibility, since both /u/ and /ü/, being contrastive for [±back], would remain visible for harmony.

A second class of cases that would clearly be excluded would be those in which all contrastive values were transparent for harmony, so that only Finnish-type noncontrastive /i,e/ would be copied from, and all other value-sources would result in last-resort insertion of a single feature-value. A third class of cases would be those in which all marked values were transparent, so that a rounding harmony language with the eight-vowel system of Kirghiz, Shor, or Altai would *only* copy [+round] from /u/, and could do so at a distance.

In some previous research on vowel harmony, beginning with Kiparsky 1981, the visibility to the Search-and-Copy procedure of particular classes of feature-values but not others has been implemented in theories of underspecification, which hold that, for example, the noncontrastive or unmarked feature-values are simply not present at the point of the representation at which harmony occurs. As discussed earlier in this chapter, underspecification models that treat skipped vowels as altogether missing a value for the harmonic feature face problems when other phonological processes demand the presence of those feature-values in the

τ is either {all values of f_i contrastive for f_i, marked for f_i}
myVals V
myPosition P
myFeatsneeded F

while F is not empty:
- Go in direction δ and update P
- **if** P of type τ for any $f, f \in F$:
  - Copy Val(P, f) to V
  - Remove f from F

Figure 3.3
Parameterized single-pass search until all features harmonize

representation. In one concrete case presented in section 3.4, Finnish /i/ must possess [−back] in order to condition the rule of coronal assibilation; in a second case mentioned there, one instance of Hungarian /i/ is transparent but two instances are not, a situation that cannot be described if /i/ has no specification at all for [±back].

Further empirical problems with underspecification as a mechanism for determining (non)participation in assimilation have been more generally discussed in Mohanan 1991, McCarthy and Taub 1992, and Steriade 1995. The general spirit of these earlier proposals, that noncontrastive or unmarked feature-values are "invisible" to the harmony process, is captured here by relativizing the search. However, the letter of underspecification proposals, that the feature-values on such segments are literally absent from the representation, cannot be maintained.

Halle, Vaux, and Wolfe (2000) discuss Uyghur data in which contrastive /ä/, when unstressed and in a medial open syllable, raises to [i], thereby becoming transparent for the purposes of subsequent suffixes added to the right. Clearly, the change from /ä/ to [i] involves height alone and should not affect the [−back] specification of the vowel, but because it now bears a noncontrastive value [−back], the vowel is skipped by subsequent harmonic searches. Echoing the conclusion drawn in the present model, Halle, Vaux, and Wolfe state that the pattern of vowels in harmony systems "derives...from their role in the phonemic inventory of the language, rather than from their derivational history" (pp. 398–399).

The most general statement of what parameterization does is that it cuts out a swath of irrelevant segments and, in so doing, opens up the possibility of long-distance harmony. There is no obvious modification of Optimality Theory approaches to harmony, such as correspondence-based identity between vowels or contiguous domains of harmonizing vowels, that can restrict this relation to elements that bear the contrastive or marked value of the harmonic feature, as the nature of Optimality Theory constraints does not allow reference to inventory properties of this sort. In the present model, the Search algorithm is (in a sense) so "dumb" in copying from the closest leftward item in the domain, that if nothing were cut out of the way, all harmony would be strictly adjacent. It is precisely the relativization of adjacency based on these inventory properties that allows the empirical fit with locality patterns of vowel harmony. The Search algorithm developed up to this point is schematized in figure 3.3.

The restrictiveness of the present theory results from the fact that items can be removed from the search only on the basis of their feature-values, coupled with the inventory-derived properties of contrastiveness and markedness. In the next chapter, we will see that if the needy segment requires anything of its donor besides contrastiveness or markedness for the harmonic feature, the stop-with-closest nature of minimal search can yield surprising results.

4 Defective Intervention: When Search Comes Back Empty-Handed

If two vowels go walking, the first does the talking.
—Theodore Clymer

4.1 The Grammatical Elements of Minimality

We have seen that the Search procedure for vowel harmony can relativize its locality in very limited ways, according to a small parametric space. The establishment of the search domain leads to an extremely myopic principle of copying from the closest element encountered. We now turn to defining and describing the conditions that determine whether an element, once found, can be copied from or not. Elements that cannot be successfully copied from—even though they are included in the search domain—are called *blockers*, especially when there are more distant elements in the domain that they block from ever being considered. The effect of blockers, seeking a harmonic value with whom fails as soon as they are encountered, is an inviolable principle of locality. Once the search halts with a defective element in its path, no more-distant elements may be considered.

Consider the following configuration: A is a needy *value-seeker* searching for a *value-source*. The elements x, y, z are in its domain.

(1) $[\ldots x \ldots y \ldots z \ldots] \leftarrow A$

Ordinarily, the search will terminate with z. However, suppose that although z is in the search domain and the *closest* element to A within that domain, it does not satisfy some additional requirement R. By virtue of not satisfying R, z is *defective*. What is most interesting about these configurations is that both y and z bear the feature [F] that A needs, but, by failing to meet R, not only is z excluded as a value-source—it also prevents y (which does meet R) from being a value-source as well. The concept of *minimality* expresses the idea that search cannot look past a defective element to a more distant one.

A syntactic example of defective intervention can be schematized with plural agreement in Icelandic.

(2) Það finnst mörgum stúdentum tölvurnar ljótar.
    there find.SG/*PL some student.DAT.PL computer.NOM.PL ugly
    'Some students find the computers ugly.'
    (Holmberg and Hróarsdóttir 2004, 654)

In (2), the *value-seeker* is the Tense node, which needs to value its ϕ-features. The closest element in its domain is the dative 'some students', which indeed has a [+plural] feature that T could potentially copy. However, there is an additional *source condition*: the source must be [+nominative]. The dative fails this condition. Not only does T thereby fail to agree with the [+plural] dative, it also fails to agree with the [+plural] nominative, which is the *next* closest element in the domain. In other words, once the closest DP is found, *there is no second chance* (Chomsky 2001).

When T cannot find a licit value-source in its domain, a last-resort operation supplies a default value for the needed feature(s). The default value for [±plural] in Icelandic is [−plural]. Default values can be determined within a given language using considerations of morphosyntactic markedness, but to some extent they are language-particular. Compare default agreement in Hindi (3), which is masculine singular, with default agreement in Russian (4), which is neuter singular.

(3) Lakshmi-ne Sumita-ko dekhaa.
    Lakshmi-FEM-ERG Sumita-FEM-OBJCTV saw.PFCTV.MASC
    'Lakshmi saw Sumita.'

(4) Ivanu nužno vrača.
    Ivan.MASC.DAT needs.NEUT doctor.MASC.ACC
    'Ivan needs a doctor.'

In (3), neither (feminine) noun phrase can be copied from for agreement, because both are nonnominative. The last-resort gender-value that is inserted in order for Hindi verbal agreement to interface with the morphology is masculine. In (4), when neither of the (masculine) noun phrases can be copied from for agreement because both are nonnominative, the Russian value of last-resort default agreement is neuter. We see, then, that when there is no licit source for feature-copying in syntactic agreement, the default value must be determined on a language-specific basis. In section 3.3, we saw that Finnish and Uyghur, two languages with contrastive [±back] harmony and identical inventories, insert different last-resort values when search fails: [−back] for Finnish and [+back] for Uyghur.

In a target-centric theory of locality, once the *search domain* is delimited, the *value-seeker* (*A* in (1)) will always halt the search with the first element (*z*) in its domain. If an additional *source condition* R is specified on the search, and *z* fails to meet this condition, search will terminate in failure, *even if there is a more-distant potential value-source* y *that does satisfy R*. This constitutes the essence of *defective intervention*. When search terminates in failure owing to defective intervention, however, a last-resort operation of default-value insertion provides the value-seeker with a value. (We can diagnose that defective intervention has occurred when a default value surfaces, even though there are nondefault values on all other elements in the domain.)

4.2 No Second Chances after Search Fails

The defective intervention constraint governing the way search operates excludes a wide class of patterns and provides a formal foundation for expressing the conditions found in *parasitic harmony* (Steriade 1981; Cole and Trigo 1988). The name "parasitic harmony" describes the fact that in order for one element to copy [±F] from another, the two elements must already bear the same value for another feature [±G], the copying thus being "parasitic" on the requirement R of sharing an orthogonal feature. One case of parasitic harmony is Yawelmani rounding harmony, which is parasitic on shared height. Yawelmani has two underlying heights, distinguishing [+high] /i,u/ from [−high] /a,o/. In order for a suffixal vowel to copy [±round] from a source vowel, the source vowel must bear the same value of [±high] as the value-seeker.

(5) *Parasitic harmony*
    Yawelmani [αhigh] suffix vowels can copy [±round] only from a source that is also [αhigh].

This is exemplified in (6) for the [−high] nondirective gerundial suffix of Yawelmani (Kuroda 1967, 14). When the vowel in the syllable immediately to the suffix's left is also [−high], copying for [±round] occurs successfully (6a–d), but when the vowel in the syllable immediately to its left is [+high], search fails (6e–g).

(6) *Yawelmani nondirective gerundial suffix seeks [±round] &
R = [αhigh]*
   a. qob-tow   'take.care.of.an.infant–NONDIR.GER'
   b. hoyo:-tow   'name-NONDIR.GER'
   c. xat-taw   'eat-NONDIR.GER'
   d. pana:-taw   'arrive-NONDIR.GER'
   e. giy-taw   'touch-NONDIR.GER'
   f. mut-taw   'swear-NONDIR.GER'
   g. wo:wul-taw   'stand.up–NONDIR.GER'

In (6e–f), the closest leftward vowel is [+high], and even when that vowel is [+round] as in (6f), it cannot be copied from, since it bears "the wrong height." Pattern (6g) exemplifies defective intervention: not only does the closest leftward vowel bear the wrong height, it also prevents the next-closest leftward vowel, which does bear the correct height, from being copied from. This exemplifies a derivational search procedure in which there is no lookahead: search immediately terminates in failure with the closest leftward element, even though only one element away there is a licit value-source. Ironically enough—because of the way the Search procedure works when orthogonal requirements R such as [αheight]-sharing are imposed on the source—in (6g), no value of [+round] at all is copied, even though both stem vowels are [+round]!^{1}

In cases of parasitic harmony, the conditional requirement R is always the requirement that the value-seeker and the value-source be identical for a feature-value orthogonal to the harmonic value. In Yawelmani, in order for [±round] to be successfully copied to the gerundial suffix, the source for that value must meet an additional subcondition that it has the same value for height as the suffix.

Mailhot and Reiss (2007) provide a useful metaphor for search-termination when a conditional requirement R is not met. Suppose I ask you to stop the first man you see with a parrot, and if the parrot is red, tell me its name. That's very different from asking you to stop the first man you see with a red parrot, and to tell me the parrot's name. In the latter case, you will search until you find a red parrot. In the former case, however, you will search only until you find a parrot, whatever its color; if that parrot happens not to be red, then the search terminates in failure. Defective intervention occurs when, once a potential value-source is found, if it does not meet the conditional requirement R, the search terminates. The essential premise of this chapter is that phonology does not allow "search for a red parrot," so to speak—in linguistic terms, there are never cases of parasitic harmony (searches for a source for the harmonic feature [F], with an additional requirement on what value of [G] licit sources must bear) that are of unbounded distance and blind to defective interveners.

Vowel harmony searches may be simple "searches for a parrot" with no additional source requirements (e.g., [±back] harmony in Finnish), or they may be "searches for a parrot, copying *if it's red*" (e.g., [±round] harmony, parasitic on [αhigh], which fails if there is any closer [−αhigh] source). However, phonology does not allow vowel harmony searches that are "searches for a red parrot" (e.g., [±round] harmony parasitic on [αhigh] that is not blocked by any closer [−αhigh] source and can look past such defective interveners).

In what follows, we will examine several types of defective intervention, subsuming the representative cases of what have traditionally been called "opaque segments" or "blockers" in the vowel harmony literature. The present model places important constraints on what can be a "blocker": (1) it must be something that is already included within the relativized search domain (i.e., it must bear the harmonic feature), and (2) it must fail to be copied from because of a property orthogonal to the harmonic feature. This orthogonal property may be subsegmental or morphological.

Subsegmental conditional requirements are for preexisting identity with an orthogonal feature: for example, shared height as in Yawelmani [±round] harmony above and in Khalkha Mongolian (section 4.5), shared roundness as in Bantu [±high] harmony (section 4.4.1), or shared [±consonantal] as in Nawuri (section 4.3). Importantly, such conditional requirements cannot refer to arbitrary properties of the source without reference to the value-seeker, nor can they demand featural *non*identity between the needy suffix and the source.

Conditional requirements also may place restrictions on the morphological affiliation of the source, as in Jingulu (section 4.7.1). Such requirements may demand that the source be in a different morphological constituent than the value-seeker in order to be copied from. Again, failure of the closest element in the domain to meet such a requirement leads to immediate defective intervention, even when licit sources for the harmonic feature exist downstream.

Importantly, these two types of conditional requirements on copyable sources cannot change the delimitation of the harmonic search domain: only the inventory-derived properties based on the harmonic feature itself may do so. Once the relativized search domain has been established, the affixes are "stuck with" defective interveners in their search path that fail to meet an orthogonal requirement on being a licit source of value-copying. Such defective interveners are really only "partially defective": crucially, they do bear the value that needs to be copied, but by lacking something else, they cause the entire search to halt.

4.3 "Opaque" Blockers of Harmony: Consonants in Nawuri

Let us examine a feature-based conditional requirement that leads to defective intervention in the [+round] harmony of Nawuri, a Kwa language of Ghana (Casali 1995). Nawuri has the following vowel inventory:

(7) *Nawuri vowel inventory*

[−back, −rd]	[+back, +rd]	[+back, −rd]	
i	u		[+high, −low, +ATR]
ɪ	ʊ		[+high, −low, −ATR]
e	o		[−high, −low, +ATR]
ɛ	ɔ		[−high, −low, −ATR]
		a	[−high, +low, −ATR]

The noun class prefix [gi-]/[gɪ-]/[gu-]/[gʊ-] copies [±round] (as well as [±ATR]) from a following vowel.

(8) *Nawuri noun class prefix copies [±round] (Casali 1995, 651)*
    a. gɪ-baː 'hand'
    b. gɪ-sɪbɪta 'sandal'
    c. gʊ-sʊ 'ear'
    d. gʊ-lɔ 'illness'
    e. gi-ɲi 'tooth'
    f. gi-keːli 'kapok tree'
    g. gu-jo 'yam'
    h. gu-kuː 'digging'

In addition to a rightward search for [±round], Nawuri imposes another source requirement in Nawuri: the closest source of [+round] must be [−consonantal], as indicated by the "& R" condition in (9).

(9) *Nawuri /gV-/ noun class prefix must:*
    ATR-Harmonize and Round-Harmonize: δ = right, F = [±ATR; ±round & R = −consonantal]

The last-resort value of [±round] is [−round] in Nawuri. The scenario for defective intervention arises because Nawuri has labial consonants (/p,b,m,f/), which in this language contain the feature [+round]. (The glide /w/ is a licit source for [+round] harmony, as it is [−consonantal] (Chomsky and Halle 1968; Clements and Keyser 1983).)²

In Nawuri, when the closest rightward source of [+round] to copy from is a [+consonantal] element such as /p,b,m,f/, the search fails, because these consonants fail to satisfy the orthogonal conditional requirement. In fact, these consonants crucially *block* rounding harmony from a downstream [+round] vowel, instantiating defective intervention: once the search for [+round] fails with the [+consonantal] element in the domain, there is no second chance to copy from the second-closest element.

(10) *Nawuri [+round] copying fails with [+consonantal, +round] nearest source (Casali 1995, 652)*
    a. gi-mu: 'heat'
    b. gi-fufuli   'white'
    c. gi-pula   'burial'
    d. gi-bo:to: 'leprosy'
    e. gʊ-wɛ   'sympathy'
    f. gʊ-wʊrʊ 'hat'

The failure of labial consonants to provide a value for [+round] results from the specific requirement of Nawuri that licit sources be [−consonantal].³ There is evidence from many languages that labial consonants can induce vowel rounding. In Tulu (Sagey 1986), both labial consonants and round vowels cause adjacent rounding of a high vowel. Conversely, in Akkadian (von Soden 1969; Odden 1994), dissimilation between labial consonants is blocked by round vowels.

A successful pattern of prefixal [+round] copying from a following labial consonant is found in Southern Igbo (Ihiunu and Kenstowicz 1994).⁴

(11) *Igbo gerundive vowel copies [+round] from following labial consonant*
    a. sì-sè   'stir, draw water'
    b. tí-tá   'bite'
    c. mú-má   'know'
    d. wù-wè   'take'
    e. fú-fá   'stuff'

While [+round] can be copied from labial consonants in Igbo, it cannot be copied from labial consonants in Nawuri.⁵ As the result of a conditional requirement that the [±round] source must be [−consonantal], any labial consonant in Nawuri causes immediate failure of the prefix vowel's harmonic search, even from a further source. Nawuri constitutes a case of "blocking" by "inert" feature-bearers that allow copying neither from themselves nor from downstream licit sources. Lack of lookahead and immediate failure of the search leads to default insertion of [−round] in such cases.

The halting of search with a [+consonantal] element in Nawuri [ɣi-mu] is illustrated by the derivation in (12)–(16).

(12) *Nawuri noun class prefix begins search for contrastive [±ATR] and all [±round], R = [−consonantal] in [gi-mu]*

$$x_1 \quad x_2 \quad \rightarrow \quad x_3 \quad x_4$$

$$\begin{bmatrix} +\text{cons} \\ \text{dors} \\ -\text{cont} \\ +\text{voi} \end{bmatrix} \begin{bmatrix} -\text{cons} \\ +\text{high} \\ -\text{back} \end{bmatrix} \begin{bmatrix} +\text{cons} \\ \text{lab} \\ \text{nas} \\ +\text{rd} \end{bmatrix} \begin{bmatrix} -\text{cons} \\ +\text{high} \\ +\text{back} \\ +\text{high} \\ +\text{ATR} \\ +\text{rd} \end{bmatrix}$$

(13) *Nawuri noun class prefix finds defective [±round]*

$$x_1 \quad x_2 \quad \nleftrightarrow \quad x_3 \quad x_4$$

$$\begin{bmatrix} +\text{cons} \\ \text{dors} \\ -\text{cont} \\ +\text{voi} \end{bmatrix} \begin{bmatrix} -\text{cons} \\ +\text{high} \\ +\text{back} \end{bmatrix} \begin{bmatrix} \mathbf{+cons} \\ \text{lab} \\ \text{nas} \\ \mathbf{+rd} \end{bmatrix} \begin{bmatrix} -\text{cons} \\ +\text{high} \\ +\text{back} \\ +\text{high} \\ +\text{ATR} \\ +\text{rd} \end{bmatrix}$$

(14) *Nawuri noun class prefix undergoes default insertion for [−round]*

$$x_1 \quad x_2 \quad \rightarrow \quad x_3 \quad x_4$$

$$\begin{bmatrix} +\text{cons} \\ \text{dors} \\ -\text{cont} \\ +\text{voi} \end{bmatrix} \begin{bmatrix} -\text{cons} \\ +\text{high} \\ -\text{back} \\ -\text{rd} \end{bmatrix} \begin{bmatrix} +\text{cons} \\ \text{lab} \\ \text{nas} \\ +\text{rd} \end{bmatrix} \begin{bmatrix} -\text{cons} \\ +\text{high} \\ +\text{back} \\ +\text{high} \\ +\text{ATR} \\ +\text{rd} \end{bmatrix}$$

(15) *Nawuri noun class prefix continues search for contrastive [±ATR]*

$$x_1 \quad x_2 \quad x_3 \quad \rightarrow \quad x_4$$

$$\begin{bmatrix} +\text{cons} \\ \text{dors} \\ -\text{cont} \\ +\text{voi} \end{bmatrix} \begin{bmatrix} -\text{cons} \\ +\text{high} \\ -\text{back} \\ -\text{rd} \end{bmatrix} \begin{bmatrix} +\text{cons} \\ \text{lab} \\ \text{nas} \\ +\text{rd} \end{bmatrix} \begin{bmatrix} -\text{cons} \\ +\text{high} \\ +\text{back} \\ +\text{high} \\ +\text{ATR} \\ +\text{rd} \end{bmatrix}$$

(16) *Nawuri noun class prefix finds and copies [+ATR]*

$$x_1 \quad\quad x_2 \quad\quad x_3 \quad \overset{\rightarrow}{} \quad x_4$$

$$\begin{bmatrix} +\text{cons} \\ \text{dors} \\ -\text{cont} \\ +\text{voi} \end{bmatrix} \quad \begin{bmatrix} -\text{cons} \\ +\text{high} \\ -\text{back} \\ +\text{ATR} \\ -\text{rd} \end{bmatrix} \quad \begin{bmatrix} +\text{cons} \\ \text{lab} \\ \text{nas} \\ +\text{rd} \end{bmatrix} \quad \begin{bmatrix} -\text{cons} \\ +\text{high} \\ +\text{back} \\ +\text{high} \\ +\text{ATR} \\ +\text{rd} \end{bmatrix}$$

$$\text{g} \quad\quad \text{i} \quad\quad \text{m} \quad\quad \text{u}$$

Although it has not been suggested before, the case of Nawuri defective intervention by labial consonants falls under the logic of parasitic harmony as well. Recall that parasitic harmony is any case in which copying of feature [F] between segments X and Y takes place only if X and Y share the same value for an orthogonal feature [G], [G] ≠ [F]. In this case, the orthogonal feature is [−consonantal], a property of both the value-seeker and any licit goal. Nawuri differs from Southern Igbo in that the latter copies [±round] from any source, whereas Nawuri requires that sources be [−consonantal] in order to be copied from.[6] The minor addition of this conditional requirement to the Search procedure developed in chapter 2 yields great divergences in the surface patterning of Igbo and Nawuri [+round] copying.

The revised Search algorithm is presented in figure 4.1, where R is a matrix of conditional requirements on each feature that is needed by the

τ is either {all values of f_i contrastive for f_i, marked for f_i}
myVals V
myPosition P
myFeatsneeded F
myConditionalRequirements(F) = R

while F is not empty:
·   Go in direction δ and update P
·   **if** P of type τ for any $f, f \in F$:
·   ·   **if** R is true of P:
·   ·   ·   Copy Val(P, f) to V
·   ·   ·   Remove f from F
·   ·   **else:**
·   ·   ·   **exit**

Figure 4.1
Parameterized single-pass search with conditional requirements

copying affix. R may be empty (i.e., when none of the needed features impose conditional requirements on their source).

The revised algorithm in figure 4.1 states that as soon as the first element P bearing the relativized feature-value is found, a check is performed: does the element P meet the source requirement for that feature? If not, the search for that feature terminates, leaving the affix to last-resort default value-insertion.

4.4 Parasitic Harmony: Conditional Requirements for [±high], [±round], and [±ATR] Copying

The discussion of Nawuri illustrated a case in which labial consonants bearing the right feature cause a crash when they intervene between a prefixal vowel and a round vowel, and we absorbed this case under the rubric of parasitic harmony: a requirement for identity with respect to an orthogonal feature. In sections 4.4.1–4.43, we will consider several classic cases of parasitic harmony that instantiate the inviolable nature of the Search procedure halting with the closest element in the domain, even if a "better" one can be found just a bit further away. Section 4.4.1 demonstrates [±high] harmony dependent on identity with respect to [±round] in Kisa. This conditional requirement is paired with a second one—[±ATR] harmony dependent on identity with respect to [±high]—in Kimatuumbi (section 4.4.2).

4.4.1 Height Harmony in Bantu

Consider the height harmony pattern shown by a majority of the Bantu languages, in which the affixal vowels /i,u/ lower when preceded by /e,o/, as found in five-vowel systems such as that of Kisa.

(17) *Kisa vowel inventory*

[−back, −rd]	[+back, +rd]	[+back, −rd]	
i	u		[+high, −low]
e	o		[−high, −low]
		a	[−high, +low]

Copying of contrastive [±high] eliminates /a/ from the search domain, because [±high] is not contrastive in the context of [+low]. Failure to find anything in the search domain results in last-resort insertion of [+high], as in (18e).

(18) *Kisa applicative suffix copies contrastive [±high] from its left (Hyman 1999, 238)*
    a. tsom-el-a   'pierce-APPL-FV'
    b. rek-el-a   'set.trap-APPL-FV'
    c. βis-il-a   'hide-APPL-FV'
    d. fuːng-il-a   'lock-APPL-FV'
    e. βaːmb-il-a   'spread.out-APPL-FV'

Up to now this is a straightforward process of contrastive feature-copying of the type seen throughout chapter 3. However, Hyman notes that Kisa (as well as many other Bantu languages, including Kinyarwanda, Kirundi, Kinyakore, Luganda, Haya, Jita, Shambaa, Shi, Bemba, Yao, and Shona) exhibits a different harmony pattern with the reversative suffix [-ul]/[-ol]. Unlike the applicative suffix [-il]/[-el], which may copy [−high] from either /e/ or /o/, the reversative copies [−high] only from /o/. This is a case of parasitic harmony: the reversative suffix can copy [±high] only from a source that has the same roundness value as itself. This difference between the two suffixes is shown in (19) and (20).

(19) *Kisa applicative suffix must:*
Height-Harmonize: δ = left, F = [c: high]

(20) *Kisa reversative suffix must:*
Height-Harmonize: δ = left, F = [c: high & R = +round]

The requirement in (20) dictates that the reversative suffix will not copy contrastive [−high] from /e/—even though /e/ bears contrastive [−high]—because /e/ fails to satisfy the conditional requirement of sharing [+round].

(21) *Kisa reversative suffix copies contrastive [±high] only when source is [+round]*
    a. tsom-ol-a   'pull.out'
    b. βis-ul-a   'reveal'
    c. fuːng-ul-a   'unlock'
    d. βaːmb-ul-a   'spread apart'
    e. rek-ul-a   'spring trap'

The failure of (21e) to copy contrastive [−high] from the preceding /e/ is a case of parasitic harmony in which the required orthogonal shared feature is [±round].[7] It is well-known from cases such as Yawelmani and from Khalkha Mongolian (to be discussed in section 4.5) that [±round] harmony may parasitically require orthogonal featural identity for

[±high]. The Kisa pattern demonstrates that this height-roundness relation can work in either direction, as [±high] harmony requires orthogonal identity for [±round].[8]

The defective intervention analysis predicts that a contrastively [−high] vowel that is not [+round] will terminate the search in failure immediately, even if there is another contrastively [−high] vowel that *is* [+round] further to the left. The Shona repetitive suffix [-urur]/[-oror] has the same requirement as the Kisa reversative suffix in (20). When this suffix attaches to disyllabic noun stems of the form [o...e],[9] we can diagnose defective intervention.

(22) *Shona repetitive suffix [-urur]/[-oror] (Fortune 1981): Search for contrastive [−high] fails with /u/*
    a. dzok-oror   'plant-REP'
    b. tsets-urur   'grind-REP'
    c. zoténg-úrúdz-a   'sell-REP'

Let us resist explaining (22) in terms of a restriction that the repetitive suffix cannot look further than one syllable to the left. Many types of harmony are unbounded and can look more than one syllable away (e.g., Sibe [+low] harmony, Finnish [±back] harmony, both discussed in chapter 3), and hence the question is, why would a putative restriction to one syllable in (22) coincide with the fact that this is a case of parasitic harmony? In other words, if it were merely an incidental property of the items in (22) that conditionally parasitic search is restricted to one syllable, we would expect to find another language where conditionally parasitic search is unbounded—for example, in which [−high] copying could look as far as needed for a [+round] source. However, no such cases exist: whenever an orthogonal featural requirement is placed on copyable sources, search halts at the first element in the domain. The logic of defective intervention provides a reason why: such systems are excluded by the theory of *no-second-chance* locality. There are no "long-distance" cases of parasitic harmony at all within the typology of vowel harmony precisely because the Search algorithm allows "search and copy [−high] from the closest [−high] vowel only if that vowel is [+round]" and does not allow "search and copy [−high] from the closest [−high, +round] vowel."

The derivation of (22c), with search terminating immediately when R is not met, is given in (23)–(25).

Defective Intervention

(23) *Shona repetitive suffix begins search for contrastive [±high],*
$R = [+round]$

$$x_1 \quad x_2 \quad x_3 \quad x_4 \quad x_5 \quad x_6 \quad \leftarrow \quad x_7$$

$$\begin{bmatrix} -\text{voc} \\ \text{cor} \\ +\text{cont} \\ +\text{voi} \end{bmatrix} \begin{bmatrix} +\text{voc} \\ -\text{low} \\ +\text{back} \\ +\text{rd} \\ -\text{high} \end{bmatrix} \begin{bmatrix} -\text{voc} \\ \text{cor} \\ -\text{cont} \\ -\text{voi} \end{bmatrix} \begin{bmatrix} +\text{voc} \\ -\text{low} \\ -\text{back} \\ -\text{rd} \\ -\text{high} \end{bmatrix} \begin{bmatrix} -\text{voc} \\ \text{dors} \\ +\text{nas} \end{bmatrix} \begin{bmatrix} -\text{voc} \\ \text{dors} \\ -\text{cont} \\ +\text{voi} \end{bmatrix} \begin{bmatrix} +\text{voc} \\ -\text{low} \\ +\text{back} \\ +\text{rd} \end{bmatrix}$$

(24) *Shona repetitive suffix finds defective instance of [±high]*

$$x_1 \quad x_2 \quad x_3 \quad x_4 \quad \leftrightarrow \quad x_5 \quad x_6 \quad x_7$$

$$\begin{bmatrix} -\text{voc} \\ \text{cor} \\ +\text{cont} \\ +\text{voi} \end{bmatrix} \begin{bmatrix} +\text{voc} \\ -\text{low} \\ +\text{back} \\ +\text{rd} \\ -\text{high} \end{bmatrix} \begin{bmatrix} -\text{voc} \\ \text{cor} \\ -\text{cont} \\ -\text{voi} \end{bmatrix} \begin{bmatrix} +\text{voc} \\ -\text{low} \\ -\text{back} \\ \mathbf{-rd} \\ \mathbf{-high} \end{bmatrix} \begin{bmatrix} -\text{voc} \\ \text{dors} \\ +\text{nas} \end{bmatrix} \begin{bmatrix} -\text{voc} \\ \text{dors} \\ -\text{cont} \\ +\text{voi} \end{bmatrix} \begin{bmatrix} +\text{voc} \\ -\text{low} \\ +\text{back} \\ +\text{rd} \end{bmatrix}$$

(25) *Shona repetitive suffix undergoes last-resort insertion of [+high]*

$$x_1 \quad x_2 \quad x_3 \quad x_4 \quad x_5 \quad x_6 \quad x_7$$

$$\begin{bmatrix} -\text{voc} \\ \text{cor} \\ +\text{cont} \\ +\text{voi} \end{bmatrix} \begin{bmatrix} +\text{voc} \\ -\text{low} \\ +\text{back} \\ +\text{rd} \\ -\text{high} \end{bmatrix} \begin{bmatrix} -\text{voc} \\ \text{cor} \\ -\text{cont} \\ -\text{voi} \end{bmatrix} \begin{bmatrix} +\text{voc} \\ -\text{low} \\ -\text{back} \\ -\text{rd} \\ -\text{high} \end{bmatrix} \begin{bmatrix} -\text{voc} \\ \text{dors} \\ +\text{nas} \end{bmatrix} \begin{bmatrix} -\text{voc} \\ \text{dors} \\ -\text{cont} \\ +\text{voi} \end{bmatrix} \begin{bmatrix} +\text{voc} \\ -\text{low} \\ +\text{back} \\ +\text{rd} \\ +\mathit{high} \end{bmatrix}$$

z   o   t   e   n   g   u

The effect of conditional requirements on the source introduced in this chapter differs significantly from the effect of relativization of the search domain introduced in chapter 3. Relativization of the search domain prunes certain elements from ever being searched for in the first place, whereas parasitic requirements on sources cannot remove elements from the domain; they merely impose strict requirements on whether copying can actually take place.

4.4.2 Kimatuumbi: Conditional [±ATR] and Conditional [±high] Harmony

Kimatuumbi has harmonic copying for two features, each of which imposes its own conditional subrequirement. Kimatuumbi has seven vowels, of which /i,ɪ,u,ʊ/ are contrastive for [±ATR] and /ɪ,ʊ,ɛ,ɔ/ are contrastive for [±high].

(26) *Kimatuumbi vowel inventory*

[−back, −rd]	[+back, +rd]	[+back, −rd]	
i	u		[+high, −low, +ATR]
ɪ	ʊ		[+high, −low, −ATR]
ɛ	ɔ		[−high, −low, −ATR]
		a	[−high, +low, −ATR]

Odden (1991, 282) notes that the harmonic copying of [±high, ±ATR] initiated by the applicative suffix in Kimatuumbi "has a peculiar condition on it, namely that the vowel ε does not cause u to assimilate," while the other [−high, −low, −ATR] vowel, /ɔ/, does allow copying from itself, as do the other [−back, −round] vowels /i,ɪ/. (The [+low] vowel /a/ does not allow copying, but it is not contrastive for [±high] or [±ATR].)

(27) *Kimatuumbi applicative suffix can copy from /i,u,ɪ,ʊ,ɔ/*
    a. tyam-ul-ya   'sneeze-APPL-INF (sneeze on)'
    b. tip-ul-ya   'break.off.maize-APPL-INF'
    c. gul-ul-ya   'wash.dishes-APPL-INF'
    d. yʊng-ʊl-ya   'answer-APPL-INF'
    e. tɪk-ʊl-ya   'break-APPL-INF'
    f. lɔnd-ɔl-ya   'find.a.witch-APPL-INF'
    g. chɛk-ul-ya   'laugh-APPL-INF'
    h. nɛm-ul-ya   'dance-APPL-INF'

Given the "rectangular" shape of high front, high back, mid front, and mid back vowels, what is unique about the pattern of defective interveners is that only one corner of the rectangle is a defective source: the mid front vowels. Why should the high front, high back, and mid back vowels participate in harmony, forming a "diagonal" natural class of participants to the exclusion of the mid front vowels? The answer, I propose, is that the Kimatuumbi applicative suffix combines two distinct types of parasitic harmony; one for each feature being copied.

Copying of contrastive [±high] requires that the source be [+round], and copying of contrastive [±ATR] requires that the source be [+high]. Kimatuumbi thus combines the same parasitic harmony rule observed in Kisa with the parasitic harmony rule observed in Canadian French, whereby [±ATR] harmony occurs only among vowels that are [+high] (Poliquin 2006); see also Menominee in section 5.3.2 for a height-parasitic [±ATR] harmony.[10] I assume that in cases in which multiple features are copied from the same source, an ordering may be imposed among the copying processes;[11] in these cases, copying of [±high] (and default insertion of [+high] in case of failure) precedes copying of [±ATR], as represented by > in (28).

(28) *Kimatuumbi applicative suffix must:*
    Height- and ATR-Harmonize: δ = left, F = [c: high & R = +round > c: ATR & R = +high]

The combination of these two distinct conditional requirements on each feature being copied means that [+round] /ʊ,ɔ/ may be copied from for contrastive [±high], and [+high] /i,u,ɪ,ʊ/ may be copied from for contrastive [±ATR]. Neither /ɛ/ nor /a/ may be copied from for either feature. Default values inserted for these features are [+high] and [+ATR], as seen in (27a,g–h).

Both of these harmony requirements are met when the source is /ʊ/, as the derivation in (29)–(31) illustrates.

(29) *Kimatuumbi applicative suffix finds /ʊ/*

$$x_1 \leftarrow x_2$$
$$\begin{bmatrix} +\text{voc} \\ -\text{low} \\ +\text{rd} \\ +\text{high} \\ -\text{ATR} \end{bmatrix} \quad \begin{bmatrix} +\text{voc} \\ -\text{low} \\ +\text{rd} \end{bmatrix}$$

(30) *Kimatuumbi applicative suffix copies contrastive [±high] from [+round] source*

$$x_1 \leftarrow x_2$$
$$\begin{bmatrix} +\text{voc} \\ -\text{low} \\ \mathbf{+rd} \\ \mathbf{+high} \\ -\text{ATR} \end{bmatrix} \quad \begin{bmatrix} +\text{voc} \\ -\text{low} \\ +\text{rd} \\ +\text{high} \end{bmatrix}$$

(31) *Kimatuumbi applicative suffix copies contrastive [±ATR] from [+high] source*

$$x_1 \leftarrow x_2$$
$$\begin{bmatrix} +\text{voc} \\ -\text{low} \\ +\text{rd} \\ \mathbf{+high} \\ \mathbf{-ATR} \end{bmatrix} \quad \begin{bmatrix} +\text{voc} \\ -\text{low} \\ +\text{rd} \\ +\text{high} \\ -\text{ATR} \end{bmatrix}$$

The derivations for other preceding vowels are summarized in (32). (I assume, on the basis of the Kimatuumbi vowel inventory, an implicational rule of the form [−high] → [−ATR].)

(32) *Summary of harmonic copying from preceding vowels in Kimatuumbi*
 ɔ [−high] copying succeeds; [±ATR] copying succeeds
 u [+high] copying succeeds; [±ATR] copying succeeds

i [±high] copying fails, [+high] inserted; [±ATR] copying succeeds
ɪ [±high] copying fails, [+high] inserted; [±ATR] copying succeeds
ɛ [±high] copying fails, [+high] inserted; [±ATR] copying fails
a [±high] copying fails, [+high] inserted; [±ATR] copying fails

We now observe that the pattern of noncopying with /ɛ/ is no longer peculiar: the fact that /ɪ/ but not /ɛ/ allows [±ATR] copying is due to parasitic harmony for height, and the fact that /ɔ/ but not /ɛ/ allows [±high] copying is due to parasitic harmony for roundness. The combination of two distinct, independently attested harmonic requirements involving the same pairs of features explains why the Kimatuumbi applicative suffix refuses to copy from /ɛ/ on two distinct counts.

4.5 Intervention and Skipping Coexist in Khalkha Mongolian [±round] Harmony

Khalkha Mongolian illustrates an interesting combination of "transparent" and "opaque" interveners in its pattern of [±round] harmony: the high vowels /u,ʊ/ are defective interveners, forcing search to terminate in failure, while the high vowel /i/ is excluded from the relativization and skipped in the search. This combination of marked-value relativization (chapter 3) and parasitic harmony (this chapter) yields the first system we have considered in which defective intervention and skipped vowels coexist. The vowel system of Khalkha is shown in (33).

(33) *Khalkha Mongolian vowel inventory (Svantesson 1985)*

[−back, −rd]	[+back, +rd]	
i	u	[+high, +ATR]
	ʊ	[+high, −ATR]
e	o	[−high, +ATR]
a	ɔ	[−high, −ATR]

Khalkha has both [±ATR] harmony and [±round] harmony. The vowel /i/ is excluded from the search domain of both of these features, but for different reasons. [±ATR] harmony is relativized for contrastive values of [±ATR], and hence all vowels except for /i/ are included in the search domain. [±round] harmony, however, is relativized for marked values, as evidenced by the inclusion of /u,ʊ/ in the search domain for [±round] harmony even though they are not contrastive for this feature.

The patterning of /i/ and /u,ʊ/ is quite different in [±round] harmony: even though none of these vowels are contrastively [±round], the latter pair blocks further leftward harmony, while the former vowel is skipped completely. In the present model, blocking can only be the result of conditional restrictions on copyable sources, and indeed in Khalkha, as in many Altaic [±round] harmony systems, we are dealing with a case of parasitic harmony based on height. These two factors in the harmony system are summarized as follows:

(34) *Khalkha [±round] harmony*
    a. Unmarked transparency
        /i/ does not bear the marked value of [±round], stays invisible.
    b. Wrong-height defective intervention
        /u,ʊ/ are [+round] but block further search.

Defective intervention can be observed in the interaction between the perfect suffix, which demands marked [±round] from a source that is [−high], and the causative suffix, which is [+high] and hence can defectively intervene between the perfect and the root, causing [+round] to fail to be copied from the root, since leftward search halts immediately.[12]

Note that each suffix has no difficulty in copying contrastive [±ATR] from the immediately closest leftward vowel.

(35) *Defective intervention in Khalkha [±round] harmony*
    a. tor-oːd   'be.born-PERF'
    b. ɔr-ɔːd   'enter-PERF'
    c. tor-uːl-eːd 'be.born-CAUS-PERF'
    d. ɔr-ʊːl-aːd 'enter-CAUS-PERF'

The harmonic requirements of the Khalkha suffixes are shown in (36) and (37).

(36) *Khalkha causative suffix must:*
    ATR-Harmonize: δ = left, F = [c: ATR]

(37) *Khalkha perfect suffix must:*
    ATR-Harmonize and Round-Harmonize: δ = left, F = [c: ATR; m: round & R = −high]

The derivation of (35d), [ɔr-ʊːl-aːd], is provided in (38)–(43).[13]

(38) *Khalkha causative suffix begins ATR-Harmonize in [ɔr-ʊːl]*

$$x_1 \quad x_2 \quad \leftarrow \quad x_3 \quad x_4$$

$$\begin{bmatrix} +\text{voc} \\ -\text{high} \\ +\text{back} \\ +\text{rd} \\ -\text{ATR} \end{bmatrix} \begin{bmatrix} -\text{voc} \\ +\text{son} \\ -\text{nas} \\ -\text{lat} \end{bmatrix} \begin{bmatrix} +\text{voc} \\ +\text{high} \\ +\text{back} \\ +\text{rd} \end{bmatrix} \begin{bmatrix} -\text{voc} \\ +\text{son} \\ -\text{nas} \\ +\text{lat} \end{bmatrix}$$

(39) *Khalkha causative suffix finds and copies [−ATR]*

$$x_1 \quad \leftharpoonup \quad x_2 \quad\quad x_3 \quad\quad x_4$$

$$\begin{bmatrix} +\text{voc} \\ -\text{high} \\ +\text{back} \\ +\text{rd} \\ -\text{ATR} \end{bmatrix} \quad \begin{bmatrix} -\text{voc} \\ +\text{son} \\ -\text{nas} \\ -\text{lat} \end{bmatrix} \quad \begin{bmatrix} +\text{voc} \\ +\text{high} \\ +\text{back} \\ +\text{rd} \\ -\text{ATR} \end{bmatrix} \quad \begin{bmatrix} -\text{voc} \\ +\text{son} \\ -\text{nas} \\ +\text{lat} \end{bmatrix}$$

$$\quad\ \ \ \mathrm{ɔ} \quad\quad\quad\ \ \mathrm{r} \quad\quad\quad\ \ \mathrm{ʊ} \quad\quad\quad\ \ \mathrm{l}$$

The next affix to begin harmony is the perfect suffix, which follows the causative in morphological structure.

(40) *Khalkha perfect suffix begins ATR- and Round-Harmonize in [ɔr-ʊːl-aːd]*

$$x_3 \quad\quad x_4 \quad \leftarrow \quad x_5 \quad\quad x_6$$

$$\begin{bmatrix} +\text{voc} \\ +\text{high} \\ +\text{back} \\ +\text{rd} \\ -\text{ATR} \end{bmatrix} \quad \begin{bmatrix} -\text{voc} \\ +\text{son} \\ -\text{nas} \\ +\text{lat} \end{bmatrix} \quad \begin{bmatrix} +\text{voc} \\ -\text{high} \\ +\text{back} \end{bmatrix} \quad \begin{bmatrix} -\text{voc} \\ \text{cor} \\ -\text{cont} \\ +\text{voi} \end{bmatrix}$$

(41) *Khalkha perfect suffix finds and copies contrastive [−ATR]*

$$x_3 \quad \leftharpoonup \quad x_4 \quad\quad x_5 \quad\quad x_6$$

$$\begin{bmatrix} +\text{voc} \\ +\text{high} \\ +\text{back} \\ +\text{rd} \\ -\text{ATR} \end{bmatrix} \quad \begin{bmatrix} -\text{voc} \\ +\text{son} \\ -\text{nas} \\ +\text{lat} \end{bmatrix} \quad \begin{bmatrix} +\text{voc} \\ -\text{high} \\ +\text{back} \\ -\text{ATR} \end{bmatrix} \quad \begin{bmatrix} -\text{voc} \\ \text{cor} \\ -\text{cont} \\ +\text{voi} \end{bmatrix}$$

(42) *Khalkha perfect suffix finds defectively [+high] instance of [+round]*

$$x_3 \quad \leftrightarrow \quad x_4 \quad\quad x_5 \quad\quad x_6$$

$$\begin{bmatrix} +\text{voc} \\ \mathbf{+\text{high}} \\ +\text{back} \\ \mathbf{+\text{rd}} \\ -\text{ATR} \end{bmatrix} \quad \begin{bmatrix} -\text{voc} \\ +\text{son} \\ -\text{nas} \\ +\text{lat} \end{bmatrix} \quad \begin{bmatrix} +\text{voc} \\ -\text{high} \\ +\text{back} \\ -\text{ATR} \end{bmatrix} \quad \begin{bmatrix} -\text{voc} \\ \text{cor} \\ -\text{cont} \\ +\text{voi} \end{bmatrix}$$

(43) *Khalkha perfect suffix undergoes last-resort insertion of [−round]*

$$\begin{matrix} x_3 & x_4 & x_5 & x_6 \\ \begin{bmatrix} +\text{voc} \\ +\text{high} \\ +\text{back} \\ +\text{rd} \\ -\text{ATR} \end{bmatrix} & \begin{bmatrix} -\text{voc} \\ +\text{son} \\ -\text{nas} \\ +\text{lat} \end{bmatrix} & \begin{bmatrix} +\text{voc} \\ -\text{high} \\ +\text{back} \\ -\text{rd} \\ -\text{ATR} \end{bmatrix} & \begin{bmatrix} -\text{voc} \\ \text{cor} \\ -\text{cont} \\ +\text{voi} \end{bmatrix} \\ \upsilon & l & a & d \end{matrix}$$

The high vowels /u,ʊ/ are defective interveners included in the search because they carry marked values for [±round]. On the other hand, /i/ is transparent for rounding harmony, excluded from the search in the first place, because it is unmarked for [−round].[14] /i/ is also transparent for [±ATR] harmony, because it is noncontrastive for this feature. Both types of skipping over /i/ are illustrated in (44g).[15]

(44) *Khalkha [+round] harmony for the comitative suffix*
    a. nar-tai   'sun-COMIT'
    b. ner-tei   'name-COMIT'
    c. ʊːl-tai   'mountain-COMIT'
    d. xun-tei   'person-COMIT'
    e. ɔd-tɔi   'star-COMIT'
    f. bičig-tei   'letter-COMIT'
    g. mɔri-tɔi   'horse-COMIT'

In (44g), contrastive [±ATR] harmony and marked [±round] harmony both skip over /i/. In (44c–d), note that with the same suffix, /u,ʊ/ fail to provide a [+round] value, even though they are indeed round. Similar effects of transparency in Khalkha are observed with the accusative suffix /-ig/.

(45) *Transparency of suffixal /i/ in Khalkha (Svantesson et al. 2005, 50)*
    a. poor-ig-o   'kidney-ACC-REFL'
    b. xɔɔlʒ-ig-ɔ   'food-ACC-REFL'
    c. mʊʊr-ig-a   'cat-ACC-REFL'
    d. suulʒ-ig-e   'tail-ACC-REFL'

The Khalkha system is of interest to locality theory because of the difference between the two high vowels /i/ and /u/. Neither ends up providing a value of [±round], but for different reasons and with different effects: /i/ because it is excluded from search in the first place, and /u/ because it is included in search but is defectively of the wrong height.

4.6 Defective Intervention Due to All-Value Relativization in Oroch

While in Khalkha, defective intervention is caused by vowels with *marked* values for [±round] of the wrong height, this is distinct from what occurs in the Tungusic language Oroch (Tolskaya 2008), in which defective intervention may be caused by *all* values of [±round] of the wrong height.[16] In Oroch, as in Khalkha, none of the high vowels /i,u,ʊ/ are contrastive for [±round] (since there are no front round or back unround high vowels in the language), but in fact all are included in search, and defectively so. Unlike in Khalkha, in Oroch the high vowel /i/ blocks further [±round] copying as well; as soon as search hits any instance of a high vowel, it halts, despite further licit instances of [+round] downstream.[17] As introduced in section 3.12, Oroch has the following vowel inventory:

(46) *Oroch vowel inventory*

[−back, −rd]	[+back, −rd]	[+rd]	
i		u	[+high, +ATR]
		ʊ	[+high, −ATR]
æ	ə		[−high, +ATR]
	a	ɔ	[−high, −ATR]

Like Khalkha, Oroch exhibits [±ATR] harmony in addition to [±round] harmony.

(47) *Oroch accusative suffix, focus suffix must:*
ATR-Harmonize and Round-Harmonize: δ = left, F = [c: ATR; ±round & R = −high]

As a result of a relativization in Oroch whereby *all* values of [±round] are visible within the search domain, any high vowel that is the closest to a [±round]-seeking suffix induces defective intervention (48b–c).

(48) *Oroch rounding harmony blocked by [+high] vowels*
 a. ɔtɔŋgo-vɔ-dɔ 'kayak-ACC-FOC'
 b. ɔtɔŋgo-dʊ-da 'kayak-DAT-FOC'
 c. ɔtɔŋgo-ɲi-dɔ 'kayak-3SG-FOC'

In Oroch [ɔtɔŋgo-ɲi-dɔ] (48c), the focus suffix searches leftward for any value of [±round], the search domain thereby including /i/. As soon as /i/ is encountered, its failure to be [−high] halts the search, which ends in failure, triggering last-resort insertion of [+round]. If only the algorithm were different, the search might have persisted in looking further for a [±round] source that was [−high]. But the derivational nature of the Search procedure is such that as soon as it hits the closest element, it stops, whether that element is a good source or not. Oroch blocking by /i/ is yet another case where the no-second-chance property of search within a domain is nonnegotiable.

4.7 Derived-Environment Effects in Harmony

4.7.1 Derived-Environment Phenomena as Defective Intervention

The majority of cases of vowel harmony discussed in previous sections are cases where an affix copies harmonic features from another morpheme, or where a root copies from within itself. As we saw in chapter 2, affixes may be fairly indiscriminate in what they copy from: either a leftward suffix or a root can provide a harmonic value, and what matters is simply what's closest in terms of immediate precedence within the search domain.

We also find languages in which root vowels harmonically copy from affixes, thereby exhibiting a left-to-right directionality in the case of suffixation (e.g., Kalenjin (section 2.9); also see Noske 2001 on Turkana, Mahanta 2007 on Assamese). In these cases as well, root vowels are indiscriminate in choosing their value-source, copying from either a root vowel or a suffix vowel, depending on phonological closeness alone once the domain has been featurally relativized.

The model of conditional requirements on sources developed thus far allows for the possibility that value-seekers will be "picky" not only about the orthogonal features a licit source may bear, but also about the source's morphological affiliation. Such cases are rare in the literature and often subsumed under derived-environment effects. However, *derived-environment effects* is largely a phenomenological term for which a variety of heterogeneous mechanisms have been proposed. Even when harmonic copying shows an apparent derived-environment requirement (namely, the requirement that the value-seeker and the value-source come from distinct morphemes; hence, their cooccurrence within the same word is *derived*), one would not necessarily expect them to show blocking effects, whereby a vowel with the wrong morphological affiliation blocks a vowel with the right morphological affiliation. By contrast, modeling the demand that the value-seeker and the value-source have distinct morphological affiliations in terms of conditional requirements on copying leads to strong predictions about defective intervention in such cases.

4.7.2 Jingulu: Morphological Requirements on Source

The [±high] harmony in Jingulu (Pensalfini 2002), a language of north-central Australia, imposes a morphological requirement on what can serve as a licit source. Jingulu has the three vowels /i,u,a/.

(49) *Jingulu vowel inventory*

    [−back, −rd] [+back, +rd] [+back, −rd]
    i   u   [+high]
                                       a   [−high]

In a three-vowel system of this sort, we can assume an implicational statement of the form [+high, −round] → [−back] (see section 2.11 for an introduction to such "redundancy" statements for languages lacking /ü/). Jingulu [−round] vowels copy marked [+high], starting from left to right.

(50) *Jingulu [−round] vowels harmonize with following affixes*
    a. ŋaɟa   ŋiɟi-mindi-yi   'see / see-1.DUAL.INCL-FUT'
    b. baḍarba   biḍirbi-ṇi   'younger brother / younger sister'
    c. kuɲarba   kuɲirbi-ṇi   'dog / dog-female'
    d. ŋarabaɟa   ŋiribiɟi-wuru-nu 'tell / tell-3PL-did'

Pensalfini (2002) characterizes the class of suffixes that may be copied from in terms of morphological domain: gender suffixes with nouns/adjectives and tense/agreement suffixes with verbs.[18] I assume that root vowels alternating between [a] and [i] are lexically marked as requiring harmony for the feature [±high], and if they fail to find a value-source, [−high] is assigned as the default value (Pensalfini 1997, chap. 2). Non-alternating root vowels are lexically [+high].

(51) *Jingulu needy root vowels must:*
    High-Harmonize: δ = right, F = [m: high & R = nonroot]

In Jingulu, root vowels requiring harmony initiate their own search iteratively, starting with the leftmost such vowel, as shown in for [ŋiɟi-mindi-yi] in (52)–(56).

(52) *First root vowel begins High-Harmonize in Jingulu /ŋaʃa-mindi/*

x_1	x_2	→	x_3	x_4	x_5	x_6
$\begin{bmatrix} -\text{voc} \\ \text{dors} \\ +\text{nas} \end{bmatrix}$	$\begin{bmatrix} +\text{voc} \\ -\text{rd} \end{bmatrix}$		$\begin{bmatrix} -\text{voc} \\ \text{cor} \\ -\text{cont} \\ +\text{voi} \\ -\text{ant} \\ +\text{distr} \end{bmatrix}$	$\begin{bmatrix} +\text{voc} \\ -\text{rd} \end{bmatrix}$	$\begin{bmatrix} -\text{voc} \\ \text{lab} \\ +\text{nas} \end{bmatrix}$	$\begin{bmatrix} +\text{voc} \\ -\text{rd} \\ -\text{back} \\ +\text{high} \end{bmatrix}$

Defective Intervention

(53) *First root vowel finds and copies [+high] on suffix vowel*

$$x_1 \quad x_2 \quad x_3 \quad x_4 \quad x_5 \stackrel{\curvearrowleft}{} x_6$$

$$\begin{bmatrix} -\text{voc} \\ \text{dors} \\ +\text{nas} \end{bmatrix} \begin{bmatrix} +\text{voc} \\ -\text{rd} \\ +\textbf{high} \end{bmatrix} \begin{bmatrix} -\text{voc} \\ \text{cor} \\ -\text{cont} \\ +\text{voi} \\ -\text{ant} \\ +\text{distr} \end{bmatrix} \begin{bmatrix} +\text{voc} \\ -\text{rd} \end{bmatrix} \begin{bmatrix} -\text{voc} \\ \text{lab} \\ +\text{nas} \end{bmatrix} \begin{bmatrix} +\text{voc} \\ -\text{rd} \\ -\text{back} \\ +\textbf{high} \end{bmatrix}$$

(54) *Second root vowel begins High-Harmonize*

$$x_1 \quad x_2 \quad x_3 \quad x_4 \rightarrow x_5 \quad x_6$$

$$\begin{bmatrix} -\text{voc} \\ \text{dors} \\ +\text{nas} \end{bmatrix} \begin{bmatrix} +\text{voc} \\ -\text{rd} \\ +\text{high} \end{bmatrix} \begin{bmatrix} -\text{voc} \\ \text{cor} \\ -\text{cont} \\ +\text{voi} \\ -\text{ant} \\ +\text{distr} \end{bmatrix} \begin{bmatrix} +\text{voc} \\ -\text{rd} \end{bmatrix} \begin{bmatrix} -\text{voc} \\ \text{lab} \\ +\text{nas} \end{bmatrix} \begin{bmatrix} +\text{voc} \\ -\text{rd} \\ -\text{back} \\ +\text{high} \end{bmatrix}$$

(55) *Second root vowel finds and copies [+high]*

$$x_1 \quad x_2 \quad x_3 \quad x_4 \quad x_5 \stackrel{\curvearrowleft}{} x_6$$

$$\begin{bmatrix} -\text{voc} \\ \text{dors} \\ +\text{nas} \end{bmatrix} \begin{bmatrix} +\text{voc} \\ -\text{rd} \\ +\text{high} \end{bmatrix} \begin{bmatrix} -\text{voc} \\ \text{cor} \\ -\text{cont} \\ +\text{voi} \\ -\text{ant} \\ +\text{distr} \end{bmatrix} \begin{bmatrix} +\text{voc} \\ -\text{rd} \\ +\textbf{high} \end{bmatrix} \begin{bmatrix} -\text{voc} \\ \text{lab} \\ +\text{nas} \end{bmatrix} \begin{bmatrix} +\text{voc} \\ -\text{rd} \\ -\text{back} \\ +\textbf{high} \end{bmatrix}$$

(56) *Implicational statement supplies [−back] for [+high, −round] vowels*

$$x_1 \quad x_2 \quad x_3 \quad x_4 \quad x_5 \quad x_6$$

$$\begin{bmatrix} -\text{voc} \\ \text{dors} \\ +\text{nas} \end{bmatrix} \begin{bmatrix} +\text{voc} \\ -\text{rd} \\ -\textbf{back} \\ +\text{high} \end{bmatrix} \begin{bmatrix} -\text{voc} \\ \text{cor} \\ -\text{cont} \\ +\text{voi} \\ -\text{ant} \\ +\text{distr} \end{bmatrix} \begin{bmatrix} +\text{voc} \\ -\text{rd} \\ -\textbf{back} \\ +\text{high} \end{bmatrix} \begin{bmatrix} -\text{voc} \\ \text{lab} \\ +\text{nas} \end{bmatrix} \begin{bmatrix} +\text{voc} \\ -\text{rd} \\ -\text{back} \\ +\text{high} \end{bmatrix}$$

ŋ a ɟ i m i

Although a root vowel requiring harmony copies marked [+high] from a rightward source, importantly, a [+high] vowel within the same root cannot provide a value for this harmony process. Naturally, because of the very restricted nature of value-parameterization outlined in chapter 3, there is no way to exclude [+high] root vowels from the search. Nonetheless, the morphological requirement that only nonroot vowels may be copied from can be encoded as a conditional requirement on the copying procedure.

A [+high] vowel in the root will *block* the copying process from a suffixal [+high] vowel. Stated differently, an underlying [+high] vowel in the root will prevent any *preceding* vowels from raising. In Jingulu, the conditional requirement R on harmonic sources is that their morphological affiliation must be [−root]. As a result, [+high] *root* vowels, although they have the required value, cannot provide a source for copying [+high]. Moreover, not only do these [+high] root vowels fail to provide a source for copying [+high], they also block copying [+high] from any further potential determinants, thereby constituting defective interveners.

(57) *Defective intervention in Jingulu [+high] harmony*
   a. waḷaku   waḷaku-ṇi   'dog/ dog-FEM'
   b. mamambiyaka   mamambiyiki-mi   'soft / soft-VEG'
   c. ŋamuḷa   ŋamuḷi-ṇi   ' big / big-FEM'
   d. aŋkila   aŋkili-ṇi   'cross-cousin /
                                         cross-cousin-FEM'

In (57a–b), the first two root vowels cannot copy from the suffixal vowel because of a closer, defective root vowel. In (57c–d), the initial root vowel cannot copy from the suffixal vowel because of a closer defective root vowel. The derivation for *aŋkili-ṇi* (57d) is shown in (58)–(63). The first root vowel's search fails as soon as it hits the [+high] second root vowel. As a consequence of defective intervention, default [−high] is inserted. The final root vowel's search then proceeds and successfully copies from a [−root] vowel. In the following diagrams, although [±root] is a morphological affiliation and not a subsegmental feature, I include it in the same column for ease of visual inspection.

(58) *First needy root vowel begins High-Harmonize in [aŋkili-ṇi]*

x_1	$\rightarrow$	x_2	x_3	x_4	x_5	x_6	x_7	x_8
$\begin{bmatrix} +\text{voc} \\ -\text{rd} \end{bmatrix}$		$\begin{bmatrix} -\text{voc} \\ \text{dors} \\ +\text{nas} \\ +root \end{bmatrix}$	$\begin{bmatrix} -\text{voc} \\ \text{dors} \\ -\text{cont} \\ -\text{voi} \\ +root \end{bmatrix}$	$\begin{bmatrix} +\text{voc} \\ -\text{rd} \\ -\text{back} \\ +\text{high} \\ +root \end{bmatrix}$	$\begin{bmatrix} -\text{voc} \\ \text{cor} \\ +\text{son} \\ -\text{nas} \\ +\text{lat} \\ +root \end{bmatrix}$	$\begin{bmatrix} +\text{voc} \\ -\text{rd} \\ +root \end{bmatrix}$	$\begin{bmatrix} -\text{voc} \\ \text{cor} \\ -\text{ant} \\ -\text{distr} \\ +\text{nas} \\ -root \end{bmatrix}$	$\begin{bmatrix} +\text{voc} \\ -\text{rd} \\ -\text{back} \\ +\text{high} \\ -root \end{bmatrix}$

Defective Intervention

(59) *First needy root vowel finds defective [+high] vowel*

$$x_1 \quad x_2 \quad x_3 \quad \nrightarrow \quad x_4 \quad x_5 \quad x_6 \quad x_7 \quad x_8$$

$$\begin{bmatrix} +\text{voc} \\ -\text{rd} \end{bmatrix} \begin{bmatrix} -\text{voc} \\ \text{dors} \\ +\text{nas} \\ +\textit{root} \end{bmatrix} \begin{bmatrix} -\text{voc} \\ \text{dors} \\ -\text{cont} \\ -\text{voi} \\ +\textit{root} \end{bmatrix} \begin{bmatrix} +\text{voc} \\ -\text{rd} \\ -\text{back} \\ +\textbf{high} \\ +\textbf{\textit{root}} \end{bmatrix} \begin{bmatrix} -\text{voc} \\ \text{cor} \\ +\text{son} \\ -\text{nas} \\ +\text{lat} \\ +\textit{root} \end{bmatrix} \begin{bmatrix} +\text{voc} \\ -\text{rd} \\ \\ +\textit{root} \end{bmatrix} \begin{bmatrix} -\text{voc} \\ \text{cor} \\ -\text{ant} \\ -\text{distr} \\ +\text{nas} \\ -\textit{root} \end{bmatrix} \begin{bmatrix} +\text{voc} \\ -\text{rd} \\ -\text{back} \\ +\text{high} \\ -\textit{root} \end{bmatrix}$$

(60) *First needy root vowel undergoes default insertion of [−high]: Implicational [−high] → [+back]*

$$x_1 \quad x_2 \quad x_3 \quad x_4 \quad x_5 \quad x_6 \quad x_7 \quad x_8$$

$$\begin{bmatrix} +\text{voc} \\ -\text{rd} \\ +\textbf{back} \\ -\textbf{high} \end{bmatrix} \begin{bmatrix} -\text{voc} \\ \text{dors} \\ +\text{nas} \\ +\textit{root} \end{bmatrix} \begin{bmatrix} -\text{voc} \\ \text{dors} \\ -\text{cont} \\ -\text{voi} \\ +\textit{root} \end{bmatrix} \begin{bmatrix} +\text{voc} \\ -\text{rd} \\ -\text{back} \\ +\text{high} \\ +\textit{root} \end{bmatrix} \begin{bmatrix} -\text{voc} \\ \text{cor} \\ +\text{son} \\ -\text{nas} \\ +\text{lat} \\ +\textit{root} \end{bmatrix} \begin{bmatrix} +\text{voc} \\ -\text{rd} \\ \\ +\textit{root} \end{bmatrix} \begin{bmatrix} -\text{voc} \\ \text{cor} \\ -\text{ant} \\ -\text{distr} \\ +\text{nas} \\ -\textit{root} \end{bmatrix} \begin{bmatrix} +\text{voc} \\ -\text{rd} \\ -\text{back} \\ +\text{high} \\ -\textit{root} \end{bmatrix}$$

(61) *Second needy root vowel begins High-Harmonize*

$$x_1 \quad x_2 \quad x_3 \quad x_4 \quad x_5 \quad x_6 \quad \rightarrow \quad x_7 \quad x_8$$

$$\begin{bmatrix} +\text{voc} \\ -\text{rd} \\ +\text{back} \\ -\text{high} \end{bmatrix} \begin{bmatrix} -\text{voc} \\ \text{dors} \\ +\text{nas} \\ +\textit{root} \end{bmatrix} \begin{bmatrix} -\text{voc} \\ \text{dors} \\ -\text{cont} \\ -\text{voi} \\ +\textit{root} \end{bmatrix} \begin{bmatrix} +\text{voc} \\ -\text{rd} \\ -\text{back} \\ +\text{high} \\ +\textit{root} \end{bmatrix} \begin{bmatrix} -\text{voc} \\ \text{cor} \\ +\text{son} \\ -\text{nas} \\ +\text{lat} \\ +\textit{root} \end{bmatrix} \begin{bmatrix} +\text{voc} \\ -\text{rd} \\ \\ +\textit{root} \end{bmatrix} \begin{bmatrix} -\text{voc} \\ \text{cor} \\ -\text{ant} \\ -\text{distr} \\ +\text{nas} \\ -\textit{root} \end{bmatrix} \begin{bmatrix} +\text{voc} \\ -\text{rd} \\ -\text{back} \\ +\text{high} \\ -\textit{root} \end{bmatrix}$$

(62) *Second needy root finds and copies [+high] from [−root] vowel*

$$x_1 \quad x_2 \quad x_3 \quad x_4 \quad x_5 \quad x_6 \quad x_7 \quad \curvearrowleft \quad x_8$$

$$\begin{bmatrix} +\text{voc} \\ -\text{rd} \\ +\text{back} \\ -\text{high} \end{bmatrix} \begin{bmatrix} -\text{voc} \\ \text{dors} \\ +\text{nas} \\ +\textit{root} \end{bmatrix} \begin{bmatrix} -\text{voc} \\ \text{dors} \\ -\text{cont} \\ -\text{voi} \\ +\textit{root} \end{bmatrix} \begin{bmatrix} +\text{voc} \\ -\text{rd} \\ -\text{back} \\ +\text{high} \\ +\textit{root} \end{bmatrix} \begin{bmatrix} -\text{voc} \\ \text{cor} \\ +\text{son} \\ -\text{nas} \\ +\text{lat} \\ +\textit{root} \end{bmatrix} \begin{bmatrix} +\text{voc} \\ -\text{rd} \\ +\textbf{high} \\ +\textit{root} \end{bmatrix} \begin{bmatrix} -\text{voc} \\ \text{cor} \\ -\text{ant} \\ -\text{distr} \\ +\text{nas} \\ -\textit{root} \end{bmatrix} \begin{bmatrix} +\text{voc} \\ -\text{rd} \\ -\text{back} \\ +\textbf{high} \\ -\textit{root} \end{bmatrix}$$

(63) *Implicational statement provides [−back]*

$$x_1 \quad x_2 \quad x_3 \quad x_4 \quad x_5 \quad x_6 \quad x_7 \quad x_8$$

$$\begin{bmatrix} +\text{voc} \\ -\text{rd} \\ +\text{back} \\ -\text{high} \end{bmatrix} \begin{bmatrix} -\text{voc} \\ \text{dors} \\ +\text{nas} \\ +\textit{root} \end{bmatrix} \begin{bmatrix} -\text{voc} \\ \text{dors} \\ -\text{cont} \\ -\text{voi} \\ +\textit{root} \end{bmatrix} \begin{bmatrix} +\text{voc} \\ -\text{rd} \\ -\text{back} \\ +\text{high} \\ +\textit{root} \end{bmatrix} \begin{bmatrix} -\text{voc} \\ \text{cor} \\ +\text{son} \\ -\text{nas} \\ +\text{lat} \\ +\textit{root} \end{bmatrix} \begin{bmatrix} +\text{voc} \\ -\text{rd} \\ -\textbf{back} \\ +\text{high} \\ +\textit{root} \end{bmatrix} \begin{bmatrix} -\text{voc} \\ \text{cor} \\ -\text{ant} \\ -\text{distr} \\ +\text{nas} \\ -\textit{root} \end{bmatrix} \begin{bmatrix} +\text{voc} \\ -\text{rd} \\ -\text{back} \\ +\text{high} \\ -\textit{root} \end{bmatrix}$$

a ŋ k i l i ɲ i

The Jingulu restriction on harmonic copying can be viewed as a derived-environment restriction: the harmony rule can only be triggered by "derived contexts," and two root-internal vowels do not constitute a derived context. But I will assimilate this case of morphological defective intervention to the subsegmental-feature cases because the logic is the same. Moreover, the mechanism through which search halts as soon as the right vowel with the wrong morphological affiliation is found will be general enough to hold even for cases in which word formation does not involve distinct derivational cycles for root and nonroot material.[19]

To summarize our progress, in this section we examined a conditional requirement on the source that is morphological in nature. In the previous sections, we examined more familiar cases of parasitic harmony, in which the source precondition is based on a subsegmental feature. Importantly, the defective-intervention rubric unites both sets of cases: once a parrot is found, if it's not red, there's no second chance to look for another. This is an inviolable principle of locality that supersedes the language-specific settings for what constitute licit sources of feature valuation.

4.8 Conclusions

Defective intervention is the result of the fact that the Search procedure inviolably stops at the first element in the search domain. The only way that items can be excluded from the domain is by failing to bear an inventory-derived property (either markedness or contrastiveness) for the harmonic feature itself. The crosslinguistic variation within harmony systems that may be based on featural properties unrelated to the harmonic feature cannot serve to exclude a segment from the search domain. When such conditions are parametrically imposed on a given set of potential value-sources, they can lead to failure of copying, but they cannot render the defective elements invisible.

I have proposed a restrictive set of conditional requirements on licit sources: they can only refer to two types of properties, namely, featural identity and morphological nonidentity.

The first type of restriction that leads to "blocking" is the requirement of orthogonal featural identity between value-seeker and value-source.[20] We have observed cases of parasitic harmony where the conditionally identical feature may be [±high], [±round], or [±consonantal]. Crucially, however, we find no cases of conditional-requirement harmony that require *nonidentity* of an orthogonal feature (see also Cole and Trigo 1988, 23); for example, there is no system in which round harmony copies *only* from an opposite height and otherwise yields defective intervention.

The second type of restriction that brings the search procedure to a halt is the requirement of morphological distinctness between value-seeker and value-source. From a functional perspective, this might be a somewhat natural type of condition to expect: failure to harmonize with segments that are already in the same morpheme. However, in chapter 2, Turkish and Finnish root harmony showed that some languages indeed engage in an active process of harmonic copying between elements within the same morpheme. More importantly, whether or not a condition that elements can only harmonize with heteromorphemic segments is functionally motivated, we would not necessarily expect this condition to yield blocking—but it does. Languages that require heteromorphemic sources for harmony cannot "keep looking" past the first element bearing the harmonic feature within the search domain.

In summary, what causes "blocking" is never markedness or contrastiveness of the harmonic feature. Blocking can only be a function of the values of orthogonal features—crucially, without respect to their markedness or contrastiveness. Only the predicate of identity between source and goal for the orthogonal feature can cause copying to succeed or fail.

Defective intervention is an empirical hypothesis about harmony systems that can be modeled in any target-centric theory of locality, possibly even within differing representations of harmonic features (Kaye, Lowenstamm, and Vergnaud 1985; Archangeli and Pulleyblank 1994; Van der Hulst and Van de Weijer 1995; Clements 2003). However, the no-lookahead property of the Search procedure seems to require a target-initiated, procedural search, which cannot obviously be replicated in declarative models.[21] The conclusion that search terminates with the closest potential source, regardless of more optimal sources downstream, is a generalization about phonological locality with parallels in other modules of linguistic computation where lack of lookahead and strict minimality lead to failure to copy a needed feature from either the closest or the second-closest source.

5 Domain Limitations on Search

Imagine you're on a search. Locality (i.e., when you stop searching) has two components: *minimality* (stopping at the closest potential element) and *boundedness* (an extrinsically defined limit on how far you can go in your search).

In syntactic theory, the principles of minimality rule out searching for an element beyond a defective one.[1] Consider *wh*-movement in (1), for example. Here, minimality demands that the matrix C's search halt with *whether*; C cannot look further to move *who*.

(1) a. [C$_{[needs:\ wh]}$ [did [you [wonder [$_{CP}$ [whether$_{[wh,\ -movable]}$ [who$_{[wh,\ +movable]}$ [danced]]]]]]]]
    b. *Who did you wonder whether t$_{who}$ danced?

Boundedness, on the other hand, rules out searching for an element past certain kinds of nodes. Consider *wh*-movement in (2). Here, the matrix C's search cannot look past *the*, regardless of what lies beyond (see Adger 2003, chap. 10, for an introductory exposition).

(2) a. [C$_{[needs:\ wh]}$ [did [you [hear [the$_{boundary}$ [recitals [of [which poem]$_{[wh,\ +movable]}$]]]]]]]
    b. *Which poem did you hear the recitals of t$_{which\ poem}$ last night?

In chapter 4, we discussed the phonological analogue of cases such as (1) within a theory of relativization and defective intervention. Here, we will develop the phonological instantiation of (2): when search "hits a wall" and ends not because a defective element of the relevant type was found, but because the search domain was bounded.

We will discuss two types of boundedness that constrain the extent of the search in vowel harmony: *distance parameters*, which regulate how far a search can proceed before giving up, and *sonority hurdles*, which impose barriers to search.

5.1 Distance Parameters Limit the Extent of Search

While a great deal of phonological theory centers on the minimality side of locality, the fact that some assimilation processes are strictly local, others are long-distance, and still others are in-between (in a way to be made precise below) is a dimension that must be developed in a more inclusive model. Just as syntactic theory does not collapse the distinction between minimality and boundedness,[2] so the study of vowel harmony must separate the delimitation of the search domain—in terms of relativized closeness—from phenomena in which certain elements simply cannot look past an extrinsically defined limit of segments or syllables. As Yamada (1983, 63) remarks, "In general, the problem of distance should be clearly distinguished from what may intervene in a phonological rule."

5.1.1 Unbounded versus Syllable-Bounded Search

Odden (1994) makes the important observation that certain assimilation and dissimilation processes have "locality bounds" that are not solely determined by relativization to a class of interveners. As Odden points out, these distance parameters impose additional constraints on the maximal distance between interacting segments. Many cases of crosslinguistic variation in the same harmony process can only be understood in these terms. Consider long-distance nasal harmony in Kikongo applicative and passive suffixes (Ao 1991; Odden 1994; Piggott 1996).

(3) *Kikongo long-distance nasalization with the suffixes [-il]/[-in] and [-ul]/[-un]*
    a. sa.ki.di.la   'to congratulate for'
    b. man.ti.**na**   'to climb for'
    c. ku.du.mu.ki.si.**na** 'to cause to jump for'
    d. ma.ki.nu.**nu**   'it was planted'
    e. wu.man.tu.**nu**   'it was climbed'

As (3) shows, the applicative suffix in Kikongo can search unboundedly, copying marked [+nasal] from up to three syllables away. If no marked [+nasal] is found, the default [−nasal] is inserted.[3] Formulating the long-distance harmony rule in Kikongo is straightforward, following the domain-relativization parameterization developed in chapter 3.

(4) *Kikongo applicative and passive suffixes must:*
    Nasal-Harmonize: δ = left, F = [m: ±nasal]

Lamba, another Bantu language exhibiting nasal harmony, imposes stricter locality demands on the search domain. Here, the search cannot look further than one syllable away from the needy suffix (I assume that resyllabification occurs immediately upon suffixation, even before the harmonic search is initiated). The failure of the Lamba reversative and perfective suffixes to copy from a [+nasal] source more than one syllable away is illustrated in (5) (Odden 1994).

(5) *Lamba syllable-bounded nasalization*
    a. fi.su.lu.ka   'plaster.REVERS'
    b. mi.nu.nu.ka   'swallow.REVERS'
    c. pa.ti.le   'scold.PFCTV'
    d. u.mi.ne   'dry.PFCTV'
    e. ma.si.le   'plaster.PFCTV'

While Lamba and Kikongo both exhibit leftward harmony for the marked values [+nasal] with the same relevant segments in the inventory, the parametric difference between these two languages must be grammatically encoded in terms of a boundedness condition. Specifically, there is a distance parameter that is set to *unbounded* in the case of Kikongo but to just *one syllable* in Lamba. In terms of implementation, the Search algorithm must be supplemented with a "counter," so that if the leftward search exceeds one syllable beyond the Lamba suffix, it halts. Every time a syllable frontier is passed, the counter is incremented. At each step along the segmental path, the syllable counter is checked to see whether it has exceeded 1. This is included as a new parameter β, expressed in (6).

(6) *Lamba perfect suffix must:*
    Nasal-Harmonize: δ = left, β = 1 syllable, F = [m: $\pm$nasal]

As soon as one syllable boundary has been crossed, the search among segments must end. This is illustrated in (7)–(12) for the distinct patterns of the two Lamba words [u.mi.ne] (where a [+nasal] vowel is encountered within one traversed syllable) and [ma.si.le] (where no [+nasal] vowel is encountered within one traversed syllable).

(7) *Lamba perfective suffix begins search for marked [+nasal] in [u.mi.ne]*

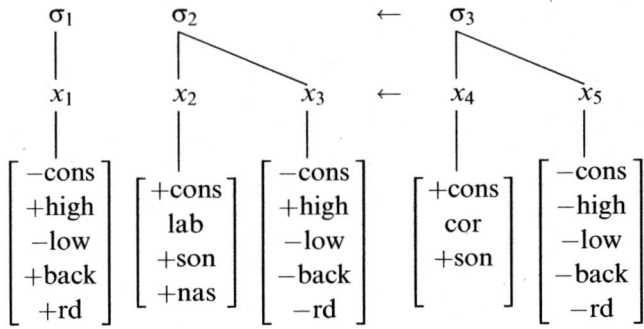

(8) *Lamba perfective suffix finds [+nasal] source*

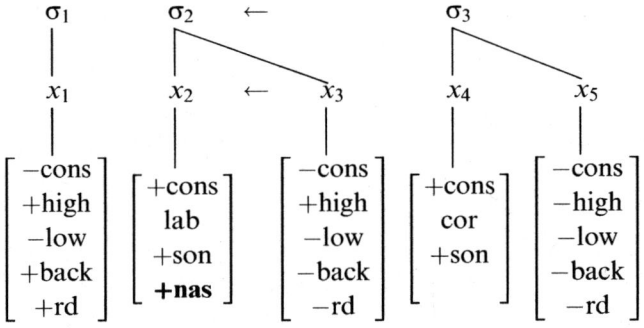

(9) *Lamba perfective suffix copies marked [+nasal]*

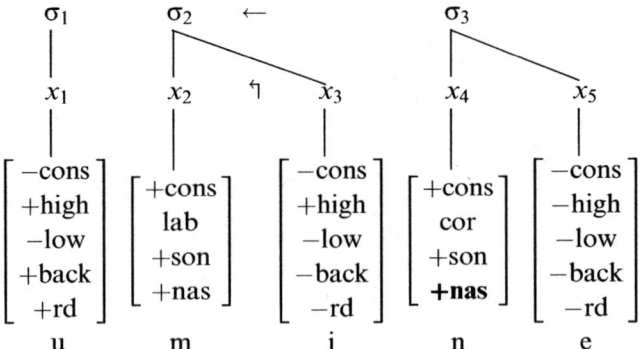

In [u.mi.ne], a [+nasal] source is encountered before the syllable-boundary counter has been incremented to 1. In [ma.si.le], however, the syllable-boundary counter is incremented to 1 before a nasal source has been found, bringing the search to an early end, indicated by ↔ in (11).

Domain Limitations on Search 153

(10) *Lamba perfective suffix begins search for marked [+nasal] in [ma.si.le]*

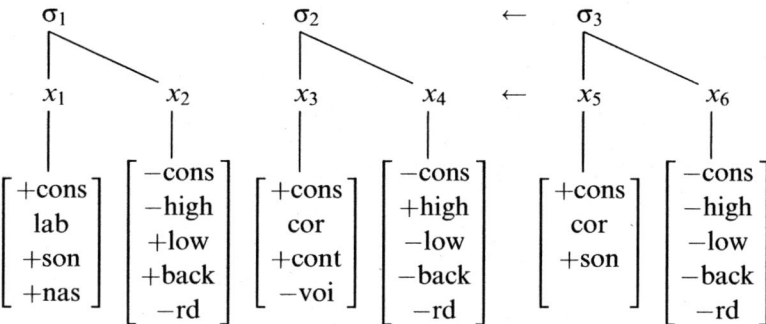

(11) *Lamba search for marked [+nasal] terminates when σ_2 crossed*

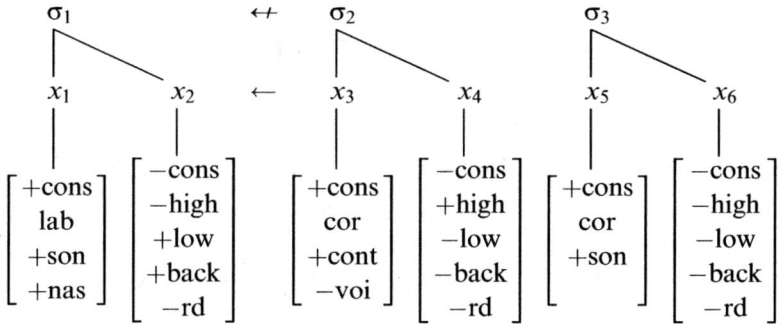

(12) *Default insertion of [−nasal] and default [+sonorant, −nasal] → [+lateral]*

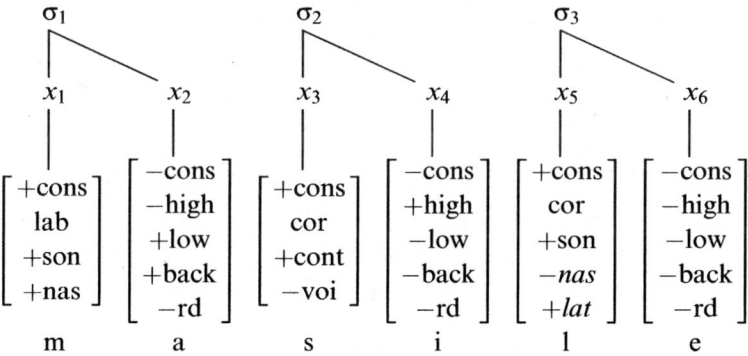

Comparing the patterns in Kikongo and Lamba reveals that the featural properties of the value-seeker and the value-source are the same in both rules. Indeed, the two languages have identical inventories in the relevant respects. Nonetheless, Lamba imposes a restriction that the harmonic search may not look beyond one syllable.

Odden (1994) has introduced a restricted set of distance parameters that I adopt here, with some modifications to be introduced below.[4] In fact, the rule of nasal assimilation in Kikongo and Lamba may be further compared with that of Chukchi (Odden 1994, 301), in which a stop assimilates to the nasality of a preceding nasal only when the two are immediately adjacent. While rules governing adjacent assimilation are not the concern of this book (which focuses on nonadjacent cases of locality), they can be accounted for by the same model as harmony, and they clearly demonstrate the need for a distance parameter that allows search to traverse just one segment (i.e., with no intervening segments allowed).

Restrictions on the length of harmonic search are formally parallel to barriers (or phase boundaries) in syntactic theory:[5] even though a harmonic source may not have been found within a relativized domain, and even though an appropriate value-source may lie just beyond that domain, the search simply ends at a given point.

Chomsky (1986), following the work of Rizzi (1982), proposes that one parameter distinguishing the syntax of English and Italian is whether the limit for *wh*-movement is crossing one IP node (English) or crossing one CP node (Italian). As (13) and (14) show, the dependency can cross only one IP node in English, whereas in Italian it can cross two.

(13) *Your brother, [IP to whom I wonder [CP what stories [IP they told *t*]]], was very troubled.

(14) Tuo fratello, [IP a cui   mi domando [CP che   storie [IP abbiano
     your brother   to whom I wonder   what stories   they.had
     raccontato *t*]]], era molto preoccupato.
     told   *t*   was very troubled

In the same way that syntactic searches may vary parametrically in whether they halt with CP or IP, phonological searches may halt with either the next segment, the next syllable boundary, or the end of the phonological word regardless of its length. In fact, phonological searches, much like *wh*-dependencies, have the option of allowing one extrinsically defined phonological barrier to be crossed, but not two, as described in (15b,d).

(15) *Possible values of β, the distance parameter, in vowel harmony*
   a. No intervening segments
   b. One intervening segment

c. No intervening syllables
d. One intervening syllable
e. No distance restrictions

The implementation of β in the Search algorithm for the parameters in (15) is shown in figure 5.1. When no {segment, syllable} is allowed to intervene, the counter that keeps track of traversed segments is incremented if no copying has taken place. In cases of strictly adjacent assimilation, the counter is incremented after the first segment is passed, halting the search. Similarly, for cases of syllable-adjacent assimilation, the counter is incremented after the first searched syllable is passed, even though no copying may have occurred. In cases where exactly one {segment, syllable} is allowed to intervene between the value-seeker and the value-source, after search has traversed two {segments/syllables} and not found

τ is either {all values of f_i contrastive for f_i, marked for f_i}
β is either $\{1, 2, \infty\}$ and γ is either {*countSylls* or *countSegs*}
myVals V
myPosition P
mySegsTraversed = 0
mySyllsTraversed = 0
myFeatsneeded F
myConditionalRequirements(F) = R

while F is not empty:
- Go in direction δ and update P
- **if** P is of type τ for any $f, f \in F$:
  - **if** $R(f)$ is true of P:
    - Copy Val (P, f) to V
    - Remove f from F
  - **else**:
    - Remove f from F
- mySegsTraversed = mySegsTraversed + 1
- **if** P is in a new Syllable:
  - mySyllsTraversed = mySyllsTraversed + 1
  - **if** ((mySyllsTraversed > β **and** γ = *countSylls*)
    or
    ((mySegsTraversed > β) **and** γ = *countSegs*) :
    - **exit**

Figure 5.1
Parameterized single-pass search with distance bounds

anything, incrementation of the counter will cause the search to halt as well.[6]

The values of the distance parameter result from the combination of three types of quantification (*none, only one, any amount*) with two types of elements (*segments, syllables*). Freely combining these and subtracting one—because allowing any number of segments is equivalent to allowing any number of syllables—generates the five distance parameters in (15), with no other possibilities. Having already discussed (15a), (15c), and (15e) with respect to nasal harmony, I now turn to exemplifying the necessity of including (15b) and (15d) in the set of universal distance parameters.

5.1.2 Distance Boundary of One Intervening Segment

Krämer (2001) provides an illustrative example of the one-intervening-segment distance parameter in Yucatec Maya, which allows leftward vowel harmony across one consonant but not two. Yucatec Maya has a five-vowel system (/i,u,e,o,a/) distinguished by [±high, ±low, ±back, ±round]. The intransitive imperfective suffix /-Vl/ and the subjunctive suffix /-Vk/ copy leftward for all four of these vowel features; they may do so across an intervening consonant, as shown in (16).

(16) *Yucatec Maya total vowel harmony across intervening consonant*
    a. ʔah-al   ʔah-ak   'wake.up-IMPF / SBJNCT'
    b. ʔok-ol   ʔok-ok   'enter-IMPF / SBJNCT'
    c. lub'-ul   lub'-uk   'fall-IMPF / SBJNCT'
    d. wen-el   wen-ek   'sleep-IMPF / SBJNCT'
    e. kiim-il   kiim-ik   'die-IMPF / SBJNCT'

However, Yucatec Maya will not allow such copying across two intervening segments (17); in such cases, the default values [−high, +low, +back, −round] are inserted, resulting in [a].

(17) *Yucatec Maya leftward vowel harmony quits after one consonant*
    a. t'oč-b'-al   'harden-IMPF'
    b. heek'-n-ak   'break-SBJNCT'

These affixes' search must give up after crossing two segments, even without having yet encountered a valid source.

(18) *Yucatec Maya imperfective, subjunctive suffixes must:*
    Total-Harmonize: δ = left, β = 2 segments, F = [±high, ±low, ±back, ±round]

An identical restriction holds for the harmony initiated by root vowels in Assamese, a language of northeast India. Assamese root vowels ordinarily copy marked [+ATR] from a rightward source (Mahanta 2007); I assume that the rightmost root vowel copies rightward first and that the first root vowel then copies [+ATR] from the second root vowel. In both cases of copying, the search may cross one intervening segment.

(19) *Assamese rightward [±ATR] harmony allows search past one intervening segment*
    a. kʰɛtɔr   kʰetori   'evil spirit, MASC / FEM'
    b. gɛrɛla   gereli   'fat, MASC / FEM'
    c. lɔg   logori   'company / companion'
    d. opɔr   upori   'above / in addition'
    e. nɔrɔk   noroki   'hell / sinful'

Vowel harmony is blocked in Assamese when more than one consonant intervenes; in such cases, the root vowels undergo last-resort insertion of [−ATR].

(20) *Assamese rightward [±ATR] search quits after two intervening segments*
    a. kɔrmɔ   kɔrmi   'work / active person'
    b. xɔbdɔ   xɔbdit   'sound / resounded'
    c. kɛtli   'kettle'
    d. sɔkrɔ   sɔkrika   'circle / platelet'
    e. tɛz   tɛzɔswi   'strength / powerful'

It is important to point out that in (20d–e), the two intervening consonants form an onset, and thus that the segmental bounding restriction is in principle independent of syllabic constituency.

Yucatec Maya and Assamese are cases in which the distance parameter allows at most one intervening segment to be crossed before the search ends. I have found no cases in which vowel harmony is specifically bounded by certain subsyllabic constituents, regardless of their size (e.g., vowel harmony that cannot cross a coda, regardless of whether it consists of one, two, or three segments, yet can cross an onset of any size). I therefore adopt the position that distance parameters are sensitive to segments or syllables, but not to constituents between these levels of structure.

5.1.3 Distance Boundary of One Intervening Syllable

The distance parameter that allows one intervening syllable in vowel harmony is found in many idiolects of Hungarian for trisyllabic stems such as *aszpirin-nek* 'aspirin-DAT'. Some background on Hungarian [±back] harmony and on the grammars that generate the *aszpirin-nek* pattern (here called *Hungarian ML*, for *more local*) is in order, before we analyze divergent patterns for these inputs in other idiolects. Once we understand the grammars in which harmonic search is constrained by one intervening syllable, we will turn to how inter- and intraspeaker variability with these same stems arises.

The pattern of Hungarian vowel harmony is to a certain extent complicated by the fact that the language has long and short vowels with different inventories and by the fact that long /a:/ alternates (in length alternations) with short /ɒ/ which is rounded. I assume that this is due to a late rule of rounding, whereby [+back] vowels become [+round] when short (Goldsmith 1985; Reiss 2003), but that the grammar of vowel harmony treats short /ɒ/ as contrastively [−back] with respect to short /ɛ/. Similarly, long /e:/ alternates with short /ɛ/, which phonologically patterns as a low vowel (Vago 1975; Hayes and Londe 2006, 62). Nonetheless, both the long and short versions of these vowels are written in the orthography with the same grapheme (*a* and *e*, respectively). The short and long inventories are shown in (21) and (22).

(21) *Hungarian short vowel inventory*

[−back, +rd]	[−back, −rd]	[+back, +rd]	[+back, −rd]	
ü	i	u		[+high, −low]
ö		o		[−high, −low]
	ɛ		ɒ	[−high, +low]

(22) *Hungarian long vowel inventory*

[−back, +rd]	[−back, −rd]	[+back, +rd]	[+back, −rd]	
ü:	i:	u:		[+high, −low]
ö:	e:	o:		[−high, −low]
			a:	[−high, +low]

Hungarian suffixes copy contrastive [+back] from the closest leftward vowel,[7] as exemplified in (23) for the [+round] vowels with the dative suffix (stress is always initial in Hungarian).

(23) *Hungarian dative suffix copies closest contrastive [±back]*
 a. mo:kuʃ-nɒk 'squirrel-DAT'
 b. ürü-nɛk 'sheep-DAT'
 c. öröm-nɛk 'joy-DAT'
 d. büro-nɒk 'bureau-DAT'
 e. ʃofö:r-nɛk 'chauffeur-DAT'

Following the definition of contrastiveness from chapter 3, the round vowels and short /ɒ,ɛ/ will be contrastive for [±back]. This relativization to contrastive values leaves the [−low, −back, −round] vowels transparent to vowel harmony.[8] The dative suffixes in (24) copy from the closest leftward vowel bearing contrastive [±back].

(24) *Hungarian dative suffix skips noncontrastive [−back] vowels*
    a. kɒvit͡ʃ-nɒk   'pebble-DAT'
    b. rɒdiːr-nɒk   'eraser-DAT'
    c. taːɲeːr-nɒk   'plate-DAT'
    d. nüɒns-nɒk   'nuance-DAT'
    e. bikaː-nɒk   'bull-DAT'
    f. boheːm-nɒk   'bohemian-DAT'
    g. müːveːs-nɒk   'artist-DAT'

While [−back] vowels are transparent to [+back] harmony across themselves in disyllabic stems such as those in (24), Farkas and Beddor (1987) and Ringen and Kontra (1989) point out that when there are two or more noncontrastively [±back] segments in a row, a pattern emerges in which suddenly [+back] harmony cannot occur.

Some speakers disallow [+back] harmony in words such as [ɒspirin-nɛk], even though they allow it in words such as [ɒktiːv-nɒk]. We will begin by focusing on these speakers/grammars; later, we will return to the other grammars, which allow [+back] harmony to search further (yielding, for example, [ɒspirin-nɒk]). Hungarian ML engages in [+back] copying when only one [−back] vowel intervenes between the suffix and a [+back] vowel (e.g., [rɒdiːr-nɒk] in (24)), but disallows such copying when *two* [−back] vowels intervene.

(25) *Hungarian ML: [+back] harmony fails when two syllables intervene*
    a. ɒ.nɒ.liː.ziʃ-nɛk   'analysis-DAT'
    b. ɒ.li.bi-nɛk   'alibi-DAT'
    c. bron.çi.tis-nɛk   'bronchitis-DAT'
    d. no.vɛm.bɛr-nɛk   'November-DAT'

The grammar of Hungarian ML with respect to vowel harmony represents an intermediate stage between the distance parameter of Lamba and that of Kikongo (section 5.1.1): while Lamba's search fails after traversing one syllable, Hungarian ML's search halts after traversing two syllables. Failure to find a contrastive value of [±back] once two syllables have been traversed results in default insertion of [−back].

(26) *Hungarian ML dative suffix must:*
   Back-Harmonize: δ = left, β = 2 syllables, F = [c: ±back]

For a word like [ɒ.li.bi], this distance parameter will terminate the search as soon as the leftward-moving syllable-pointer finishes the syllable /li/, never permitting the search to reach the contrastively [+back] /ɒ/. This is illustrated in (27)–(29).

(27) *Hungarian ML [c: back] search begins in [ɒ.li.bi-nɛk]*

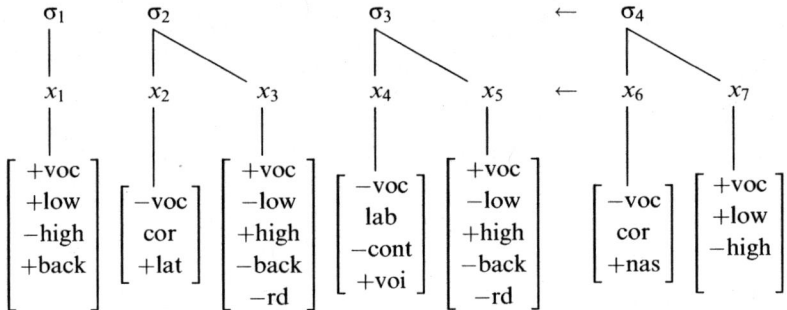

(28) *Hungarian ML [c: back] search ends when two syllables are crossed in [ɒ.li.bi-nɛk]*

(29) *Hungarian ML suffix undergoes last-resort insertion in [ɒ.li.bi-nɛk]*

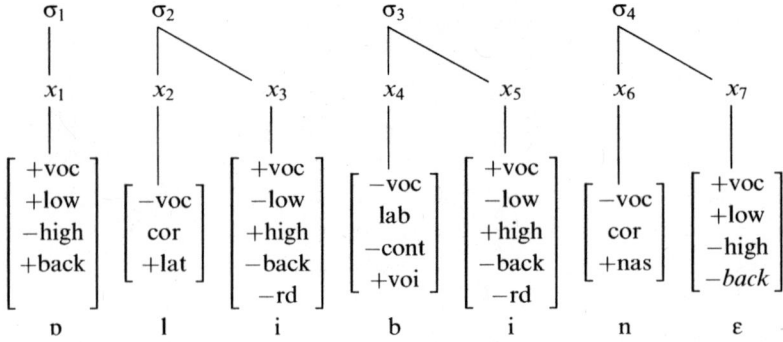

In contrast, the grammar of Hungarian ML generates a successful result in the derivation of a word such as [ɒk.tiːv-nɒk]: the syllable counter does not surpass two syllables before the contrastive [+back] value is found on /ɒ/, and therefore the suffix successfully copies [+back]. The difference in harmonic [+back] copying for these two patterns of words in Hungarian ML provides evidence for the existence of a one-intervening-syllable distance parameter. While transparent [−low, −back, −round] vowels are not included in the domain of the Search-and-Copy procedure, the additional boundedness on this process tracks two syllables as the maximum that can be traversed before search must end prematurely, leading to default insertion.[9]

Having accounted for Hungarian ML in terms of the intervening-syllable parameter, we turn to a grammar of Hungarian that diverges from Hungarian ML with respect to these trisyllabic back + transparent + transparent words. I will refer to this grammar as *Hungarian MD* (for *more distant*).[10] The harmony pattern of Hungarian MD differs from that of Hungarian ML only in that the former has an unbounded setting of the distance parameter.

(30) *Hungarian MD dative suffix must:*
 Back-Harmonize: δ = left, F = [c: ±back]

In Hungarian MD, [+back] copying succeeds both in words such as [ɒktiːv-nɒk] and in words such as [ɒlibi-nɒk], whose pattern is shown in (31).

(31) *Hungarian MD: [+back] harmony succeeds when two vowels intervene*
 a. ɒnɒliːziʃ-nɒk 'analysis-DAT'
 b. ɒlibi-nɒk 'alibi-DAT'
 c. bronçitis-nɒk 'bronchitis-DAT'
 d. novɛmbɛr-nɒk 'November-DAT'

Crucially, Hungarian ML and Hungarian MD pattern alike with respect to words in which there is only one intervening syllable, such as [ɒktiːv-nɒk]. The theory of distance parameters makes a strong prediction: while Hungarian ML and Hungarian MD pattern alike for [ɒktiːv-nɒk] and differently for [ɒlibi-nɛk~ɒlibi-nɒk], there could never be idiolectal variation between two grammars in which the opposite held (patterning differently for [ɒktiːv-nɒk~ɒktiːv-nɛk] but alike for [ɒlibi-nɒk]). The reason such a pattern of dialectal microvariation is not possible is that the distance parameters are defined in terms of the value-seeker, and any grammar that allowed finding a [+back] source three syllables away would also allow finding a [+back] source two syllables away. However, as we have seen with Hungarian ML versus Hungarian MD, a grammar that allows finding a [+back] source two syllables away does not necessarily allow finding a [+back] source three syllables away.

Our restricted set of distance parameters also predicts that while dialectal variation can arise such that two grammars may be identical with respect to their pattern for copying from two syllables away but differ in their ability to copy from three syllables away, there can be no dialectal variation such that two grammars are identical with respect to their pattern for copying from three syllables away but differ in their ability to copy from *four* syllables away. The greatest distance allowed that is short of unbounded copying is one intervening syllable, and the possibility of a grammar that allows copying from a source maximally two intervening syllables away is explicitly ruled out.

To summarize so far, the five distance parameter settings listed in (15) have been exemplified with the following cases:

(32) *Examples of the five possible values of β*
   a. No intervening segments: Chukchi nasal copying
   b. One intervening segment: Yucatec Maya total copy, Assamese [±ATR] copying
   c. No intervening syllables: Lamba nasal copying
   d. One intervening syllable: Hungarian ML [±back] copying
   e. No distance restrictions: Hungarian MD [±back] copying, Kikongo nasal copying

In chapter 3, we discussed microvariation in Kirghiz, Yoruba, and Finnish with respect to differences only in the value-relativization parameters. In a similar way, distance parameters should be expected to govern not only crosslinguistic variation between typologically unrelated languages, but also microvariation within dialects and idiolects of a single language.

An important question to be raised is, how can microvariation in a single parameter with drastically different surface effects on harmony emerge within a linguistic community? One of the most pervasive sources of within-language variability is parametric ambiguity within the predominant vocabulary and primary linguistic data. Recall that Finnish interspeaker variation arises with loanwords containing mixed contrastive [±back] values, a pattern not encountered within the core vocabulary. Similarly, divergence between the Hungarian ML and MD grammars arises only when noun stems are trisyllabic or longer, items that are loanwords and that, taken on the whole, are less frequent in the input than shorter words, as estimated if token frequency decreases with word length.

The primary "diet" of harmony patterns on the basis of which Hungarian learners must set parameters consists of words that are parametrically ambiguous between an unbounded-distance value and a one-intervening-syllable value. Learners attempting to fix a value for the distance parameter may choose one or the other, or may choose on the basis of a default setting for this parameter (if unbounded is the default (Schein and Steriade 1986, 696)). Alternatively, learners enountering parametrically ambiguous data might end up with a grammar that stochastically chooses between both values. Crucially, stochastic choice between unbounded-distance and one-intervening-syllable values will always generate the same result for [ɒktiːv-nɒk]. Only upon encountering longer words will one be able to tell that a stochastic setting of this parameter is present.

The structural property of Hungarian that leads to variation in back + transparent + transparent words is not simply the fact that the input is stochastic to begin with; rather, it is the fact that back + transparent words are ambiguous between different parametric settings of boundedness restrictions, an ambiguity inherent in any parameterized theory of allowable distance between interacting segmental elements.

5.1.4 Dahl's Law Microvariation as an Extension

By now, we have seen how distance parameters can regulate the extent to which a search for a subsegmental feature can be restricted by considerations of phonological distance alone. As an interesting confirmation that these parameters circumscribe a space of possible variation, we will examine [−voice] dissimilation in the Bantu languages, a process known as Dahl's Law (Davy and Nurse 1982). In this process, prefixal velar consonants take the value [+voice] when a stem contains a marked [−voice] segment. This is a language-specific instance of featural markedness (perhaps explaining the rarity of [−voice] dissimilation). Bennett (1967) suggests that Dahl's Law results from an earlier stage of Bantu that contrasted aspirated and unaspirated voiceless stops, in which case the [−voice] stops derive from earlier marked aspirated stops. The markedness relationship between the members of this laryngeal opposition has been preserved in contemporary Bantu as marked [−voice].

It turns out that the distance parameters developed above predict exactly the attested within-language variation in Dahl's Law dissimilation, thus offering a possible extension of the model of distance parameters to other intersegmental dependencies. This process will be exemplified with Gikuyu (note that the name *Gi-kuyu* itself exemplifies Dahl's Law). The application of Dahl's Law can be observed when the gerund prefix becomes [+voice] because a [−voice] segment is present in the stem. (A further implicational rule in Gikuyu that [+voice, −sonorant] → [+continuant] yields lenition).

(33) *Gikuyu dissimilation occurs before the voiceless segments /s,t,k/*
    a. ko-ruɣa   'GERUND-cook'
    b. ko-niina   'GERUND-finish'
    c. ɣo-siara   'GERUND-give.birth'
    d. ɣo-tɛɣa   'GERUND-trap'
    e. ɣo-kama   'GERUND-milk'

While we have not treated dissimilation-at-a-distance in any detail up to now, for the purpose of exemplifying the formal parallel with distance parameters in harmony, we can model dissimilation as a case of search-and-copy in which the *opposite* value is copied from the source. The rightward search seeks a marked value of [±voice], but copies the opposite value onto the needy element.

(34) *Gikuyu prefixes must:*
    Voice-Dissimilate: δ = right, F = opposite([m: voice])

The question of formally unifying vowel harmony and long-distance consonantal dissimilation is addressed further in chapter 6. For present purposes, let us consider the involvement of the distance parameter in this dissimilation process. When there is only one prefix directly concatenated to the stem, the structural analysis is ambiguous between various limits of boundedness. Dissimilation will be compatible with the distance parameter set to any possible value: adjacent-syllable, one-intervening-syllable, or unbounded.

(35) *Gikuyu distance parameters for dissimilation in /ko-ikia/ 'to throw'*
    a. The value-seeker and the value-source must be in adjacent syllables: generates [ɣwii.kia].
    b. The value-seeker and the value-source must be separated by no more than one intervening syllable: generates [ɣwii.kia].
    c. The value-seeker and the value-source may be at unbounded distance: generates [ɣwii.kia].

This happy convergence among all three parameter settings begins to diverge when a word contains two dorsal-initial prefixes. I assume that copying for [−voice] follows the order of prefix concatenation, so that the object prefix closer to the root attempts dissimilation before the more distant tense prefix does. According to Davy and Nurse (1982), Gikuyu speakers allow two different ways for Dahl's Law to apply in /a-kaa-ke-ikia/, resulting in either [a.ɣaa.ɣii.kia] or [a.kaa.ɣii.kia]. This microvariation can be modeled as depending on which distance parameter was chosen.

(36) *Gikuyu distance parameters for dissimilation in /a-kaa-ke-ikia/ 'he(1)-will-it(7)-throw'*
   a. The value-seeker and the value-source must be in adjacent syllables: generates [a.kaa.ɣii.kia].
   b. The value-seeker and the value-source must be separated by no more than one intervening syllable: generates [a.ɣaa.ɣii.kia].
   c. The value-seeker and the value-source may be at unbounded distance: generates [a.ɣaa.ɣii.kia].

In (36a), the object prefix finds an instance of [−voice] within the adjacent rightward syllable and dissimilates to [+voice]. The next outward affix, the tense prefix, does not find an instance of [−voice] in the adjacent rightward syllable and hence surfaces with default [−voice]. In the grammar exemplified by (36b), the object prefix finds an instance of [−voice] within the adjacent rightward syllable and dissimilates to [+voice]. Next, the tense prefix finds an instance of [−voice] two syllables to the right and also dissimilates to [+voice]. The same derivation holds for (36c).

Importantly, although there are two dorsal-initial prefixes in (36), and hence four logical possibilities for whether dissimilation happens or not, Gikuyu speakers only allow two possibilities: dissimilation of the closest prefix or dissimilation of both prefixes. When there are three dorsal-initial prefixes, although we might logically expect eight possibilities, only three are attested: exactly the three allowed by the set of syllable-based distance parameters in (15).

Given an input with an object prefix, a tense prefix, and a subject prefix, all of which begin with a dorsal segment, Davy and Nurse (1982) report that speakers generate three different options: for example, for /ka-kaa-ke-ikia/ 'he(12)-will-it(7)-throw', they generate [ɣa.kaa.ɣii.kia], [ka.ɣaa.ɣii.kia], or [ɣa.ɣaa.ɣii.kia].[11]

(37) *Gikuyu distance parameters for dissimilation in /ka-kaa-ke-ikia/ 'he(12)-will-it(7)-throw'*
   a. The value-seeker and the value-source must be in adjacent syllables: generates [ɣa.kaa.ɣii.kia].
   b. The value-seeker and the value-source must be separated by no more than one intervening syllable: generates [ka.ɣaa.ɣii.kia].

c. The value-seeker and the value-source may be at unbounded distance: generates [ɣa.ɣaa.ɣii.kia].

In (37a), the object prefix finds [−voice] in the adjacent syllable and dissimilates to [+voice]; the tense prefix does not find [−voice] in the adjacent rightward syllable and hence surfaces with default [−voice]; and finally the outermost subject prefix finds [−voice] in the adjacent syllable and hence dissimilates to [+voice]. This yields an "alternating" pattern of dissimilatory voicing, as shown in the derivation in (38)–(44) (vowel length not represented).

(38) *Innermost prefix begins rightward search in Gikuyu [ɣa.kaa.ɣii.kia]*

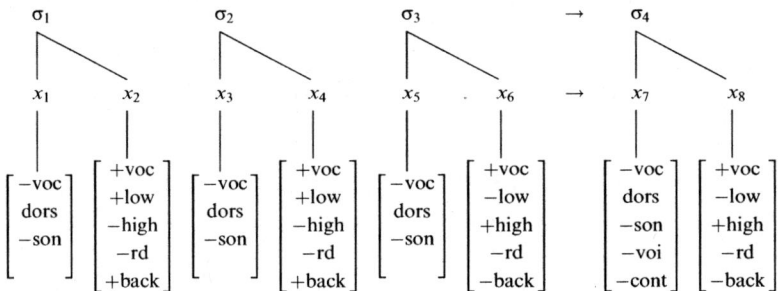

(39) *Innermost prefix finds marked [−voice] and copies opposite value*

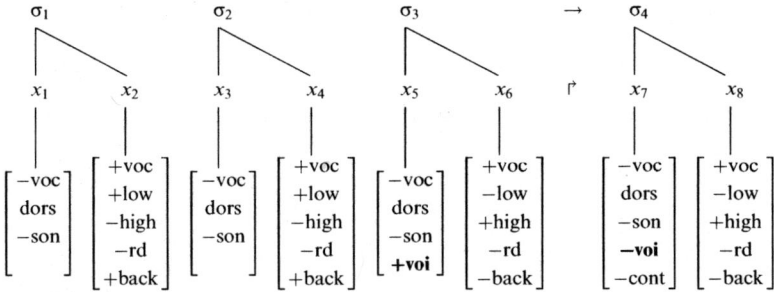

(40) *Second prefix begins search for [−voice]*

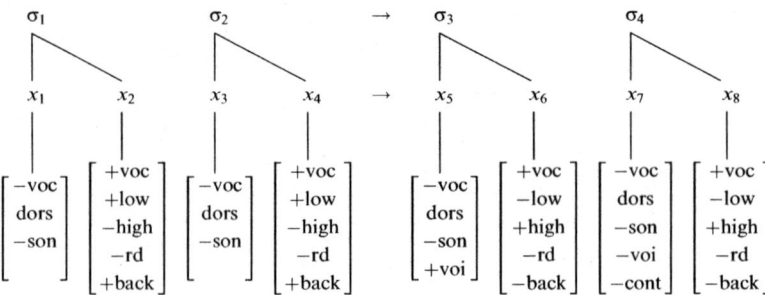

Domain Limitations on Search

(41) *Second prefix passes adjacent syllable and must terminate search for [−voice]*

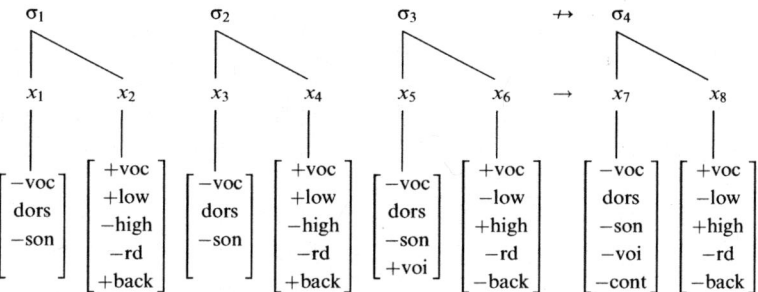

(42) *Second prefix undergoes last-resort [−voice] insertion*

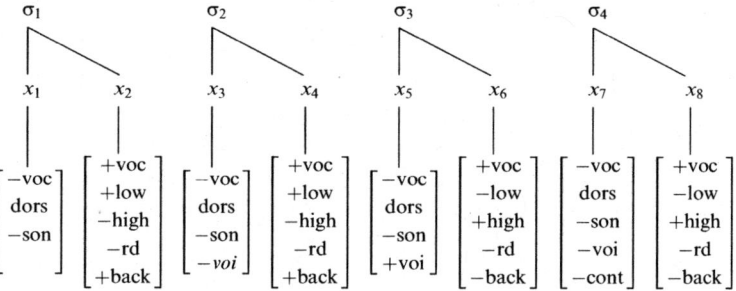

(43) *Outermost prefix begins search for [−voice]*

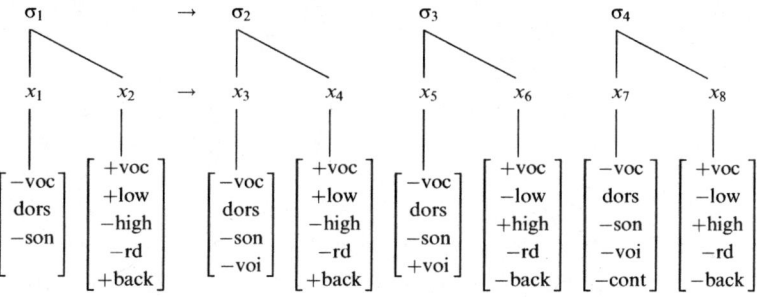

(44) *Outermost prefix finds [−voice] and copies opposite value*

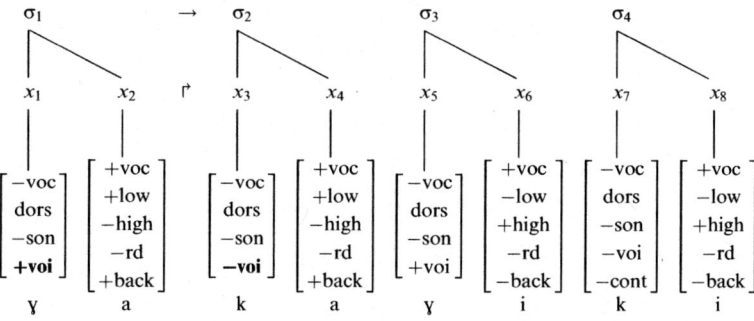

The grammar of Gikuyu under adjacent-syllable distance-boundedness will generate an alternating pattern, no matter how many prefixes are attached. The "myopic" adjacent-syllable search by the second prefix does not manage to find the [−voice] segment two syllables to the right. The second prefix undergoes last-resort insertion and in turn provides a [−voice] value for the derivationally subsequent prefix to its left.

In the grammar exemplified by (37b) [ka.ɣaa.ɣii.kia], when the distance parameter is set to one-intervening-syllable, the object prefix finds [−voice] in the adjacent syllable and dissimilates to [+voice]. Next, the tense prefix finds [−voice] within the one-intervening-syllable limit and hence dissimilates to [+voice]. Finally, the subject prefix does not find [−voice] within the one-intervening-syllable limit, surfacing with default [−voice]. This yields a "rightmost-two" pattern of dissimilatory voicing, no matter how many prefixes are attached.

In (37c) [ɣa.ɣaa.ɣii.kia], when the distance parameter is set to unbounded, the object prefix finds [−voice] in the adjacent syllable and dissimilates to [+voice]. Next, the tense prefix finds [−voice] within an unbounded distance and hence dissimilates to [+voice]. Finally, the subject prefix finds [−voice] within an unbounded distance, thereby dissimilating to [+voice]. This yields an "everything dissimilates" pattern of dissimilatory voicing, no matter how many prefixes are attached.

These three options are the only ones for Gikuyu speakers, and they represent a small subset of the logically possible options, following exactly the restrictive parameters of distance-sensitivity developed for harmony in (15). While Gikuyu speakers allow multiple possibilities and exhibit intraspeaker variation in words with three dorsal-initial prefixes, this variation is not random: it is the result of a highly constrained set of options for the boundedness of the search. This variation obtains only with longer sets of potentially dissimilating elements, but no optional or stochastic behavior results when there is only one dissimilable element. Dahl's Law in Gikuyu supports a model in which parametrically ambiguous inputs (such as the one in (35), compatible with all three distance-settings) give rise to divergent grammars that are only disambiguated in words that span greater distances.

5.2 Sonority Peaks Are Barriers

Boundedness in phonological locality is not determined only by the extent of the search path traversed. In this section, we will see that certain elements can halt the search as a result of their inherently high sonority. These sonority peaks should be excluded from the search domain because of their noncontrastive value, but they pose a hurdle beyond which search cannot proceed.

Ross (1984) discusses syntactic restrictions whereby benefactive and locative prepositional phrases cannot be extracted across negative elements, even though this clearly does not constitute a minimality violation (Frampton 1991).

(45) a. *For whom didn't you enter the race?
b. *Down the road Sanford doubts we will zoom.

Ross points out that many relative and operator constructions are also blocked by negation.

(46) a. *All these samples don't have to do is contain ytterbium and we're saved.
b. *The papers are ready for you not to put relish on.

The intuition among syntacticians is that the negative elements create an "island," imposing a boundary across which an A-bar relation simply cannot be established, even though the negative elements need not form a homogenous class in terms of the lexical category they belong to (cf. (45a–b)).

In this section, we will see that high-sonority vowels create similar boundaries across which harmonic searches cannot proceed, even though no minimality-based locality is at stake. We thus have two types of extrinsic limits on search: limits of *extent* (elements "too far" to cross) and *hurdles* (elements "too high" to cross). The syntactic case of crossing two IPs in (13) is a limit of extent, and that of negative elements is a hurdle (island). The same two limits on the length of search arise in vowel harmony: copying from an element too far away, as expressed by distance parameters, and copying past an element that is too high, as I will argue for sonority peaks.

As the result of case studies from Classical Manchu, Finnish, Wolof, and Hungarian, I will develop the following implicational generalization:

(47) Given two relativization-excluded (e.g., noncontrastive/nonmarked) vowels ϕ and ψ, where ϕ is of higher sonority than ψ, it will never be the case that ϕ is transparent while ψ is not. (In other words, transparency of ϕ implies transparency of ψ.)

For example, in Wolof, while /iː,uː,aː/ are all noncontrastive for [±ATR], only /aː/ acts as a hurdle in harmony. Similarly, while in Classical Manchu /ə,u/ are both unmarked for [±ATR], only /ə/ acts as a hurdle in harmony. The claim in (47) is that the opposite cannot occur in natural language: sonority induces a particular asymmetry among the vowels outside of the relativized-value domain. High-sonority vowels may act as hurdles to the exclusion of low-sonority vowels, but never vice versa.

Cases in which sonority can turn elements otherwise expected to be transparent into blockers for vowel harmony have been discussed by Ultan (1973) and Anderson (1980); that this phenomenon might have a perceptual basis has been proposed by Harms (1987).[12] In this section, I attempt to systematically formalize the effects of sonority in a variety of harmony patterns and to develop a strong prediction about the effects of vowel height on vowel harmony, one general enough to apply independently of the features involved or the value-relativization.

Before proceeding further, I would like to point out that while high sonority (e.g., lower vowel height) is often correlated with duration, the effect of sonority hurdles considered in the case studies below cannot be reduced to the effects of duration. For example, although Hungarian long /iː/ has a greater duration than all the short vowels in the inventory (Magdics 1969), it is transparent. Similarly, Hungarian long /eː/ is transparent while short /ɛ/ is not, even though /eː/ is over 35% greater in duration than /ɛ/.[13] Careful examination of the patterns of transparency in languages with long/short vowel distinctions reveals that the relevant factor in the hurdle effects discussed below is vowel height itself (i.e., high sonority).

I adopt the scale of sonority levels in (48) (based on work by Parker (2002)).[14] In this scale, I assume an inherent sonority ranking among the segments themselves; the relevant features are shown to the right. Not every language may phonologically encode a [±ATR] (or even a [±low]) contrast; nonetheless, /a/ will be more sonorous than /i/ in such languages, as determined by the feature [±high].[15] The features listed in (48) are thus provided for a "ten-vowel" (e.g., three heights with a [±ATR] contrast) system; the values provided alongside the vowels will be referred to throughout this chapter.

(48) *Sonority levels*

Segments	Sonority level	Relevant features
a,ä,ɒ	8	[+low, −ATR]
ə	7	[+low, +ATR]
ɛ,ɔ	6	[−low, −ATR]
e,o	5	[−low, +ATR]
ɪ,ʊ	4	[+high, −ATR]
i,u	3	[+high, +ATR]
y,w	2	[+high, +ATR, −voc, −cons]
sonorant consonants	1	[+son, +cons]

I adopt Gouskova's (2004) proposal whereby each language selects a cut-off point in the sonority hierarchy to which its grammar is sensitive. Under this view, the locus of crosslinguistic variation is the threshold above which certain sonority elements cannot be passed, although the relative ordering in the scale in (48) is itself crosslinguistically invariant.

The ultimate effect of sonority hurdles, like the effect of distance bounds, is that they halt the search as soon as they are met. This effect is implemented by a variable maintaining the allowable sonority threshold, as shown in the revised Search algorithm in figure 5.2.

τ is either {all values of f_i, contrastive for f_i, marked for f_i}
myVals V
myPosition P
myFeatsneeded F
mySonorityTolerance ζ (0 = allows anything)

while F is not empty:
- Go in direction δ and update P
- **if** Sonority(P) > ζ:
  - **if** P has any value for f:
    - Copy Val (P, F) to V
  - **exit**
- **else-if** P is of type τ for any value for $f, f \in F$:
  - Copy Val (P, F) to V
  - Remove f from F

Figure 5.2
Single-pass search with sonority thresholds. (Distance bounds omitted for conciseness.)

While their ultimate effect is to halt the search, there is an important difference between the role of extrinsic bounding imposed by distance parameters and that of sonority hurdles. When search halts because it reaches a sonority hurdle, the sonority hurdle's value for the harmonic feature is copied, *even if the high-sonority segment is not included within the relativized search domain.* Copying a feature-value from a sonority hurdle is a kind of "penultimate resort": the high-sonority hurdle manages to provide a harmonic value before default/last-resort insertion can take place.

Let us examine the effect of sonority hurdles in two [±ATR] harmony systems and two [±back] harmony systems: Classical Manchu, Finnish, Wolof, and Hungarian. Individual analyses of these languages could easily include unrelated special statements for the exceptional patterns of /ə/, /ä/, /aː/, /ɛ/, respectively. Within the present analysis, however, these cases are unified under the generalization about sonority: each "exception" is the lowest vowel in the set of excluded elements.

As early as Jespersen 1904, the fundamental effects of sonority on phonotactic sequences and intersegmental relations were confirmed. Sonority plays an important role in a number of phonological processes in which vowels are adjacent. Sonority determines the syllabification of vocalic sequences in Spanish (Harris 1983), Berber (Dell and Elmedlaoui 1985; Prince and Smolensky 1993), and Tahitian (Bickmore 1995), wherein vowels of lower height are the ones affiliated to the syllabic nucleus. Sonority also may dictate hiatus persistence—that is, which vowel stays around in hiatus when one of two vowels must be deleted (Casali 1998), wherein the choice of which to keep is determined not by linear order, but by sonority.

Sonority interacts with relative prominence among vowels (i.e., stress) in two directions of causality. Sonority may determine stress placement above and beyond syllable weight and directionality, as argued for Kobon by Kenstowicz (1997); thus, high sonority demands stress. Conversely, vowels may undergo lowering when they have already been assigned stress in Chamorro (Crosswhite 1998); thus, stress demands high sonority.

The existence of sonority hurdles within vowel harmony thus falls within a broad class of prominence-based asymmetries in which syntagmatic interactions are sensitive to vowel height.

5.2.1 Classical Manchu

In Classical Manchu, two vowels, /ə/ and /u/, are excluded from the domain of value-relativization. Only one of them manages to wedge its way into the vowel harmony search, and it is the more sonorous of the two. Classical Manchu has a [±ATR] harmony system and the following vowel inventory (Zhang 1996):

(49) *Classical Manchu vowel inventory*

[−back, −rd]	[+back, +rd]	[+back, −rd]	
i	u		[+high, +ATR]
	ʊ		[+high, −ATR]
		ə	[−high, +ATR]
	ɔ	a	[−high, −ATR]

Classical Manchu displays velar/uvular alternations based on the [±ATR] value of immediately preceding vowels. The velars [k,g,x] occur before [+ATR] [i,ə,u], while the uvulars [q,ɢ,χ] occur before [−ATR] [a,ɔ,ʊ] (Zhang 1996; Vaux 1999).

(50) *Velar/Uvular alternations conditioned by [±ATR] value of preceding vowel*
  a. ətu-ku   'clothing'
  b. xərə-ku   'ladle'
  c. kimu-nggə   'harboring enmity'
  d. urgu-nggə   'joyous'
  e. dərgi-kən   'somewhat above'
  f. taci-qʊ   'school'
  g. ɢɔsin   'pity'
  h. ilχa   'flower'
  i. nuχa-qan   'somewhat easy'
  j. ɢʊnin   'thought'
  k. fɔχɔlɔ-qan   'somewhat short'

The consonantal alternations show that Manchu exhibits a [±ATR] contrast with two distinct natural classes of vowels.[16] The marked value is [−ATR], and the vowels contrastive for [±ATR] are /ə,a/ and /u,ʊ/. Though to a large extent the distribution of /u,ʊ/ is influenced by preceding dorsal consonants, there are minimal pairs demonstrating their phonemic status (Zhang 1996, 43).

(51) *Minimal pairs demonstrating Classical Manchu contrast between /u/ and /ʊ/*
  a. butun   'hibernation'   bʊtʊn   'crock, large jar'
  b. mungku   'a frozen fish'   mʊnggu   'bird's nest'
  c. ulən   'irrigation ditch' ʊlən   'house'

Vowel harmony in Classical Manchu is initiated by a variety of suffixes and yields alternations in the suffixal vowels between /u/ and /ʊ/ as well as between /ə/ and /a/. The vowel /i/ is noncontrastive for [±ATR] and is transparent for [−ATR] copying across it. The results of [±ATR] harmony in the adjectivalizing, verbalizing, and diminutive suffixes are provided in (52) and (53).

(52) *Classical Manchu [−ATR] suffixal variants (Zhang 1996, 49)*
    a. algin-ngga   'famous'
    b. malxʊ-ngga   'frugal'
    c. aga-ngga   'rainy'
    d. ilxʊ-ngga   'lying straight'
    e. farxʊ-kan   'somewhat dark'
    f. gʊrgi-la   'to flame'
    g. bakci-la   'to oppose'
    h. bakta-kʊ   'internal organs'
    i. banji-shʊn   'having money'

(53) *Classical Manchu [+ATR] suffixal variants (Zhang 1996, 48)*
    a. xəhə-ngɡə   'female'
    b. xətu-kən   'somewhat stocky'
    c. dərgi-kən   'somewhat above'
    d. icə-lə   'make new'
    e. juwə-lə   'lean to two sides'
    f. xərə-ku   'ladle'
    g. sidərə-shun   'hobbled / lame'

These suffixal alternations are the result of a leftward search for marked [−ATR].

(54) *Classical Manchu adjectivalizing, verbalizing, and diminutive suffixes must:*
    ATR-Harmonize: δ = left, F = [m: ATR]

As the following stems illustrate, the last-resort value in case nothing is found is [−ATR].

(55) *Suffixes undergo default [−ATR] insertion when attached to all-/i/ stems (Zhang 1996, 56)*
    a. fili-kan   'somewhat solid'
    b. ici-ngga   'having direction'
    c. iji-shʊn   'obedient'
    d. sifi-kʊ   'hairpin'

In the inventory of Classical Manchu, both /u/ and /ə/ are contrastive for [±ATR] and unmarked for [±ATR]. However, unlike /ə/, /u/ can cooccur with [−ATR] vowels in roots and allows [−ATR] copying across itself. The transparent behavior of [+ATR] /u/ is exemplified by the following cases:

(56) *Classical Manchu transparent /u/ in harmony (Zhang 1996, 49)*
    a. dacu-kan   'somewhat sharp'
    b. gʊsu-la   'tie up with thick rope'
    c. xʊdu-ngga 'speedy'

The transparent patterning of /u/ is entirely expected given the relativization to marked values in (54).[17] However, of the two contrastive and unmarked [+ATR] vowels, while /u/ may be skipped in search, /ə/ may not. The fact that search halts with /ə/ (but not with /u/) cannot be explained by relativization to contrastive or marked values: in terms of harmonic feature-values, there is no way to exclude /u/ from the domain without also excluding /ə/.

The relativization of Classical Manchu [±ATR] harmony to only marked values means that search should continue past [+ATR] vowels. As we have seen, however, search does not pass over /ə/, despite its unmarked value. The fact that search halts with /ə/ must be due to its high sonority.

(57) *Classical Manchu adjectivalizing, verbalizing, and diminutive suffixes must:*
    ATR-Harmonize: δ = left, F = [m: ATR], ζ = 6

In Classical Manchu, the search for [±ATR] harmony is extrinsically bounded by all vowels of sonority greater than 6, as shown by the threshold parameter ζ in (57). As soon as the search reaches an element exceeding that cutoff (such as /ə/), it halts whether it has encountered a potential value-source or not.

However, given that the purpose of a vowel harmony search in the first place is to provide a suffix with a value for the harmonic feature, the sonority hurdle is copied from, even though it is outside the domain of value-relativization. In other words, although the search is relativized to marked [−ATR] values, when a barrier is encountered, the search ends. In examples such as [juwə-lə] 'lean to two sides', the search reaches an element of sonority > 6, and the hurdle is copied from, as shown in (58)–(60). (The sonority level of each element is included next to its height feature for the reader's convenience.)

(58) *Classical Manchu verbalizing suffix begins marked [−ATR] search in [juwə-lə]*

$$
\begin{array}{cccc}
x_1 & x_2 & \leftarrow\ x_3 & x_4 \\
\begin{bmatrix} -\text{voc} \\ \text{lab} \\ +\text{high} \\ +\text{back} \\ +\text{rd} \end{bmatrix} &
\begin{bmatrix} +\text{voc} \\ -\text{high; son} = 6 \\ +\text{back} \\ -\text{rd} \\ +\text{ATR} \end{bmatrix} &
\begin{bmatrix} -\text{voc} \\ \text{cor} \\ +\text{son} \\ -\text{nas} \\ +\text{lat} \end{bmatrix} &
\begin{bmatrix} +\text{voc} \\ -\text{high} \\ +\text{back} \\ -\text{rd} \end{bmatrix}
\end{array}
$$

(59) *Classical Manchu verbalizing suffix encounters sonority hurdle in [juwə-lə]*

$$
\begin{array}{cccc}
x_1 & x_2 & \leftrightarrow\ x_3 & x_4 \\
\begin{bmatrix} -\text{voc} \\ \text{lab} \\ +\text{high} \\ +\text{back} \\ +\text{rd} \end{bmatrix} &
\begin{bmatrix} +\text{voc} \\ \mathbf{-\text{high; son} = 6} \\ +\text{back} \\ -\text{rd} \\ +\text{ATR} \end{bmatrix} &
\begin{bmatrix} -\text{voc} \\ \text{cor} \\ +\text{son} \\ -\text{nas} \\ +\text{lat} \end{bmatrix} &
\begin{bmatrix} +\text{voc} \\ -\text{high} \\ +\text{back} \\ -\text{rd} \end{bmatrix}
\end{array}
$$

(60) *Classical Manchu verbalizing suffix copies from sonority hurdle in [juwə-lə]*

$$
\begin{array}{cccc}
x_1 & x_2 & x_3 & x_4 \\
\begin{bmatrix} -\text{voc} \\ \text{lab} \\ +\text{high} \\ +\text{back} \\ +\text{rd} \end{bmatrix} &
\begin{bmatrix} +\text{voc} \\ \mathbf{-\text{high; son} = 6} \\ +\text{back} \\ -\text{rd} \\ \mathbf{+\text{ATR}} \end{bmatrix} &
\begin{bmatrix} -\text{voc} \\ \text{cor} \\ +\text{son} \\ -\text{nas} \\ +\text{lat} \end{bmatrix} &
\begin{bmatrix} +\text{voc} \\ -\text{high} \\ +\text{back} \\ -\text{rd} \\ \mathbf{+\text{ATR}} \end{bmatrix} \\
\text{w} & \text{ə} & \text{l} & \text{ə}
\end{array}
$$

By the lights of the inventory and the relativization to marked [−ATR], /ə/ should not be copied from, but its low height and the sonority threshold of Classical Manchu cause the search to terminate with and copy from it.

5.2.2 Finnish

A pattern formally identical to that of Classical Manchu—in which there is relativization to the marked value of a feature but one member of the unmarked set nonetheless participates in harmony—is found in Finnish B (recall section 3.11). The Finnish vowel inventory is repeated in (61).

(61) *Finnish vowel inventory*

[−back, −rd]	[−back, +rd]	[+back, +rd]	[+back, −rd]	
i	ü	u		[+high, −low]
e	ö	o		[−high, −low]
ä			a	[−high, +low]

Recall that in Finnish B, loanwords with mixed contrastive [±back] vowels yield [+back] harmony in the suffixes. This led us to conclude that Finnish B copies [±back] from marked sources (namely, those with [+back]).

(62) *Finnish B partitive suffix must:*
  Back-Harmonize: δ = left, F = [m: back]

The harmony procedure in (62) results in transparency of the contrastively [−back, +round] vowels /ü,ö/ (in addition to the transparency of /i,e/).

(63) *Finnish B shows transparency of /ü,ö/*
  a. marttüüri-a   'martyr-PARTIT.SG'
  b. klorofülli-a   'chlorophyll-PARTIT.SG'
  c. sutenööri-a   'pimp-PARTIT.SG'
  d. amatööri-a   'amateur-PARTIT.SG'

While the relativization to *marked* values of [±back] explains the transparency of /ü,ö/ in (63), Campbell (1980, 251) notes an interesting asymmetry among the contrastive [−back] vowels: "... *sutenööriä* and *amatööriä* are perfectly acceptable [alongside *sutenööria* and *amatööria*]. However, *hydrosfääria* and the like are impossible." In other words, /ä/ does not allow [+back] to be copied across itself, in any dialect or register. As all three of /ü,ö,ä/ are unmarked for [±back], it is perhaps surprising that Finnish B (the dialect that allows skipping over /ö/ in [sutenööri-ä]) *must* copy [−back] from /ä/. The fact that /ä/ stubbornly remains a copy-source for [±back] harmony despite being excluded from value-relativization calls for a parameterization in terms of sonority hurdles.

(64) *Finnish B partitive suffix must:*
  Back-Harmonize: δ = left, F = [m: back], ζ = 7

Since the sonority threshold in (64) requires all [+low] vowels to halt the harmony search, items such as [hüdrosfääri-ä] will require suffixal harmony to stop dead in its tracks as soon as /ä/ is encountered. The [−low] vowels /ü,ö/, on the other hand, are tolerated by the sonority threshold and excluded from the domain of value-relativization. The search passes them right by, eventually copying marked [+back] from a leftward vowel that lies beyond them.

Campbell's observation—that Finnish loanwords with mixed contrastive [±back] vowels allow copying of [+back], except when the [−back] vowel is [+low]—finds a natural account in terms of sonority hurdles. All of the [−back] vowels are excluded by marked-value relativization, but the [+low] vowel imposes a boundary that prevents search from looking beyond it. It is striking that a formally identical interaction between marked-value relativization and unmarked low vowels holds in Finnish as in Classical Manchu, even though the harmonic feature is different ([±ATR] in Classical Manchu and [±back] in Finnish) and the "stubborn" vowel is different as well (/ə/ in Classical Manchu and /ä/ in Finnish). The explanatory power of including sonority hurdles in the theory is that they allow a unified account of these otherwise disparate phenomena.

5.2.3 Wolof

Sonority-based asymmetry in vowel harmony is further exemplified by the [±ATR] system of Wolof, a West Atlantic language spoken in Senegal. Wolof has slightly different inventories of long and short vowels. The short vowel inventory is shown in (65) and the long vowel inventory in (66). Notice that long /aː/ has no [+ATR] counterpart and is thus non-contrastive for the harmonic feature.

(65) *Wolof short vowel inventory*

[−back, −rd]	[−back, −rd]	[+back, +rd]	
i		u	[+high, −low, +ATR]
e		o	[−high, −low, +ATR]
ɛ		ɔ	[−high, −low, −ATR]
	ə		[−high, +low, +ATR]
	a		[−high, +low, −ATR]

(66) *Wolof long vowel inventory*

[−back, −rd]	[−back, −rd]	[+back, +rd]	
iː		uː	[+high, −low, +ATR]
eː		oː	[−high, −low, +ATR]
ɛː		ɔː	[−high, −low, −ATR]
	aː		[−high, +low, −ATR]

Suffixes harmonize for [±ATR], including the instrumental/locative [-e]/[-ɛ], participant [-le]/[-lɛ], past tense [-oːn]/[-ɔːn], benefactive [-əl]/[-al], possessive [-əm]/[-am], and comitative [-əndoː]/[-andɔː] (Ka 1994). The

Domain Limitations on Search 179

following examples illustrate these suffixes copying contrastive [±ATR] from the nearest leftward source:

(67) *Wolof suffixes copy closest contrastive [±ATR]*

a.	doːr-e	'to hit with'	xɔːl-ɛ	'to look with'
b.	reːr-e	'to be lost in'	dɛm-ɛ	'to go with'
c.	gən-e	'to be better in'	xam-ɛ	'to be known in'
d.	doːr-e	'to help hit'	jɔx-le	'to help give'
e.	reːr-le	'to lose one's property'	dɛː-le	'to lose a relative'
f.	yəg-le	'to announce'	takk-lɛ	'to help tie'
g.	reːr-oːn	'was lost'	reːr-ɔːn	'had dinner'
h.	now-oːn	'came'	jɔx-ɔːn	'gave'
i.	bəgg-oːn	'wanted'	takk-ɔːn	'tied'
j.	leːb-əl	'to tell stories for'	bɛy-al	'to cultivate for'
k.	foːt-əl	'to launder for'	wɔːr-al	'to fast for'
l.	jənd-əl	'to buy for'	wax-al	'to speak for'
m.	sofoːr-əm	'his driver'	nɛlaw-am	'his sleep'
n.	genn-əndoː	'to go out together'	dɛnd-andɔː	'to be neighbors'
o.	tox-əndoː	'to smoke together'	tɔpp-andɔː	'to imitate'
p.	dəkk-əndoː	'to live together'	wax-andɔː	'to say together'

We find a sonority hurdle in the long vowel /aː/, which is noncontrastive for [±ATR] but not transparent. In the apt words of Kenstowicz (1994, 354), "[aː] finds its confreres only among the [−ATR] set." The Wolof long [+low] vowel, even though noncontrastive, provides an immediate [−ATR] value-source for vowels to its right.

(68) *Wolof /aː/ imposes a sonority hurdle*

a.	yobbu-waːlɛ	'to carry away also'
b.	genn-aːlɛ	'to go out with also'
c.	doːr-aː-tɛ	'to hit usually'
d.	jeːm-əntu-waːl-ɛːti	'to try also without conviction once more'
e.	indiw-aːlɛ	'to bring in addition'
f.	seytaːnɛ	'devil' (from Arabic)
g.	kumaːsɛ	'to start' (from French)

The parameterization of Wolof [±ATR] harmony sensitivity to high-sonority peaks is provided in (69). (Note that the cutoff at $\zeta = 7$ will cause the search to halt not only with /aː/, but also with short /ə,a/, though the hurdle effect with these vowels is indistinguishable from contrastive-value copying from them.)

(69) *Wolof instrumental, benefactive, past tense, possessive, and comitative suffixes must:*
ATR-Harmonize: $\delta =$ left, F = [c: ATR], $\zeta = 7$

Importantly, the [+high] vowels are also noncontrastive for [±ATR]. Nonetheless, unlike /aː/, they are transparent to [+ATR] copying across them (Ka 1994, 27–30; Archangeli and Pulleyblank 1994, 231).

(70) *Wolof noncontrastive [+high] vowels skipped in [±ATR] harmony*
    a. tɛkki-lɛːn   'untie'
    b. moytu-lɛːn   'avoid'
    c. watu-lɛːn   'have haircut'
    d. lettu-leːn   'braid hair'
    e. soːbu-leːn   'plunge'
    f. gəstu-leːn   'research'
    g. toːxi-leːn   'go and smoke'
    h. sɔppiwu-lɛːn   'you have not changed'
    i. tɛːruwɔːn   'welcomed'
    j. barigɔ   'barrel'
    k. kamisɔl   'robe'
    l. kɔritɛ   'Muslim holiday'
    m. kaːritɛ   'butter'
    n. warugar   'obligation'

We may conclude that the patterning of /aː/ in Wolof harmony is unique among the three noncontrastive vowels, /aː/ being the only one that is not skipped in the search by contrastive-value relativization. Archangeli and Pulleyblank (1994) propose that [±ATR] harmony must interface with the articulatorily grounded cooccurrence restrictions *[+high, −ATR] and *[+low, +ATR]. While these may represent valid crosslinguistic tendencies, what is missing from such a proposal is an implicational predictive connection between the effects of these two constraints. The sonority hurdles account predicts that whenever [+low] vowels are transparent to [−ATR] harmony across them, [+high] vowels must also be transparent to [+ATR] harmony across them. Put differently, whenever the sonority threshold is set very tolerantly and allows search to pass by noncontrastive vowels of higher sonority, it will also allow search to pass by noncontrastive vowels of lower sonority. Wolof long /aː,uː,iː/ are all noncontrastive for [±ATR], and the sonority hurdles model predicts that if only one of them fails to be transparent, it will be the most sonorous one.

The patterning of [+low] /aː/ as a nontransparent sonority hurdle is widespread throughout the [±ATR] vowel harmony systems of West Africa (Ladefoged 1968, 36–38). This sonority effect is found in all dialects of Yoruba (Baković 2000; Ola Orie 2001), regardless of whether they parameterize visibility to all or only contrastive values of [±ATR] (see section 3.9).

Wolof is an important case study for confirming the role of sonority because the long vowels show the sonority asymmetry, reflecting the conclusion that it is not duration but vowel height that brings an early end to vowel harmony searches. As we will see in section 5.2.4, the effect of vowel height on noncontrastive long vowels creates an asymmetry in Hungarian as well, explaining the differences in transparency among /ɛ,eː,aː/ there. The advantage of the sonority hurdles model is that it relates the bounding effect of /aː/ in Wolof, a [±ATR] system, to the bounding effect of /aː/ in Hungarian's [±back] harmony, precisely because of the role played by sonority.

5.2.4 Hungarian

Many of the case studies in this book have included instances of variability within a single language, arising from two distinct parameterizations that speakers may employ. For example, the marked-versus-contrastive value-relativization parameter in Finnish (section 3.11) and the one-intervening-syllable versus unbounded-distance parameter in Hungarian (section 5.1.3) generate within-language variability. In this section, we will examine yet another phenomenon in which the space of parametric options for vowel harmony provides insight into a pattern of "vacillating" behavior: whether or not Hungarian suffixes copy from the low [−back] vowel /ɛ/.

Recall that one of the intricacies of the Hungarian vowel inventory is that the short vowels /a,e/ alternate according to [±back] harmony, while at the same time long and short *e,é* and *a,á* alternate with each other according to length-modifying processes. In the following examples, these vowels are represented in terms of their surface phonetic values; in particular, following Vago (2006), short /a/ is phonetically [ɒ].[18]

(71) *Hungarian shortening alternation with the plural or verbalizing suffix (Siptár and Törkenczy 2000, 53)*

    a. viːz   vizɛk   'water, SG / PL'
    b. ɒnɒliːziʃ   ɒnɒlizaːl   'analysis / analyze'
    c. tüːz   tüzɛk   'fire, SG / PL'
    d. miniɒtüːr   miniɒtüriza:l   'miniature / miniaturize'
    e. uːt   utɒk   'road, SG / PL'
    f. uːr   uriza:l   'gentleman / play the gentleman'
    g. pɒstöːröz   pɒstörizɒl   'pasteurize'

h. loː   lovɒk   'horse, SG / PL'
i. ɒgoːniɒ   ɒgonizaːl   'agony / agonize'
j. keːz   kɛzɛk   'hand, SG / PL'
k. preːmium prɛmizaːl   'bonus / award a bonus'
l. ɲaːr   ɲɒrɒk   'summer, SG / PL'
m. kɒnaːliʃ kɒnɒlizɒl   'canal / canalize'

In addition to morphologically conditioned shortening, Hungarian exhibits a process of vowel lengthening that affects the last vowel of any morpheme when it precedes a suffix.

(72) *Hungarian morphological [ɛ,ɒ] lengthening (Siptár and Törkenczy 2000, 170)*
    a. ɒlmɒ   ɒlmaːt   'apple / apple.ACC'
    b. tɒrcɒ   tɒrcaːk   'he holds it / they hold it'
    c. kucɒ   kucaːul   'dog / like a dog'
    d. oːrɒ   oːraːjɒ   'watch / his watch'
    e. ɛpɛ   ɛpeːʃ   'bile / bilious'
    f. vittɛ   vitteːk   'he carried it / they carried it'
    g. ɛʃtɛ   ɛʃteːrɛ   'evening / by evening'
    h. mɛʃɛ   mɛʃeːjɛ   'tale / his tale'

The evidence to the learner is that, on the one hand, /ɛ/ should be a low vowel, since it alternates with /ɒ/; on the other hand, /ɛ/ should be a mid vowel, since it also alternates with /eː/. The conundrum is resolved once we realize that what /ɛ,ɒ/ have in common is being [−ATR] (Reiss 2003), that what /ɒ,aː/ have in common is being [+low], and what /ɛ,eː/ have in common is being [−low]. A revised analysis of the Hungarian vowel inventory incorporates these feature assignments (this revision does not affect the analysis of distance bounds in section 5.1.3).

(73) *Revised features for the Hungarian vowel inventory*

[−back, +rd]	[−back, −rd]	[+back, +rd]	[+back, −rd]	
ü,üː	i,iː	u,uː		[+high, −low, +ATR]
ö,öː	eː	o,oː		[−high, −low, +ATR]
	ɛ			[−high, −low, −ATR]
		ɒ	aː	[−high, +low, −ATR]

The revised feature values in (73) account for the fact that /ɛ,ɒ/ share the same [−ATR] specification and thus are closer in sonority than /eː/ and /ɒ/, while maintaining the conventional wisdom reflected in the orthography and in length alternations that /eː,ɛ/ are of the same height in terms of [−low] and that /ɒ,aː/ are of the same height in terms of [+low].

The revised inventory in (73) has significant consequences for the statement of Hungarian vowel harmony in terms of a copying procedure for contrastive values of [±back]. Only the short and long versions of /ü,u/ and /ö,o/ will be contrastive for [±back]; all other vowels lack a contrastive [±back] counterpart by the definition of contrastiveness in chapter 3. A relativization of the harmonic search in Hungarian limited to contrastive values would thus exclude all of the following vowels from search:

(74) *Noncontrastive [±back] vowels in Hungarian*

[−back, +rd]	[−back, −rd]	[+back, +rd]	[+back, −rd]	
	i,iː			[+high, −low, +ATR]
	eː			[−high, −low, +ATR]
	ɛ			[−high, −low, −ATR]
		ɒ	aː	[−high, +low, −ATR]

In fact, among the vowels in (74), the [−low, +ATR] vowels /i,iː,eː/ are excluded from the search domain and are fully transparent to harmony (see (24)). The [+low, −ATR] vowels /ɒ,aː/ intrude into the search process by way of a sonority hurdle, halting the search and providing a [+back] value as soon as they are encountered. /ɛ/, however, is variable, patterning with neither of these groups.

Vago (1975) discusses "vacillating" stems in Hungarian, so called because speakers vary in whether the suffixes attached to these stems exhibit [+back] or [−back] harmony. Stems with a [+back] vowel in the initial syllable(s) and the [−ATR, −back] vowel /ɛ/ in the final syllable vacillate in which vowel they copy from.

(75) *Hungarian dative suffix variably copies [+back] from vacillating stems*
 a. ɒgnɛʃ-nɒk *or* ɒgnɛʃ-nɛk   'Agnes-DAT'
 b. joːʒef-nɒk *or* joːʒef-nɛk   'Joseph-DAT'
 c. sɒlɒmɒndɛr-nɒk *or* sɒlɒmɒndɛr-nɛk   'salamander-DAT'
 d. hotɛl-nɒk *or* hotɛl-nɛk   'hotel-DAT'
 e. puːdɛr-nɒk *or* puːdɛr-nɛk   'powder-DAT'

I propose that suffixes vacillate in how they execute the Search-and-Copy procedure with these stems because grammars can vary in their sonority thresholds. One grammar has a more *restrictive sonority* (RS) threshold, forcing search to quit when sonority 5 is exceeded (hence with the [−low, −ATR] vowel /ɛ/).

(76) *Hungarian RS dative suffix must:*
  Back-Harmonize: δ = left, F = [c: back], ζ = 5

The effect of Hungarian RS's low sonority threshold is that /ɛ/ will halt the search immediately (even though it is not contrastive) and thereby impose [−back] as the value to be copied. The alternative pattern is generated by a slightly more *tolerant sonority* (TS) threshold; here, search breezes past /ɛ/ (because it is noncontrastive), and only the "lowest of the low"—namely, /ɒ,aː/—will halt the search and impose [+back].

(77) *Hungarian TS dative suffix must:*
Back-Harmonize: δ = left, F = [c: back], ζ = 6

Speakers who generate [ɒgnɛʃ-nɛk] are therefore using the grammar of Hungarian RS when they do so, whereas those who generate [ɒgnɛʃ-nɒk] are using the grammar of Hungarian TS. The inter- and intraspeaker variation results from a different parametric value for the sonority threshold, and the choice of which to use—Hungarian RS or Hungarian TS—is conditioned by a variety of lexical and sociolinguistic factors. However, since the sonority hierarchy is strictly ordered, there can be no idiolect or register of Hungarian in which, say, /iː/ blocks [+back] harmony across itself but /ɛ/ does not. A setting of the sonority threshold low enough that /iː/ will halt the search automatically requires all vowels of equal or greater sonority to halt the search as well.

5.3 Implicational Sonority Thresholds

This latter portion of the chapter has explored a locality principle that trumps the exclusion of nonrelativized elements from the search, by the high sonority of elements along the search path.[19] The discovery of this principle came about because, despite the extensive empirical coverage afforded by relativization to only marked or contrastive visibility, there remain a number of cases in which a noncontrastive (or nonmarked) vowel unexpectedly intrudes into the search, and this vowel is consistently the highest-sonority vowel in its class. Research focused solely on Wolof could explain its pattern by assuming that /aː/ is specially marked as lexically linked to [−ATR] (as Ka (1994) does). Research focused solely on Hungarian could explain why noncontrastive /aː/ is opaque, but noncontrastive /iː/ is not, again by assuming that [+back] vowels intrude into the search in Hungarian (though clearly Hungarian harmony is contrastively relativized, as evidenced by [ʃoføːr-nɛk] 'chauffeur-DAT'). Finally, research focused solely on Classical Manchu could assume that given the two [+ATR] vowels /u,ə/, the effect of [+ATR] in /u/ is somehow weaker because of its [+round] specification (e.g., Zhang and Dresher 1996). While each of these analyses might perhaps be reasonable within the context of a single language, a broad typological survey repeatedly reveals cases of asymmetric behavior in harmony between higher and lower vowels.

In the rest of this section, we will briefly focus on three cases in which low vowels are transparent to harmony across themselves.[20] Consistent with the predictions of the implicational generalization in (47), repeated in (78), a higher vowel must be transparent as well.

(78) Given two relativization-excluded (e.g., noncontrastive/nonmarked) vowels ϕ and ψ, where ϕ is of higher sonority than ψ, it will never be the case that ϕ is transparent while ψ is not. (In other words, transparency of ϕ implies transparency of ψ.)

5.3.1 Kinande

Kinande has ten surface vowels, [i,u,ɪ,ʊ,e,o,ɛ,ɔ,ə,a], and a system of [±ATR] harmony. Harmony copies the marked value (which is [+ATR]) from a following high vowel. That [+ATR] is the marked value is clear because, aside from [+high] vowels, [±ATR] contrasts are neutralized in roots, except as the result of harmony. Broadly consistent with this position, Archangeli and Pulleyblank (2002, 149) analyze [−ATR] roots such as [ɛrɪ-lɪma] as lacking an underlying specification for ATR altogether, with [−ATR] arising by default and [+ATR] arising in the case of harmony with a following high vowel.[21]

(79) *Kinande verbal roots copy [+ATR] from a following [+high] vowel*
    a. ɔ-mu-lib-i   ɛ-ri-lib-a   'cover-AGENT/INF'
    b. ɔ-mu-huk-i   ɛ-ri-huk-a   'cook-AGENT/INF'
    c. ɔ-mu-lim-i   ɛ-rɪ-lɪm-a   'cultivate-AGENT/INF'
    d. ɔ-mu-hum-i   ɛ-rɪ-hʊm-a   'beat-AGENT/INF'
    e. ɔ-mu-hek-i   ɛ-rɪ-hɛk-a   'carry-AGENT/INF'
    f. ɔ-mu-boh-i   ɛ-rɪ-bɔh-a   'tie-AGENT/INF'
    g. ɔ-mu-kər-i   ɛ-rɪ-kar-a   'tie-AGENT/INF'

While some research on Kinande had suggested that /a/ was transparent to [+ATR] harmony across itself (Schlindwein 1987), Gick et al. (2006) and Kenstowicz (2008) provide instrumental evidence that /a/ undergoes [±ATR] harmony, alternating with [ə]. In short, all vowels in the inventory initiate-and-copy [±ATR] harmony, consistent with the prediction in (47).

5.3.2 Menominee

Menominee is an Algonquian language spoken in Wisconsin and Michigan. In Menominee vowel harmony, as described by Bloomfield (1962) and Milligan (2000), /a/ is transparent to harmony, while /ä/ blocks harmony across itself. While it is sometimes misunderstood in papers on Menominee harmony, /æ/ is actually a low vowel (/æ/) rather than a mid vowel (/ɛ/).[22] By all accounts (Bloomfield 1962; Miner 1979; Hockett 1981; Milligan 2000), this vowel is a *low* vowel; however, Bloomfield's transcription with epsilon (ɛ) led some scholars to interpret this vowel as the mid [−ATR] vowel /ɛ/, with occasional obfuscatory consequences for subsequent understanding of the process. The features underlying the Menominee vowel inventory are shown in (80).

(80) *Menominee vowel inventory*

[−back, −rd]	[+back, +rd]	[−back, −rd]	
i	u		[−low, +ATR]
ɛ	ɔ		[−low, −ATR]
æ			[+low, +ATR]
		a	[+low, −ATR]

The basic process of vowel harmony in Menominee is illustrated in (81): [−low] long vowels copy [+ATR] from the right, as shown in the second example of each pair.

(81) *Menominee vowel harmony: [−low] long root vowels copy [+ATR] from the right*
    a. aːtqnɔːhkæw   'he tells a sacred story'
        aːtqnuːhkuwæw   'he tells him a sacred story'
    b. nɛːmɔw   'he dances'
        niːmit   'when he dances'

Following Archangeli and Pulleyblank (1994) and Milligan (2000), I analyze the Menominee vowel harmony process as [±ATR] harmony. Milligan provides an acoustic study of Menominee, stating that the [−low] vowels /ɛ,ɔ/ may be realized as [ɪ,ʊ] when short, which is consistent with their maintaining [−ATR] while undergoing a change in height. The low vowel /æ/ exhibits extensive surface variability in its height; as Doug Pulleyblank has suggested (personal communication), there may be more variability in the realization of vowels with feature-values that are articulatorily antagonistic, such as [+low, +ATR].

As the following pair shows, [+ATR] harmony is blocked by an intervening /æ/, but may skip across an intervening /a/:

(82) *Menominee vowel harmony blocked by /æ/ but not /a/ (Cole and Trigo 1988)*
 a. kɛːwæːtuaq 'when they go home'
 b. muːskamit 'if he emerges'

I propose that Menominee vowel harmony is a parasitic harmony process among [−low] vowels, searching for the marked value of [+ATR].

(83) *Menominee long root vowels must:*
 ATR-Harmonize: δ = right, F = [m: ATR & R = −low]

As a result, [−ATR] /a/ will be invisible, since it is excluded by the domain of relativization. By contrast, [+ATR] /æ/ will be a defective intervener, being included in the search domain but being of the wrong height. Although /a/ is transparent to harmony while /æ/ blocks it, these vowels crucially have a different status with respect to relativization of the harmonic value: [−ATR] /a/ is excluded from search altogether, whereas [+ATR] /æ/ is included in search but fails to meet a conditional requirement on its value for [±low]. As a result, the fact that of the two Menominee low vowels, one is transparent to harmony and one is a defective intervener is irrelevant for the predictions of (47). The implicational generalization in (47) is applicable for cases in which both vowels under comparison have the same status with respect to the value-relativization in the language (as in Wolof, Classical Manchu, Hungarian, and Finnish, above). Menominee simply has parasitic harmony.

5.3.3 Londengese

Londengese (Leitch 1996) is a seven-vowel Bantu language spoken in the Congo that has [±ATR] harmony affecting its [−high, −low] vowels.

(84) *Londengese vowel inventory*

[−back, −rd]	[+back, +rd]	[+back, −rd]	
i	u		[+high, −low, +ATR]
e	o		[−high, −low, +ATR]
ɛ	ɔ		[−high, −low, −ATR]
		a	[−high, +low, −ATR]

Londengese morphemes copy contrastive [±ATR] from the closest leftward source. Under the relativization to contrastive values, /a/ is transparent and skipped over by harmony.

(85) *Londengese /a/ transparent to [ɔ: ATR] harmony (Leitch 1996, 138)*
    a. t-ok-ak-e   'n'écoute pas'
    b. t-o-ya-k-e   'ne viens pas'
    c. t-ɛnj-ak-ɛ   'ne tire pas'
    d. t-ɔngw-ak-ɛ   'ne vole pas'
    e. tɛ-lɛ-k-ɛ   'ne mange pas'
    f. a-yo-tepy-ak-e   'qu'il aille parler continuellement'
    g. a-y-ɔs-ak-ɛ   'qu'il aille prendre continuellement'

The sonority threshold in Londengese is set to 1, essentially imposing no extrinsic barriers on the search for contrastive [±ATR]. Additional evidence that /a/ is transparent comes from a pattern of consonant reduplication formed by a CV prefix with the fixed vowel /a/. The diminutive plural prefix /to-/ copies [±ATR] from the closest contrastive source to the right, skipping right past /a/.

(86) *Londengese reduplicant /a/ transparent to diminutive prefix harmonizing across it (Leitch 1996, 139)*
    a. to-fu-fumbe   'esclave'
    b. to-ba-bo   'amende'
    c. tɔ-wa-wɔ   'bras'
    d. tɔ-ya-yɛ   'feu'
    e. tɔ-sa-sɛ   'querelle'
    f. tɔ-ta-twɔ   'prix'

The most fortuitous example of transparency across /a/ is found with the prefix /ya-/, which means 'action at a distance' (Leitch 1996, 140) and allows the eponymous process to occur across its high-sonority vowel.

(87) ɛ-sɔmba ɛ-ya-ndɛ njale
    'Le bateau remonte la rivière là-bas.'

When we apply the implicational generalization in (47), we see that it demands that the noncontrastive vowels must also be transparent to [±ATR] harmony in Londengese. There are not many high-vowel affixes in the Zone C branch of Bantu, and as Leitch reports, "There is not a single example of a form with an overt intervening high vowel and retraction after it" (p. 141). However, there is indirect evidence to support the conclusion that high vowels are transparent in Londengese. The causative morpheme (historically /-is-/) is expressed as palatalization of the root-final consonant, and in Babole and other Zone C languages, this palatalized consonant blocks [−ATR] harmony across itself by the following suffix. In other words, in Babole [±ATR] harmony is set to "all values." However, in Londengese, these same consonants are transparent to [+ATR] copying across themselves by the final vowel, as the following alternations illustrate:

(88) *Londengese palatalized consonants (the reflex of [+high, +ATR]) transparent to [−ATR] harmony (Leitch 1996, 141)*
    a. sin-y-e   'faire écrire'
    b. somb-y-e   'faire acheter'
    c. amb-y-e   'faire raconter'
    d. sɔk-y-ɛ   'fatiguer'
    e. bots-e (root: bot-)   'faire engendrer'
    f. pits-e (root: pit-)   'faire abîmer'
    g. kɛnj-ɛ (root: kɛnd-) 'faire aller'

In Babole, [±ATR] copying is relativized to all values, while in Londengese it is relativized to contrastive values of [±ATR]. The transparency of Londengese palatalized consonants (and the high glides in (85)–(87))—in comparison with what we find in other Zone C languages, in which neither these nor /a/ is transparent—constitutes a case in which [±ATR]-noncontrastive /a/ is transparent, according to relativization of the search. As (47) predicts, transparent noncontrastive /a/ implicationally requires the transparency of all lower-sonority noncontrastive segments.

5.4 General Conclusion: Extrinsic Bounds on Search

This chapter has introduced two types of extrinsic bounds on search, one of *extent*, in which crossing too many nodes on the search path causes search to halt, and one of *hurdles*, in which crossing a node of very high sonority imposes a barrier on further search. I have proposed that the distance parameter that limits the extent of intersegmental dependencies such as vowel harmony has five possible settings, and that the sonority threshold imposed on search barriers must follow the universal scale of sonority, with implicational and predictive consequences and implications for possible and impossible harmony patterns.

    As we have seen, the empirical terrain of distance bounds on search can exhibit considerable within-language variability. I have demonstrated that the variable patterning of *aszpirin*-type words in Hungarian and multiple-dorsal prefixes in Gikuyu may be understood as a case of microparametric variation in distance bounds, whereas the variable patterning of *Agnes*-type words in Hungarian may be understood as a case of microparametric variation in sonority thresholds. In both cases, the *within*-language variability tracks the same restricted possibilities as variation *between* languages.

The parallels with syntactic search run deep: as Ross's (1967) discovery of islands (along with other research) demonstrated, a complete theory of long-distance dependencies in syntax must incorporate parameterization of its limits. While agreement and *wh*-movement may often create relations between two positions separated by a host of irrelevant intervening nodes, certain boundaries simply cannot be crossed.

Harmony failures—cases in which search is unsuccessful because of extrinsic locality bounds—provide important limits that rein in what may normally be a very long-distance process. While chapter 3 focused on how far vowel harmony can travel and its apparently nonlocal aspects, the study of locality would not have been complete without considering its limits.

Our focus on vowel harmony—a long-distance assimilation process par excellence—as the starting point for the model means that simpler cases of strictly adjacent assimilation might be treated as very bounded cases of harmony. In addition, we saw in section 5.1.4 that long-distance iterative dissimilation may be tightly modeled using the distance parameters independently developed for harmony, raising the question of how much of the computation serving these two processes might be shared. We turn to these and other potentially far-reaching implications of the parameterized Search procedure for vowel harmony in the next chapter.

6 Minimalist Computation of Vowel Harmony: Implications

We are now ready to review and highlight the broader theoretical relevance of the formal model of vowel harmony developed in previous chapters. As the discussion proceeds, I will attempt to identify areas of potential future collaboration with other branches of linguistics and cognitive science.

I have proposed a principles-and-parameters theory of possible vowel harmony systems in human language, with four components:

1. An invariant *Search procedure*, according to which a value-seeking element initiates a search for the feature it needs, stops as soon as it finds the closest element bearing the relevant feature, and copies the value of that feature to itself.
2. The *relativization parameter* that determines what counts as "relevant." Following Calabrese (1995), we saw that the three parametric possibilities are (a) *all* values of the harmonic feature, (b) only the *contrastive* values, or (c) only the *marked* values.
3. *Conditional requirements* on licit sources of feature-copying. In addition to the requirement that the donor must bear the relativized value of the harmonic feature, a subrequirement of identity between source and goal is demanded.
4. *Bounding parameters*, divided into a set of extrinsic limits on absolute distance of search and a set of tolerance thresholds determining whether high-sonority elements can be skipped or not.

Our inquiry into the locality of vowel harmony has provided empirical arguments for a recipient-initiated search, based on split-source harmony and bidirectional searches. It has also illustrated how microvariation within a language can be insightfully modeled in terms of different settings of a single parameter. The treatment of defective intervention in chapter 4 places significant restrictions on what can be a possible "blocker," by restricting the conditions blocking search to orthogonal feature identity and heteromorphemicity, along with a nonnegotiable principle of "no second chance" in search. Chapter 5 explained how two new adjacency parameters added to the ones proposed by Odden (1994) expand the typology of boundedness, and it established a novel implicational generalization about the role of sonority in blocking harmony.

All of these contributions to the understanding of vowel harmony might be viewed as advancements in phonological theory. Nonetheless, this book's raison d'être is not only to provide extensive empirical coverage and unify a wide number of disparate harmony cases under a single model, but also to explore an important and often-neglected question of higher-order synthesis: does phonology instantiate any procedures of "minimalist" computation of the type argued to exist in syntax?

The Minimalist Program (Chomsky 1995) represents a major shift in linguistic theory in the way that language is viewed, namely, as an "optimal solution" to design features and interface considerations. Whether or not phonological computations also instantiate optimal solutions to interface conditions has yet to be fully addressed. I hope to convince phonologists not only that viewing vowel harmony through the lens of minimalism opens the potential to unify different levels of linguistic representation and different domains of empirical inquiry under the same foundational framework, but also that the specific implementation of a theory of the locality of dependencies represents a step forward in understanding constraints on possible harmonic languages.

6.1 Expanding the Terrain of Minimalist Inquiry

Contrary to the title and conclusions of Bromberger and Halle's (1989) article, phonology may not be as "different" as it seems. One of my goals in this book has been to bring empirical phenomena within phonology closer to the attention of minimalist theorists, whose training and research is largely focused on syntactic problems. Because Optimality Theory constraints and autosegmental representations do not resemble the primitives of syntactic theory, opportunities for unification and crossfertilization have remained limited simply because of apparent disparities in representational vocabulary. However, by framing vowel harmony in the context of the mechanism of Agree and demonstrating that the logic of closest search within a relativized domain can apply in phonology under the relation of precedence in the same way that it applies in syntax under the relation of dominance, we increase the prospects for syntacticians and cognitive scientists more generally to view subsegmental dependencies and phrase-structural dependencies as manifestations of the same cognitive architecture.

The Minimalist Program makes two central claims about the design of human language. The first claim is that computations are derivational and efficient and that they follow principles of least effort in order to satisfy feature-valuation. We have found that the Search procedure is greedy (see section 2.11) and myopic (see chapter 4).[1] The second claim is that minimalist computations are interface-driven. Vowel harmony lies at the interface between two components of human cognition: the lexicon and phonetic realization. The defining property of harmonizing morphemes is that they lack a value for the harmonic feature. These segments require a value for the harmonic feature in order to be interpreted by the articulatory component of language and perceived by the interlocutor. Vowel harmony seems to be a perfect solution to the problem of supplying a feature-value for a needy vowel: derivationally initiated feature-copying that stops with the closest possible source.

While many lines of cognitive science question whether syntactic or phonological computations are language-specific (e.g., Langacker 1987; Lieberman 2000; Marcus 2008), much less work has been devoted to the relationship *between* linguistic modules *within* the faculty of language. Hockett's (1960) very notion of "duality of patterning"—the existence of combinatorial generation and restrictions at both the phonological and syntactic levels—suggests that a formal isomorphism may be at work. Rather than claiming that phonology is domain-general or part of generalized cognition, I would like to suggest that it bears a closer relation to other linguistic modules than was perhaps previously understood. This view may be traced to notions predating generative treatments of vowel harmony: Hjelmslev (1948) formulated an "analogie du principe structurel," according to which the units and structural properties that describe one aspect of language (such as syntactic relations within sentences) should be expected to be fundamentally the same as those required by the analysis of other aspects of language (see Bermúdez-Otero and Honeybone 2006 for discussion). While Government Phonology (e.g., Kaye, Lowenstamm, and Vergnaud 1985; Charette 1991; Pöchtrager 2006) embraces the notion that syllable structure follows a binary-branching and headed pattern like that of syntactic constituency, far too little attention has been paid to long-distance dependencies in phonology as a direct structural analogue of syntactic agreement.

One could counterfactually imagine a language faculty in which syntactic agreement targeted the most distant element in the domain, while vowel harmony targeted the closest one, or vice versa. Similarly, one could imagine a phonological component without defective intervention, in which defective elements simply let search go right by them. But I have identified three formal properties of syntactic search-and-copy that are identical to properties of vowel harmony: relativized minimality, defective intervention, and the minimality/boundedness distinction. These algorithmic properties of Harmonize and Agree arguably are due to the same underlying procedure, simply operating over different data structures. While syntactic Agree operates over c-command, Harmonize operates over precedence; while Agree copies ɸ-features such as gender and number, Harmonize copies subsegmental features such as [±round] and [±ATR]. I contend that the existence of recurrent identical operative principles in both domains is due to the fact that the two use the same procedure.

Anderson (1992) discusses the lack of active crossmodular comparison between syntax and phonology, concluding that excessive modularization can lead to theoretical parochialism and "ill-supported notational alternatives" (p. 3). I would argue that the autosegmental formalism of the No-Line-Crossing Constraint, as applied to vowel harmony, is a parochial notation that ultimately obscures the formal identity of relativized locality in syntax and phonology.[2] If the hypothesis of Crossmodular Structural Parallelism is to be pursued, it is clear that the literally geometric statement of the No-Line-Crossing Constraint is an absurd means for expressing relativized minimality in syntax. By comparison, the Search-and-Copy algorithm is flexible enough to compute closeness over either dominance (in Agree) or precedence (in vowel harmony), while providing a tight fit to the empirical terrain of locality restrictions.[3]

Once a single algorithm is in place for syntactic agreement and for phonological vowel harmony—the only difference being the data structures the algorithm operates over—language acquisition potentially becomes considerably easier. The learnability challenges arise only in acquiring the specifications of each syntactic head and the ɸ-features it needs or bears or the specifications of each morpheme and the agreement features it needs or bears, and the parametric specifications of where and how far the heads or morphemes can look. The notion of "microparameters" is that linguistic variation is determined only by the specifications of each node entering into computation. This proposal was introduced into syntactic theory by Borer (1984), was brought to the fore within the Minimalist Program by Chomsky (1995), and has been characterized in terms of a restricted schema of parameters for a given syntactic node by Longobardi (2005).

The reformulation of the notion "parameter" within the Minimalist Program as a set of featural requirements on individual lexical items dovetails well with the locus of parametric variation between harmony patterns in the current model. Recall that the only ways that languages differ with respect to their vowel harmony patterns are in (1) what features they search for, (2) whether conditional subrequirements are imposed on licit copying, (3) which direction they look, and (4) how much extrinsic bounding they tolerate. In fact, there is a fairly rich tradition of work proposing parameterized systems of vowel harmony.

The autosegmental and metrical research tradition for vowel harmony, including works spanning from Steriade 1981 to Archangeli and Pulleyblank 1994, often employed a restricted set of parameters along which harmony patterns could differ; more directly, the proposals of Odden (1994) and Calabrese (1995) form the basis for the parameters that chapters 3 and 5 expand upon. However, in these previous proposals, the parameters largely focused on the harmony pattern of a language as a property of the language as a whole, rather than as properties of specific morphemes. As a consequence of viewing parametric variation as a property of vowel harmony in a language as a whole, morphemes that did not undergo harmony required special lexical marking. By contrast, the present model views parametric specifications as a property of each morpheme, and if a particular morpheme does not undergo harmony, nothing special—in fact, nothing at all—needs to be said about it.

Within all microparametric theories in which the locus of variation is individual morphemes, an important question is the role of inductive biases toward uniformity of the parameter settings for broad classes of items. Although we saw in chapter 1 that Turkish suffixes may differ from each other in that one requires back harmony and round harmony, another requires back harmony and round harmony for only one of its vowels, another requires back harmony only, and yet another requires no harmony at all, we have also seen cases where virtually all suffixes in a language harmonize in the same way (e.g., Wolof). Goodman (1955) introduces the notion of "overhypothesis": if you see that many bags contain marbles of a uniform color (e.g., some bags contain all red marbles, some contain all green marbles), you will eventually try to guess the entire contents of each new bag of marbles just by seeing one marble from it.

While the color of the marbles in each bag may be generated by its own independent "rule," an overhypothesis is a guess that the rules for all the bags will be uniform.

Questions about the uniformity of affixal patterning (into "classes of morphemes") may be ideally investigated through studies of first- and second-language acquisition. Microparametric theories of generative grammar have not fully tackled the empirical question of whether language learners quickly generalize from one morpheme's parametric settings to another's. Existing data on language acquisition in Turkish and Finnish indicate that children master vowel harmony quickly and with few errors (Aksu-Koç and Slobin 1985; Leiwo, Kulju, and Aoyama 2006). These data indicate that once children learn that a few suffixes are parametrically set to "needy" for feature [±F] in their language, they may efficiently generalize to other suffixes, but do not exhibit the incorrect overgeneralization that would be expected if "leftward [±back] vowel harmony" were a parameter of the language as a whole. Within the domain of syntactic acquisition, Lightfoot and Westergaard (2007) argue that children do not overgeneralize the featural requirements of complementizers from one clause-type to another and that they correctly distinguish declaratives and exclamatives with respect to verb-second. Language acquisition research bearing on the question of "overhypotheses" with respect to microparameter setting is in its early stages empirically and in terms of modeling,[4] and questions about the realistic nature of microparametric grammars for phonology and syntax should proceed in tandem, with frequent cross-dialogue.

In conclusion, I would argue that the hypothesis of Crossmodular Structural Parallelism embraces much more than analogical similarities between the syntax of agreement and long-distance vowel harmony, and that it can be taken literally as a claim that the same Search procedure, with its properties of no-lookahead and halting with the first element in the relativized domain, is "reused" across different levels of linguistic structure. Once the basic Search-and-Copy algorithm is in place within the language faculty, it can be applied to any alphabet of data structures situated at the interface between two components that require an efficient means of feature-valuation.

6.2 Are Assimilation and Dissimilation Subroutines of Harmony?

Our investigation of vowel harmony in this book was anchored on two pillars: (1) vowel harmony is the best place among phonological phenomena to observe long-distance intersegmental relations that are comparable to syntactic long-distance relations, and (2) vowel harmony displays a wide enough range of crosslinguistic variation to present a nontrivial learning problem, therefore a testing ground for a principles-and-parameters approach. In developing a formally explicit parameterized algorithm for vowel harmony, one consequence is that certain routines involved in the process can also serve to carry out the computations for local assimilation or for dissimilation. Let us review the Search algorithm depicted in figure 5.1.

Minor modifications to this basic algorithm can yield assimilation and dissimilation. For example, as soon as the distance parameter is set to $\beta = 1$, we have segmental adjacency. As soon as the value to be copied for feature f is multiplied by $*-1$, we have dissimilation. These parametric modifications to the algorithm reveal that once long-distance harmony is accurately handled within a formally explicit theory, assimilation and dissimilation may become special subcases of intersegmental feature relations.

The important questions, however, are empirical: although we can model dissimilation as "opposite-value harmony" and local assimilation as "very bounded harmony," do we still expect the full range of parametric options of long-distance vowel harmony, developed in chapters 3–5, to reveal themselves in these processes?

Consider the notion of parasitic harmony as applied to local assimilation. What is the typology of cases of assimilation for a feature [±F] that occurs only if both segments already bear the same value for an orthogonal feature [±G]? There are certainly clear cases of assimilation that do require identity with regard to a separate feature in order for feature-copying to occur. An example from English is the [±anterior] assimilation that only occurs between adjacent segments that are both [+continuant] (e.g., *this shoe* → [ðɪʃ ʃu]). This pattern can be treated within the logic of parasitic harmony as a case of assimilation dependent on a conditional requirement of identity.

The possibility of treating orthogonal feature requirements as a prerequisite for local assimilation has not been thoroughly explored to date, and it may prove revealing; if, on the other hand, parasitic assimilation is not robustly found, then perhaps extending the harmonic Search-and-Copy procedure to local assimilation is the wrong move. Research on this question has extensively formalized implicational conditions on the manner, place, and directionality of assimilation undergoers (e.g., Cho 1990; Jun 2004) but has not unearthed a typology of cases in which the value-source and the value-seeker must share an orthogonal feature.

Besides studying the extent to which parasitic assimilation exists, we can ask questions about other conditions on vowel harmony that apparently have not yet been documented with respect to local assimilation. For example, does context-sensitive markedness enter into assimilation in the same way it does in, say, Kirghiz B [±round] harmony (section 3.8.2)? If it does, we would expect patterns of assimilation where only the marked source of a feature may be copied from for local assimilation. A schematic example would be a case where a preceding consonant could copy the marked [+round] feature of /ü/ but not /u/, so that /nü/ → [mü] but /nu/ ↛ [mu]. While such predictions certainly seem unlikely, the effects of context-sensitive markedness in Kirghiz vowel harmony were also surprising when first encountered. Only when a hypothesis is on the table that such phenomena might exist does one begin to actively look for them.

Should it turn out, upon empirical comparison, that long-distance vowel harmony and assimilation are accomplished by different mechanisms because the latter lacks the full range of effects of parasitic requirements and relativization to marked values, a parallel question should be raised in syntactic theory. The Agree formalism was developed for cases of verbal agreement at a distance with noun phrases, and it is appropriate to ask whether the same mechanism underlies the very local agreement between adjectives and noun phrases, known as Concord.

Concord seems to be insensitive to hierarchical considerations, and it is initiated by all elements within a noun phrase; there are no known cases of defective intervention or feature-relativized locality for DP-internal concord.[5] Moreover, Concord only copies gender and number features, never person; is this lacuna fundamental to the nature of how Concord works, or merely incidental? Further research should focus on the twin questions of whether verbal agreement and DP-internal concord should be formally dissociated and whether long-distance harmony and local assimilation should be formally dissociated, ideally with cross-dialogue between these enterprises. While we pursue answers, I will suggest that although the subroutine of vowel harmony *can* be used in a limiting case to execute local assimilation, the two phenomena may not actually *be* accomplished through the same procedure. Indeed, they may serve different interfaces: vowel harmony occurs upon the concatenation of two morphemes, while much of local assimilation may be a consequence of postcyclic articulatorily driven processes.

At first blush, the claim that dissimilation is the inverse of vowel harmony fares better: similar to long-distance vowel harmony, there are cases of dissimilation that are (1) clearly long-distance, (2) clearly restricted by contrastiveness, and (3) clearly "myopic." The extended analysis of Dahl's Law in section 5.1.4 illustrated marked-feature relativization. A well-known dissimilation involving contrastive-value relativization occurs with the Latin adjectival suffix, which searches for the closest contrastive value of [±lateral] and copies the opposite value.

(1) *Latin liquid dissimilation (Gildersleeve and Lodge 1895)*
    a. nav-alis   'naval'
    b. mort-alis   'mortal'
    c. ven-alis   'venal'
    d. caud-alis   'caudal'
    e. milit-aris   'military'
    f. lun-aris   'lunar'
    g. consul-aris   'consular'
    h. vulg-aris   'common'
    i. flor-alis   'floral'
    j. sepulchr-alis   'funereal'
    k. litor-alis   'of the shore'

The alternation in the suffix between [r] and [l] (i.e., [±lateral]) is asymmetrically dependent on the value of [±lateral] for the closest leftward [+consonant, +sonorant, −nasal] element in the stem: when /l/ is the closest, the suffix is [-aris], and when /r/ is the closest, the suffix is [-alis]. We can model this process as copying of the *opposite* value of the closest contrastive [±lateral].

(2) *Latin adjectival suffix must:*
    Lateral-Dissimilate: δ = left, F = opposite([c: lateral])

Search indeed looks for the *closest* value of [±lateral], as shown by (1i–k), where both /l/ and /r/ occur in the stem, and the suffix copies [+lateral] because the [−lateral] element is closer.

The Latin lateral dissimilation process illustrates the potential for long-distance dissimilation to be based on the same Search procedure as vowel harmony. Nonetheless, one is struck by how few of the vowel harmony parameters are active in dissimilation.

Certainly the value-relativization parameters of chapter 3 are applicable in delimiting the typology of possible dissimilation patterns. The long-distance [±voice] dissimilations found in Dahl's Law in Gikuyu and Lyman's Law in Japanese (Ito and Mester 2003) present robust cases of long-distance dissimilation for the marked value of a feature. Moreover, as Suzuki (1998) has demonstrated, many of the distance parameters relevant for harmony in Odden 1994 are attested within the typology of dissimilation.

On the one hand, the breadth of dissimilation phenomena involving value-relativization and distance-relativization looks promising for the attempt to unify harmony and dissimilation (for such an attempt, see Nevins 2004). Analyses that employ the metrics of locality defined by the No-Line-Crossing Constraint have no clear no way of presenting a unified theory of assimilation and dissimilation, since dissimilation doesn't involve any "lines" to begin with. As a result, the formal unity of harmony and dissimilation was barely considered while phonological theory adopted the autosegmental framework. However, once the locality of vowel harmony is treated as relativized locality along the dimension of the precedence relation and as a copying process, it suddenly becomes possible to express dissimilation with the same mechanism. Indeed, in an experimental study of adults' ability to learn artificial grammatical patterns, Pycha et al. (2003) found that subjects could learn vowel harmony (requiring the same value for [±F]) and disharmony (requiring the opposite value for [±F]) equally as well.

On the other hand, despite the promise of treating dissimilation as a kind of "opposite-value" harmony process, the paucity of robust cases of iterative dissimilation is striking. A characteristic property of vowel harmony, as exemplified by the thirteen successive harmonizing Turkish suffixes in chapter 1, is its iterative nature: one morpheme, M_j, harmonizes with the morpheme to its left, M_{j-1}, and M_j subsequently becomes a source of copying for the next morpheme, M_{j+1}. In the realm of dissimilation, Dahl's Law appears to be the only case where dissimilation iterates (recall the dialect of Gikuyu that generates [ɣa.kaa.ɣii.kia], where each morpheme dissimilates in [±voice] from the one to its immediate right, iteratively).

If dissimilation involved just the flipping of a switch from the basic harmony procedure (whether to copy the same or the opposite value), the question would be why we don't observe more cases of iterative dissimilation. Similar questions can be raised for other dissimilation phenomena that we might expect if dissimilation were simply a special subcase of harmony. For example, are there any cases of "parasitic dissimilation"— dissimilation for [±F] only if there is already (non)identity for an orthogonal feature [±G]? A concrete case of parasitic dissimilation would be one where dissimilation of aspiration (the feature [+spread glottis]) occurred only between obstruents that had the same value for [±voice], for example, /bʰu-gʰa/ → [bʰu-ga], but /bʰu-kʰa/ → [bʰu-kʰa]. Parasitic dissimilation of this sort would be expected to even yield defective intervention, so that /bʰu-kʰe-gʰa/ → [bʰu-kʰe-gʰa]. I know of no cases of defective intervention in dissimilation, and one wonders whether this is a principled lacuna or simply due to the small sample size. Moreover, if dissimilation were simply the flip side of vowel harmony, we might expect that sonority hurdles could affect dissimilation, blocking long-distance dissimilation with a high-sonority element.

An important consideration in studying whether dissimilation really implicates the same mechanism as harmonic Search-and-Copy is that while syntax is replete with cases of long-distance Agree, there are no cases of syntactic Dis-Agree—that is, syntactic dissimilation in which the opposite value of a feature is copied.[6]

Perhaps more disturbing than the absence of parasitic dissimilation, sonority-thresholded dissimilation, and defective-intervention dissimilation, and the rarity of iterative dissimilation, is a more pressing question: why is there so little vowel dissimilation? There are a few instances of [+low] dissimilation among vowels (e.g., Woleaian, Kera (Suzuki 1998)), but there are no cases of dissimilation for other vowel features. I know of no cases of [±back], [±round], [±ATR], or [±nasal] dissimilation among vowels.

Nespor, Peña, and Mehler (2003) suggest that the relative rarity of vowel dissimilation must be linked to the relative rarity of consonant harmony. While of course there are a significant number of cases of consonant harmony (e.g., Karaim, chapter 3; Kikongo, chapter 5; sibilant harmony (Poser 1982)), especially documented in Hansson 2001, it is generally agreed that consonant harmony is more limited than vowel harmony. Nespor, Peña, and Mehler offer the broad-brush observation that, in terms of long-distance interactions, vowels like to assimilate and consonants like to dissimilate. These observations form part of a far-reaching hypothesis about the nature of vowels and consonants, and their distinctive functional roles.

The observations that Nespor, Peña, and Mehler (2003) synthesize draw on diverse evidence supporting the general claim that consonants must remain distinctive and contrastive whereas vowels need not bear any burden of lexical contrast. For example, almost all languages have more consonants than vowels; or, to put it differently, few if any languages have more vowels in their inventory (excluding diphthongs) than they have consonants. Compare the consonant-to-vowel ratios of the following randomly chosen languages: Malay, 20C:5V; Italian, 24C:7V;

Hausa, 32C:5V; Arabic, 29C:3V; Igbo, 27C:8V; Sindi, 46C:10V; Hawaiian, 8C:5V. Nespor, Peña, and Mehler argue that this asymmetry reflects a principled division of labor in which consonants are responsible for filling out the distinctive combinatorics of the lexicon.

In the Semitic languages, the lexical content of a word is borne by the consonants, which form a lexical skeleton, while the vowels contain inflectional and grammatical information (McCarthy 1985; Arad 2005). Importantly, no "Inverse Semitic"—in which the vowels form lexical skeleta and the consonants make up the variable grammatical morphemes—is known to exist. Moreover, the Semitic languages are replete with restrictions that seek to avoid the same feature occurring multiple times in a single consonantal root (Greenberg 1950; Frisch, Pierrehumbert, and Broe 2004). Nespor, Peña, and Mehler (2003) point out that similarity-avoidance effects are almost always focused on consonants; tongue-twisters, for example, are crosslinguistically based on the difficulty of repeating certain consonants, and largely do not manipulate vowels.

It seems that vowels are "cheaper" to modify than consonants; notice, for example, that vowel reduction is a widespread phenomenon, but that nothing nearly as systematic exists among consonants (e.g., no languages have processes that neutralize all coda consonants to a single segment, say, [t]). Experimental evidence also reveals that modifying vowels is apparently easier than modifying consonants. Cutler et al. (2000) provided subjects with a task in which they were allowed to change one phoneme to make a word from a nonword. When native speakers of Spanish and Dutch were given a nonword such as *kebra*, they altered the vowel more frequently than the consonant, producing *cobra* more often than *zebra*. Even Voltaire is quoted as saying, "Etymology is a science in which the vowels count for nothing, and the consonants for very little" (Müller 1994, 238). Whether or not Voltaire was right about the absolute quantities, at least he correctly identified the direction of the asymmetry: consonants are much more reliable backbones of lexical structure than vowels. Surendran and Niyogi (2003) found that consonants carry a functional load (i.e., carry informational content relevant for lexical distinctiveness, even relativized to frequency) three times greater than that of vowels in Mandarin, English, German, and Dutch.

Nespor, Peña, and Mehler (2003) develop the idea that vowels and consonants have fundamentally different functional roles: consonants exist in order to generate the lexicon (i.e., the paradigmatic component of syntax), whereas vowels exist in order to facilitate parsing of the speech stream into distinct morphosyntactic constituents. On this view, vowel harmony and consonantal dissimilation may serve fundamentally different interfaces: consonantal dissimilation may be a computation whose purpose is to facilitate lexical access to open-class items (i.e., *homonym avoidance*), whereas vowel harmony may serve the purpose of parsing the morphosyntactic words in phrases (i.e., *oronym avoidance*). Other researchers adopt a "carrier"/modulation view of vowels versus consonants (see Traunmüller 1994; Harris and Urua 2001), and experimental studies such as Owren and Cardillo's (2006) find that vowels are used much more for talker recognition and indexical cues than consonants, while consonants are used much more for word recognition and meaning recovery than vowels.

The diachronic sources of vowel harmony and consonantal dissimilation may be fundamentally different as well. Suomi (1983) proposes that vowel harmony arises from perceptual reanalysis of words with weak noninitial (more broadly, nonroot) vowels as being asymmetrically dependent on initial syllables for their backness specification. By contrast, Ohala (1981) proposes that the diachronic source for dissimilation is fundamentally hypercorrection: a listener encounters a form like Latin *quinque* [k^{w}i$^{(w)}$nk^{w}e] with rounding on the two consonants that abut a vowel, notices rounding on the vowel, and attributes the rounding to coarticulation on an underlying form with only one source of rounding: /kink^{w}e/, later becoming Italian *cinque*. If these two distinct perception-based accounts for the emergence of vowel harmony and consonantal dissimilation, respectively, are correct, they point to these two phenomena having crucially different origins in the (mis)learning process itself.

The observations and explanations I have offered here regarding the potential differences between harmony and dissimilation are preliminary and will require a great deal of research. My purpose has been more to raise more questions than to provide answers, in the hope of inspiring continued comparison of these two phenomena. On the one hand, long-distance dissimilation and vowel harmony share a number of formal properties, such as distance parameters and relativization to contrastive or marked values. On the other hand, dissimilation is a syntagmatic process with essentially no analogue in syntax; it has no formal instantiation of defective intervention; and in terms of its substantive properties, it virtually never operates on vowel features.

The relative weight of the evidence in these two directions merits serious continued attention in terms of both empirical research and theoretical development, in particular because the proposed Search-and-Copy formalism allows—for the first time in generative phonology—the potential to formally unite harmony and dissimilation under one algorithmic procedure.

6.3 Vowel Harmony and Impossible Languages

Truth is more likely to emerge from error than from vagueness.
—T. H. Huxley

Can there be a set of conditions that determine whether a language would be impossible to learn? The aim of generative grammar and the principles-and-parameters context posits that certain aspects of human language are universal and inviolable (the principles), while other aspects may vary in limited ways (the parameters).[7] The Search procedure's core mechanism is a principle, while value-relativization, conditional requirements on sources, distance bounds, and sonority hurdles are parameters, which can vary in strictly limited ways. The resulting harmony patterns represent a tiny fraction of the logically possible ones. A wide range of conceivable harmony patterns would not be allowed by the system of principles and parameters I have proposed. The following are a few harmony languages excluded by the current model.

(3) *Impossible harmony languages*
    a. Copying from the vowel furthest away from the value-seeker
    b. Copying only from vowels noncontrastive for the harmonic feature; excluding others
    c. Copying only from vowels unmarked for the harmonic feature; excluding others
    d. Long-distance parasitic harmony: absence of defective intervention when there is a conditional requirement on sources
    e. Search that can look past two intervening syllables, but not three
    f. Noncontrastive and transparent /a/ in the same language as noncontrastive but nontransparent /i/

The impossible languages in (3) are excluded either by the inviolable requirement of halting with the closest element or by the small space of allowable value-relativization parameters, distance bounds, and sonority hurdles. The claim that the harmony patterns in (3) are impossible constitutes a strong and falsifiable prediction: discovery of any language that possesses one of these patterns will require revising the theory.

Any contribution to the study of Universal Grammar should delimit the set of unlearnable languages. In my view, the function of what's called

Universal Grammar isn't to provide *a grammar*, but to provide *constraints on what can and can't be a possible grammar*. Put differently, the function of Universal Grammar in aiding the learner faced with a harmony pattern is not to produce a magic formula for the answer—in fact, as cases of optionality and intraspeaker variation show, the learner may *never* learn a uniquely correct answer—but to *prevent* the learner from ever considering a host of irrelevant answers. And I do mean *prevent*. On this view, the closest analogue to Universal Grammar in another species would be the "templates" of songbird learning.

W. H. Thorpe's attempt to teach chaffinches the songs of the tree pipit and observing their failure to learn them (although the songs were sensorily perceptible and motorally executable) led him to conclude that "the chaffinch has the inborn blueprint conferring on it a tendency to learn to pay attention to certain kinds of sounds and certain types of phrase only" (1958, 84; as cited in Marler 1997, 506). This statement, and indeed Thorpe's views generally, emphasize that the defining feature of songbird learning is what the birds cannot and do not try to learn, because they simply cannot attend to certain kinds of sound patterns. This constitutes a strong view of the chaffinch's "blueprint," and of Universal Grammar: the languages that Universal Grammar excludes are simply unlearnable; they are grammatical hypotheses that are excluded from the set of possibilities that the learner considers.

With this perspective in mind, what is more realistic than discovering a language with a heretofore unknown pattern violating the predictions in (3) is the possibility of testing these predictions in an experimental paradigm. The artificial grammar learning (AGL) paradigm is an experimental technique whereby participants (infants, adults, or animals) are taught a "miniature language" that the experimenters construct with specific properties (see Gómez and Gerken 2000 for an overview).[8] After a brief implicit exposure to words and/or sentences of this artificial language, participants are asked to discriminate and/or produce utterances that would be allowable according to the pattern of this language.

Should an excluded harmony system of the type in (3) arise, either through artificial construction in the laboratory or through an intermediate stage of radical language contact (e.g., pidginization), the proposed model predicts that learners would reshape the system in order to be consistent with principles given by Universal Grammar. In other words, in a real-life situation or an "iterated learning" AGL experiment (Kalish, Griffiths, and Lewandowsky 2007), in which one generation of speakers or subjects provides input to the next, we would expect a scenario similar to the regularization of non-UG-compatible grammars attested in the development of Nicaraguan Sign Language (Senghas 1995). Alternatively, we might observe all-out failure to learn an impossible grammar (e.g., one with noncontrastive-only relativization or only low-sonority hurdles), an outcome parallel to that reported by Smith and Tsimpli (1995), who attempted to teach a linguistic idiot savant (a person with lower-than-average general intelligence, but phenomenal languages-learning ability) a non-UG-compatible language ("Epun," in which the sentential-focus marker always appeared on the third word) and found that he failed to generalize.

Pycha et al. (2003), Koo and Cole (2006), and Bonatti et al. (2005) have carried out revealing experiments using the AGL paradigm to test questions about possible and impossible patterns of subsegmental dependencies such as vowel harmony and dissimilation. Pycha et al. (2003) studied whether experimental participants could learn harmony (identical-feature copying), disharmony (opposite-feature copying), or a random pattern of suffix allomorphy with equal ease, and found that harmony and disharmony were equally learnable by the participants, none of whom had such patterns in their native languages, but that random patterns were not. Koo and Cole (2006) studied whether experimental participants could learn consonant harmony, consonant disharmony, vowel harmony, and vowel disharmony with equal ease, and found that vowel disharmony was hardest for participants to learn. Bonatti et al. (2005) tested whether French-speaking participants could learn triconsonantal "frames" of the Semitic type as easily as learning trivocalic frames, and found that consonantal skeleta were easier to extract from continuous data streams. In summary, experiments of this sort have already established the potential for revealing generalizations about participants' ability to learn typologically "natural" and "unnatural" patterns, and demonstrated that the AGL methodology is sensitive enough to allow experimental comparison between harmony and disharmony and between consonantal and vocalic dependencies.

The AGL methodology could be used to test any of the languages in (3). The prediction is that human participants would be much less able to learn the patterns in (3) than those in (4).

(4) *Possible harmony languages*
    a. Copying from the closest vowel to the value-seeker
    b. Copying only from vowels contrastive for the harmonic feature; excluding others

c. Copying only from vowels marked for the harmonic feature; excluding others
d. No-second-chance parasitic harmony: presence of defective intervention when there is a conditional requirement on sources
e. Search that can look past one intervening syllable, but not two
f. Noncontrastive and transparent /i/ in the same language as noncontrastive but nontransparent /a/

All of the patterns in (4), in contrast to those in (3), are allowed within the vowel harmony space I have proposed. Vowel harmony is a search-and-copy process that is greedy and economical; it can relativize what matters on the basis of salient inventory properties such as contrastiveness and markedness; it can count to 1 but not to 2; and it can be blocked by high-sonority elements. We have repeatedly considered the possibility that these properties are the inevitable result of a minimalist computational architecture.

An exciting research direction would be to conduct AGL experiments testing impossible harmony patterns, in tandem with brain-imaging techniques. As Moro (2008) suggests, even if subjects manage to learn a non-UG-compliant "impossible" language, we want to know if they do so using the same neural mechanisms used to process ordinary human language, as opposed to employing clever nonlinguistic memorization or auditory encoding as an alternative means for dealing with input that the linguistic computation system simply cannot handle. Moro 2008 contains a very illuminating discussion of how the convergence of formally explicit theoretical models and experimental methodology allows the testing of "impossible languages," by observing the neural circuitry that humans use to deal with patterns that are not permitted by the highly specialized computations of human language. Even more revealing as confirmation of the hypothesis of Crossmodular Structural Parallelism would be the finding that violations of the possible harmony systems in (4) generate brain responses identical to those generated by violations of syntactic locality.

Conclusive brain-imaging results from AGL studies of harmony may be difficult to obtain, because of the extreme care needed in designing AGL experiments, particularly in controlling for potential bias from the speakers' first language.[9] A second concern in designing AGL experiments relates to the "ecological validity" of the AGL paradigm for teaching vowel harmony: How does one train subjects to learn that something is an affix asymmetrically dependent on the root, or indeed to perform morphological segmentation at all? How does one encourage subjects to generalize vowel harmony patterns to new roots and treat vowel harmony as a productive process, rather than a static fact about the words they have heard? Peperkamp, Skoruppa, and Dupoux (2007) have developed creative methodologies for implicit pattern learning through a distractor or ecologically valid task, and such approaches will continue to provide solutions to these concerns.

In summary, our lengthy discourse has traversed the locality conditions on harmony patterns where the harmonic feature is [±high], [±low], [±back], [±round], [±ATR], or [±nasal], from over thirty languages spoken in the Americas, Africa, Europe, Australia, the Indian subcontinent, and Asia. The conclusions that emerge overshadow which feature the harmony involves or where the languages are spoken. Facing locality in linguistic structure, humans do not compute distance as the crow flies, nor do they perform a global optimization. The search for the closest donor vowel may exclude a swath of irrelevant interveners, or it may halt with the first defective vowel it finds, even though a better one lies just beyond. These generalizations are affirmed repeatedly across diverse alphabets and sequences.

Typological research on understudied languages must continue, and as our knowledge of the world's languages increases, we may find vowel harmony patterns that call for revising the theory. Importantly, even if such languages are never found in natural linguistic communities, the predictions of a formally explicit principles-and-parameters model of vowel harmony are clear enough to be tested experimentally. These predictions will ultimately bear on the nature of what computations of locality are biologically possible.

Notes

Chapter 1

1. Moreover, Przezdziecki (2005) found near-significant coarticulatory effects for the vowel [a], even though in no dialect of Yoruba does [a] categorically participate in harmony. Thus, it seems that if harmony is a phonologization of existing phonetic coarticulatory tendencies, cognitive and symbolic aspects of phonological computation step in to "filter" and extract from those tendencies. Finally, since Adetugbo (1967) and Bamgboṣe (1967) argue that Proto-Yoruba had the tense/lax contrast between /i,u/ and /ɪ,ʊ/, the Central Ede dialects do not represent an innovation (see Adetugbo 1967, 158); rather, the full range of this contrast seems to have been lost in different ways throughout Yoruba.

2. The exposition here follows Reinhart and Reuland's (1993) discussion of co-argumenthood as being what makes a noun phrase relevant for binding. For a more detailed and technical exposition of binding theory, see Büring 2005.

3. Mailhot and Reiss (2007) pursue a number of convergent ideas for vowel harmony, from the perspective of learnability, making points of contact with certain aspects of the model proposed here.

4. The work of Calabrese (1995, 2005) has set the stage for these types of "visibility parameters" in the theory proposed here.

5. The "distance parameters" of chapter 5 are inspired by Odden's (1994) work on harmony.

6. For example, Cassimjee and Kisseberth (2001, 350ff.) discuss high tone movement in Nguni, whereby a high tone associated with a prefix moves to the antepenult of a toneless verb stem. Although Nguni has depressor consonants that inhibit the local association of high tones, depressor consonants do not block the long-distance process of high tone movement.

Chapter 2

1. I adopt the features proposed in Odden 2003, with two modifications. First, designated articulators such as Labial, Coronal, and Dorsal are unary features (see Halle 2005); vowels are always Dorsal. Second, two features are used to

classify vowels, glides, and consonants: [±vocalic] and [±consonantal]. Glides are [−vocalic, −consonantal], vowels are [+vocalic, +consonantal], and consonants are [−vocalic, +consonantal]; see Nevins and Chitoran 2008 for discussion.

2. I depart from Turkish orthography and represent the back unround vowel as /ɨ/ for visual perspicuity.

3. Throughout this book, I follow my sources directly where they use [a] for a nonfront unrounded low vowel, even when the authors explicitly note that the vowel in question is [+back] (and hence in certain cases might in fact be more accurately transcribed as [ɑ]). As many of these languages have only one nonfront unrounded low vowel, some variation in realization is to be expected, and as it is not always clear whether an author has chosen [a] over [ɑ] for typographic convenience, I retain [a] as a matter of consistency in the transcriptions.

4. In the case where partial orders among segments are empirically necessary (perhaps in analyses of metathesis), so that both x and y precede z but there is no lexically specified precedence relation between x and y, the algorithm could be generalized so as to allow traversal of parallel paths, with a mechanism for resolving contradictory feature-values among the closest elements on each path.

5. The only prefixation in Turkish is reduplicative: for example, [cip-ciliz], [dop-doluz], a process used for intensifying adjectives (Kelepir 2000). As the prefix includes a full copy of the initial root vowel, this process would never induce alternations in the root.

6. See Kabak and Vogel 2009 for a similar approach to disharmonic root vowels.

7. The semantics of the features [±high] and [±low] is that they are binary predicates true or false of a given articulatory configuration, where [−F] means ¬[+F].

(i) *Semantics of vowel height features*
    a. [+high]: true iff tongue body is raised beyond a certain critical point P_h above the midline
    [−high]: true iff tongue body is not raised beyond a certain critical point P_h above the midline
    b. [+low]: true iff tongue body is lowered beneath a certain critical point P_h below the midline
    [−low]: true iff tongue body is not lowered beneath a certain critical point P_h below the midline

8. Hyman (1998) analyzes a formally similar process of bidirectional height harmony in the Bantu language Yaka, in which [±high] harmony of the first vowel of the perfective suffix copies [−high] only when both the closest vowel to its left and the closest vowel to its right are [−high].

9. Notice that the harmony process does not determine a value for [±back] for the theme vowel. This particular empirical question awaits decisive evidence from phonological processes about whether the low vowel /a/ of Woleaian is [+back]. The answer to this question does not bear on the illustration of harmony at hand, however, as there is no other [−high, +low] nonround vowel that contrasts with /a/ and no other [−high, −low] nonround vowel that contrasts with /e/.

10. It does not matter which vowel is "reached earlier," if, for example, there are more irrelevant consonants to traverse on one side than the other.

11. This can be implemented either by saying that a constraint banning [−low] is what ultimately forces [+low] to surface just in case harmony fails, or as a case of a genuine Plan B process taking place as a rule of insertion. The choice between these two implementations can't and won't be made here.

12. Looking at similar data from Turkana (e.g., [a-bun-ɛ-rɛ] 'come, SG'), Noske (2001, 803–804) concludes that nonfinal alternating (i.e., needy) suffixes must be specified as harmonizing to their right. Convergent evidence for this conclusion from Nilo-Saharan is presented by Levergood (1984, 278), who determines that Maasai suffixes must copy from their right; a relevant examples is [ɛ-ta-raŋ-iʃ-e] '3SG-PAST-sing-INTR-PAST', where the nonfinal suffix copies [+ATR] from its right, rather than [−ATR] from its left.

13. In the case of epenthesis, however, it looks like the direction of search must be inherently specified. One possibility within the derivational character of the current model is that in the case of sonority-driven epenthesis, given an iterative left-to-right syllabification algorithm, the closest visible source of valuation will be to the left. A review of the handful of cases in Kawahara 2004 reveals that Kolami copy-epenthesis is furnished from the left, whereas Winnebago and Fula loanwords that include word-initial onset-liquid clusters copy from the right. In short, these data are consistent with the possibility that copying from the left is a universal default, except when there is nothing to the left.

14. A related effect in syntactic theory has been formulated as the Earliness Principle (Pesetsky 1989; Collins 2001), requiring that features be valued as soon as possible, even if this will ultimately lead to a suboptimal outcome. For example, in *John seems that [t_{John} is nice], the valuing of the case-feature of John in the embedded clause cannot be deferred until the matrix clause, leading to inability to satisfy the requirements of the higher tense node.

15. In discussing the Turkish harmony cases where a [−back] liquid intercepts [+back] harmony, Padgett (2002, 94) notes that when harmony is formalized as the initiative to spread features from donors, an output form like [meʃgul^j-düm] must violate this harmony requirement three times. This seems to be a further indication that "spreading" by potential donors is insufficient to model the locality of vowel harmony.

16. This rule deletes [±distributed] on a [coronal, +continuant, −voice] segment before [±distributed] on another [coronal, +continuant, −voice] segment.

17. There is some debate about whether local apicalization itself is a cyclic or postcyclic rule. Given that nonfinal [±distributed] deletion is a postcyclic rule, there are two possibilities. The first, as in the text, is that local apicalization follows postcyclic deletion. The second is that local apicalization is a cyclic rule and that the deletion rule is more sensitive in its foci: it deletes all nonfinal [±distributed] values except those that immediately precede a [−distributed] segment. This escape from deletion could be implemented as a condition on deletion that protects segments that have undergone local apicalization (see Kiparsky 1993). Given the complications of the deletion rule under this second possibility,

for clarity I adopt the first possibility in the text, where the primary focus of discussion is the interaction of deletion with harmony.

Chapter 3

1. Finnish orthography uses *y* where I use /ü/; I use /ü/ to emphasize the parallelism among contrastively [−back] /ü,ö,ä/.

2. The definition of contrastiveness here departs from that of Calabrese (1995), who makes crucial use of universal filters and deactivation statements. Baković (2003, 6) proposes a definition of harmonic pairing similar to the one in the text.

(i) *Harmonic pairing*
A vowel x in a language L with a harmonic feature [±hf] is harmonically paired iff there is another vowel y in L's inventory and y differs from x only in terms of [±hf].

3. Sagey (1988) demonstrates that the association lines of the autosegmental formalism must be interpreted as temporal overlap, rather than simultaneity (as was originally proposed in Goldsmith 1976). Gafos (1996) shows that since autosegmental association encodes temporal overlap between feature and segment, then—assuming in addition that segments are temporally ordered on their own—locality must be strict. As demonstrated in a number of phonetic studies (Bessell 1998; Walker 1999; Shahin 2002; Nevins and Vaux 2003), locality is not strict; as a result, autosegmental approaches to locality cannot be upheld. See Hansson 2001 for an extensive critique of Gafos's (1996) claims about the nonexistence of various harmony types.

4. This particular rule is subject to certain restrictions in Finnish, as discussed extensively by Anttila (2003), who points out the role of metrical conditioning.

5. In both Finnish and Votic, the process sensitive to the [−back] nature of /i/ is a local consonant-vowel interaction, and for these processes to be conveniently ordered after harmony in both languages would be a highly fortuitous coincidence. See Steriade 1995 for a similar conclusion.

6. The short version of /a/ is rounded, and the long version of /e:/ is higher than the short version. I return to these facts in chapter 5.

7. In fact, even the positionally relativized aspect of excluding noncontrastive values in Karaim can be argued to be (trivially) at work in Turkish and Finnish as well: those two languages simply lack the positional distributional restrictions of Karaim. That is, all languages with contrastive relativization for harmony may in fact be analyzed as involving relativization to positionally contrastive values of [±F]. Section 3.11 explores the consequences of parametric ambiguity of this sort.

8. See Anderson 1985 for an enlightening overview of the historical development of ideas about markedness and neutralization in phonological theory.

9. See Calabrese 2005, 376, for discussion of this distinction.

10. The other two [+low] vowels in Sibe, /ɛ/ and /ö/, did not exist in Classical Manchu (CM). They were created in initial syllables in Sibe by an umlaut process

(e.g., CM /omi/ → Sibe /ömi/ 'to drink', CM /alin/ → Sibe /ɛlin/ 'mountain'). Since these low vowels were in the initial, stressed syllable in Sibe, they were not subject to markedness reduction.

11. Whether there is a [+round] or [−round] vowel in the suffix is determined by the roundness value of the closest root vowel. Since the suffix vowel is a high vowel, it participates in [±round] harmony, as in Turkish.

12. Odden (1980) discusses a parallel process of long-distance uvularization in Classical Mongolian, in which a dorsal suffixal consonant may copy marked [+back] (the feature responsible for uvularization in Classical Mongolian) across an intervening vowel: [biči-g] 'write-NMLZ', [ide-g] 'eat-NMLZ' versus [jori-ʁ] 'intend-NMLZ', [jiru-ʁ] 'draw-NMLZ'.

13. The lowering rule does not apply root-internally (cf. [ɛdki] 'neighbor', [üχa] 'to itch'). This harmony process is thus more specific than a general left-to-right spreading from low vowels to dorsal consonants, hence the formulation here in terms of needy suffixes. The present analysis differs from that of Halle, Vaux, and Wolfe (2000) in this regard.

14. As the Sanjiazi Manchu inventory reveals, the front round high vowel /ü/ is not contrastive for [±low], as it has no [+low] counterpart in the seven-vowel system. However, Li 1996 contains no example of suffix alternations for a word in which /ü/ follows a [+low] vowel. Bing Li (personal communication) reports that his field notes contain no such verb roots. The prediction here is that /ü/ should be transparent in such contexts (since it is not contrastive for [±low]) and allow either value of [±low] to be copied across itself.

15. In section 4.5, we will return to "parasitic harmony," whereby the value-source must be of the same height as the value-seeker—a pattern that, in combination with marked-value harmony, fills out a large portion of the rounding harmony typology in Altaic.

16. Korn (1969, 102) describes a dialect of Kazakh in which only [−back] vowels are sources for [+round] harmony.

(i) *Kazakh [+round] harmony: Only [−back, +round] vowels are marked sources*
   a. üj-dö   'house-LOC'
   b. köl-dö   'lake-LOC'
   c. som-dan   'rubble-ABL'
   d. kul-da   'servant-LOC'

Apparently, only (51a) is active among the context-sensitive marking statements in this language. However, Vaux (1993) notes that Kazakh has a contrast between the [−high, −round] vowels /e,ä/; perhaps (51b) may only be active in two-height systems distinguished by [±high].

17. Other loanwords with this [+back] before contrastively [−back] pattern include [klorofülli], [miniatüüri], [maniküüri], [molekülli], [parfüümi], [pseudonüümi], [vampürri], [amatööri] (Campbell 1980, 250).

18. As with many instances of interspeaker variation, loanwords such as [marttüüri] exhibit some *intra*speaker variation as well. I adopt the general approach

to intraspeaker variation taken within generative grammar: such speakers have "multiple grammars" (i.e., allow for more than one setting of a given parameter (Kroch 1989; Roeper 1999; Yang 2003)), the choice among them being determined by factors such as lexical item, style, register, and rate of speech.

19. Huave, with the five-vowel inventory /i,u,e,o,a/, provides a further argument that "redundant" specifications are needed for vowels beyond what is required to differentiate the inventory as in the Successive Division Algorithm. According to underspecification analyses, it is redundant/predictable to have both [±round] and [±back] in the inventory among the [−low] vowels. Nonetheless, [±round] and [±back] are both phonologically active in Huave, allowing us to conclude that full specification for both of these features is needed.

The evidence that [±round] is active in Huave comes from the process of labial dissimilation, whereby /w/ and /f/ delete when preceded by the round vowels /o,u/. The Huave 3rd person plural suffix is /-f/: for example, [a-rang-af] 'they make it', where the vowel preceding the suffix is a copy of the stem vowel. Labial dissimilation causes /-f/ to dissimilate to the glottal fricative [j] when preceded by a round vowel (Kim 2008, 79–80): for example, [a-xum-uj] 'they find it', [a-nol-oj] 'they have an issue'.

The evidence that [±back] is active comes from vowel+coda restrictions that result in "vowel breaking," a process of diphthongization (Kim 2008). Specifically, the [−back] vowels /i,e/ cannot surface before nonpalatalized consonants, and the [+back] vowels /u,o,a/ cannot surface before palatalized consonants (Kim 2008, 104–108). In both cases, diphthongization occurs, creating an offglide with the [±back] value of the following coda consonant: for example, /a-nchip/ → [a-nchiop] 'she approaches' but /a-sap^j/ → [a-saip^j] 'she gives a gift'.

In conclusion, Huave's process of labial dissimilation requires [±round], while its process of diphthongization before coda consonants requires [±back]. The phonology of consonant-vowel interactions in Huave thus presents evidence that even when these features can be predicted one from the other, both still need to be fully specified.

20. Yamada's paper followed in the wake of a debate between Jensen (1974) and Odden (1980) regarding Jensen's attempt to define a "Relevancy Condition" for what may intervene transparently in terms of major class features (such as [±vocalic]); however, as Odden pointed out, the existence of harmonic features copied from vowels onto consonants across intervening segments clearly renders the appeal to major class features irrelevant. See Yamada 1983 for empirical problems with subsequent attempts to revise the Relevancy Condition, such as the proposal in Battistella 1982.

21. However, Yamada's proposal made no appeal to contrastiveness or markedness and thus had to contain subconditions such as "If a complement defined in the Class Complement Constraint contains a neutral vowel, *then no other vowel than this* may intervene between focus and determinant" (1983, 56; italics added), which clearly run afoul of the spirit of the current proposal, namely, to *derive* neutrality from properties of the inventory.

22. In Nevins 2007, I demonstrate the application of these same paradigmatically based parameters of domain-relativization to syntactic agreement to capture

attested and unattested versions of the Person-Case Constraint, a family of co-occurrence restrictions on clitic clusters.

Chapter 4

1. An example related to Yawelmani [+round] harmony's requirement that the needy segment and the valuesource have the same value for [±high] can be found in Kachin Khakass (Korn 1969, 103), in which [+high] suffixes copy [+round] only from a source that meets the conditional requirement of being [+high].

(i) *Kachin Khakass failure to copy [+round] from [−αhigh] vowels*
   a. kün-nu   'day-ACC'
   b. küs-tüŋ   'bird-GEN'
   c. öd-ir   'kill-INF'
   d. ok-tiŋ   'arrow-GEN'

A reviewer cites the pattern of Eastern Khanty (Finno-Ugric), described by Kiparsky and Pajusalu (2003), as another potentially relevant case of defective intervention conditioned by height-identity: it is claimed that the unpaired vowel /i/ blocks [±back] harmony between a [+low] vowel in a suffix and [+back] /a/ in a root. A straightforward application of the current model would be to say that [±back] harmony includes all values of [±back] in the search, but that it is parasitic on shared values of height, such that [−low] /i/ would cause the search to end and the default value ([−back] to be inserted, as in Uyghur (section 3.3). Kiparsky and Pajusalu 2003 provides only diagrammatic patterns of the form *[[a . . . i] . . . ä]*, without any actual examples from Eastern Khanty, and contains the claim that "in all the languages [considered in the paper], the vowel *i* is neutral (unpaired)" (p. 226).

Two exhaustive sources on Eastern Khanty, Abondolo 1998 and Filchenko 1979, contain descriptions of the inventory in which /i/ is not at all neutral, but paired with [+back] /ɨ/. According to Filchenko (1979, 4), /i/ occurs word-initially, -medially, and -finally (e.g., [iɣeta] 'to hang', [wɨj] 'craftiness', [jir] 'sacrifice', [qəli] 'corpse') and forms minimal pairs with /ɨ/ (e.g., [il] 'front' vs. [ɨl] 'down/bottom'; p. 9), as well as alternating in harmony (e.g., [wär-i-tä] 'to fish with a dam' vs. [at-ɨ-ta] 'to fence off'; p. 10). The picture of Eastern Khanty vowel harmony that Abondolo (1998) and Filchenko (1979) paint is one of an unremarkable system of harmony in which /i,ɨ/ fully participate in [±back] harmony, yielding a pattern formally identical to that of Turkish. Against this background, there is unclarity surrounding Kiparsky and Pajusalu's (2003) description of the *[[a . . . i] . . . ä]* pattern, and as attractive as it may be to apply a defective-intervention analysis in terms of shared height, the available Eastern Khanty data do not provide sufficient support for it.

2. Except where discussing glides, I have used the feature [±vocalic] in discussions and in diagrams. I adopt the feature system whereby glides and vowels are [−consonantal] and glides and consonants are [−vocalic]; see Nevins and Chitoran 2008 for discussion.

3. Casali (1995) shows that the failure to copy from [+round] consonants is not due to a dissimilation effect (whereby [+round] vowels would become [−round] before labial consonants), as there is no root-internal derounding in words like [kufe], [kuba], [kuːpu].

4. A related pattern in Igbo is described by Hyman (1975, 53).

5. Labial consonants also interact with [±round] harmony between vowels in Warlpiri (Nash 1980, 87ff.). The relationship between [+round] vowels and labial consonants could instead be mediated by assuming language-specific representations in which a feature [+labial] underlies both round vowels and labial consonants, and to which either vowels or consonants may be sensitive. Such a move, however, would require harmonizing vowels to be searching for [+labial] (and not [+round]) in languages such as Tulu, Igbo, and Nawuri, and a subsequent implicational statement that [+labial] on a vowel requires [+round] in these languages. To keep matters both simpler (avoiding a language-specific search for [+labial] by vowels) and more nearly parallel with other cases of rounding harmony, I will adopt the proposal that labial consonants are [+round] in Tulu, Akkadian, Nawuri, Igbo, and other languages that display consonant-vowel interactions of this sort, acknowledging that the phonetic implementation of [+round] may be either labial tension or labial constriction. An alternative possibility, based on proposals by Hyman (1975, 53–54, 154), is an implicational feature statement on [−consonantal] segments that [+round] ↔ [+labial]; in this case, the search in Nawuri and Igbo would be for [±labial], and successful copying would entail [+round].

6. Nawuri has a rounding contrast on labial and nonlabial consonants (/p^w,b^w,f^w,m^w/ and /$k^w,č^w,s^w$/, respectively). I follow Casali (1995) in analyzing these segments as bisegmental sequences of consonant followed by glide. Coupled with the bisegmental analysis, the defective-intervention approach correctly predicts that /p^w,b^w,f^w,m^w/ block rounding harmony owing to the defective [+round] feature on the [+consonantal] segment, while /$k^w,č^w,s^w$/ bear [+round] only on the [−consonantal] glide and therefore allow for copying to the prefix: compare [sʊ-s^wa] 'to grease', in which rounding harmony occurs, with [gɪ-b^waːrːuː] 'water yam' (Casali 1995, 656). Note that the failure of rounding harmony to occur when /p,b,f,m/ intervene cannot be accounted for in terms of contrastive [±round] alone (i.e., by positing that /p,b,f,m/ are [−round] while /p^w,b^w,f^w,m^w/ are [+round]), pace Halle, Vaux, and Wolfe (2000), since *nonlabial* unrounded consonants do not block harmony (see [gu-kuː] 'digging' and [kʊk^wɪ] 'to be sufficient'; Casali 1995, 656).

7. Hyman (1999) also discusses the pattern of vowel height harmony in Pende, in which, unlike in many other Bantu harmony patterns, /e/ copies [−high] from the low vowel /a/. In Pende as well, /o/ cannot copy [−high] from /a/, even though both are [+back], confirming that [±round] really is the feature on which parasitic harmony depends.

8. Given that [±high] harmony can depend on source values for [±round] (in Kisa) and that the reverse situation can exist as well (in Yawelmani), the idea that parasitic harmony derives from asymmetric dependence of one feature on another (e.g., Van der Hulst and Smith 1989) cannot be maintained.

9. Beckman (1997) discusses the height harmony within Shona roots, yet does not include harmony with [+round] suffixes. Additional disyllabic verb roots cited in Beckman's article that could potentially induce defective intervention with the [+round] repetitive suffix include [kobodek] 'become empty' and [bover] 'collapse inward'.

10. A similar case may be Maasai glide-induced harmony, which Cole and Trigo (1988) analyze as a special case of [±ATR] harmony parasitic on [+high].

11. Müller (2010) proposes that certain syntactic cases require ordering among the features that are satisfied on a single node.

12. A similar type of defective intervention occurs in Bashkir, in which [±round] harmony requires the source to be [−high] (e.g., [tön-ö] 'night-POSS', [qol-o] 'slave-POSS' vs. [ət-ə] 'dog-POSS', [at-ʌ] 'horse-POSS'). While /u,i,ü/ do not occur in noninitial syllables and thus cannot be used to test defective intervention, Poppe (1964, 20) reports that the [+high, +round, −vocalic] glide /w/ yields defective intervention for leftward [+round] harmony, because of its wrong height: [töðöwsə] 'builder', [qorowlʌ] 'loaded'.

13. Vowel length is omitted from the representations.

14. Hansson (2007a), exploring the role of segmental similarity in harmony, discusses predictions for hypothetical cases of vowel harmony and argues that "an opaque segment must always be more similar to the target than any transparent segment within the same system" (p. 405). The current model gives teeth to this notion of similarity: an opaque segment is included in the domain of relativization, while a transparent segment is not.

15. The comitative suffix appears as [-tai], [-tei], and [-tɔi]; according to Svantesson (1985), the diphthong /oi/ is not allowed in Khalkha on the surface, and [ei] appears where [oi] is expected. Arguably, [+ATR, +round] copying takes place at the point of harmony, as this suffix is further copied from for [+round]: [ovs-tei-go:] 'grass-ABL-REFL'.

16. Svantesson et al. (2005, 51) note that the Ulaanbaatar dialect of Mongolian is developing a variable process whereby /i/ blocks harmony, in which case its analysis becomes identical to that of Oroch in the text.

17. Kaun (1995, 72) presents additional Oroch examples in which high vowels are reported to block rounding harmony: [oggiča] 'dried out', [dokčina] 'to hear' (no morpheme boundaries provided for either). Kaun (1995, 77) also reports similar cases where /i/ blocks rounding harmony for the Tungusic language Ulcha.

18. Pensalfini (2002) suggests that the only suffixes the root may copy from are those that are spelled out in the same morphological cycle as the root.

19. Hualde (1989) discusses a derived-environment condition on raising of Basque suffixal /a/ by a preceding [+high] root or suffixal vowel, which does not apply within roots. Polgárdi (1998, 64) discusses [±ATR] harmony in Korop (a Benue-Congo language of Cameroon), for which prefixes (but not roots) need to copy rightward. As Łubowicz (2002) points out, in these cases it may be that only affixal vowels need to harmonize.

20. Rose and Walker (2004) also discuss the role of orthogonal identity as a prerequisite for harmony, although they explicitly exclude blocking effects from this rubric.

21. I leave open whether derivational versions of Optimality Theory, such as McCarthy's (2007), are able to model the procedural nature of search halting in failure at the first element it encounters, when that element is defective.

Chapter 5

1. See Fitzpatrick 2002 for an overview and comparison of different approaches to minimality-based locality within minimalist syntax.

2. Abels (2003) provides an interesting attempt to assimilate syntactic cases of boundedness as a type of minimality.

3. An insertion rule supplying [+lateral] by default in the case of [+sonorant, −nasal] segments is also necessary.

4. Suzuki (1998) has developed a theory for distance parameters in dissimilation, concluding that distance bounds for dissimilation and harmony vary in fundamentally similar ways.

5. See Boeckx and Grohmann 2007 for a comparison of barriers and phase boundaries as extrinsic locality restrictions.

6. An interesting case is what happens when δ is bidirectional (as in Woleaian, section 2.8) and β is set to one intervening segment, for forms in which the searching vowel has a single intervening consonant on one side but two or more intervening consonants on the other side. Does the failure to find a value-source on one side cause the entire bidirectional search to crash, or does the search still copy the value that was successfully found on the other side? This question is part of a larger research issue in phonology investigating whether structural descriptions may be met universally or existentially in cases of multiple environments (see, e.g., Raimy 2000 for discussion of a uniformity parameter governing the interpretation of structural descriptions in gemination and reduplication). It could be fruitfully answered using artificial grammar experiments of the type discussed in chapter 6, if no extant languages with the relevant combination of properties are found.

7. I do not provide a treatment for Hungarian stems such as /hiːd/ 'bridge' that have a [−back] vowel in the stem but require harmonizing suffixes to copy [+back] from them. Within the Agree-based approach to vowel harmony, these stems are akin to "epicene" nouns such as French *sentinelle* that are semantically masculine but require syntactic agreement with them to be feminine (Wechsler and Zlatić 2003), necessitating a distinction between inherent features available to the interpretive interface and the feature available for copying in syntagmatic dependencies. See Ringen and Vago 1998 and Krämer 2003 for similar approaches to agreement with such stems.

8. We will return in section 5.2.4 to a discussion of the [+low] vowels in Hungarian [±back] harmony.

9. The pattern in which Hungarian ML suffixes surface with [−back] when preceded by two noncontrastive [−back] vowels, but not one, seems crucially different from the "bisyllabic trigger requirement" of Classical Manchu (Zhang and Dresher 1996; Walker 2001). In Hungarian ML, harmony with the relativized value occurs as usual when one [−back] vowel intervenes, but fails when two intervene. In Classical Manchu, suffixes *fail* to harmonize when one [+round] vowel precedes; they harmonize only when two [+round] vowels with the relativized value precede. We can say that the suffixes of Classical Manchu are required to find two instances of [+round] in their search, a requirement consistent with a target-centric approach.

10. A single individual may simultaneously exhibit both of these patterns, with lexical and sociolinguistic conditioning, which can be accommodated in models of intraspeaker variability with multiple parameters such as those of Kroch (1989), Roeper (1999), and yang (2003). Hayes and Londe (2006, 77n12) entertain the possibility of coexisting harmony processes, one that allows a single intervening syllable and one that is unbounded.

11. I verified the Gikuyu data with two native speakers, Paul Njoroge and Sam Gakindi of Cambridge, MA.

12. See also Ringen and Heinämäki 1999 for remarks on sonority in Finnish vowel harmony and Hayes and Londe 2006, 83n19, for remarks on sonority in Hungarian vowel harmony.

13. In a study of coarticulatory effects in Hungarian [±back] harmony using EMMA magnetometry and ultrasound imaging, Benus and Gafos (2007) found that some cases of noncontrastive /i,iː,eː/ in Hungarian [+back] harmony words are produced with a significantly backed articulation, suggesting a susceptibility to coarticulation of the same type that Öhman (1966) and others have found for languages without harmony. Benus and Gafos (2007, 290) note a puzzling finding with respect to duration:

Long vowels have more time to achieve their target and are thus less prone to contextual coarticulatory influences than their short counterparts.... In the transparent vowels used in our experiments, there were two long vowels, [iː] and [eː], and one short vowel [i]. In the EMMA data, [eː] was affected by harmonic type the most. In the ultrasound data, it was the other long vowel [iː] that was affected the most. Therefore, long vowels were affected by harmonic type more than short vowels.

While Benus and Gafos (2007) do not provide an explanation for this finding, it seems to confirm that duration is irrelevant to understanding harmony in Hungarian.

14. The sonority of /ə/ in this hierarchy is relevant for cases in which it is phonemic, and not for purely allophonic, reduced, unstressed instances.

15. The software implementation of the algorithm in figure 5.2 includes the option to treat all phonologically inactive values as present for the purposes of computing the sonority values in (48).

16. A height-based explanation of the contrast between [u] and [ʊ] and between [ə] and [a] (e.g., Ard 1984) cannot account for the velar/uvular alternations: /ə/, a [−high] vowel, takes the velar alternant, while /ʊ/, a [+high] vowel, takes the uvular alternant.

17. There is some variation in the data for the transparency of /u/; for certain attestations, /u/ does participate in harmony. There is thus one pattern of Classical Manchu that allows copying from /u/; this pattern consistently copies from /ə/ and consistently skips /i/. Entirely parallel to the analysis of microvariation within Kirghiz in section 3.8.2, I propose that there are two grammars of Classical Manchu: the one specified in (57) in the text, relativized to marked values of [±ATR], and another, "Classical Manchu B," with the value-relativization parameter set to *contrastive* values.

(i) *Classical Manchu B adjectivalizing, verbalizing, and diminutive suffixes must:*
ATR-Harmonize: δ = left, F = [c: ATR]

Classical Manchu B is no less worthy of study than the variant in the text. However, the one in the text allows us to diagnose the effect of a sonority hurdle, which cannot be detected in Classical Manchu B, since both /ə/ and /u/ *are* included in its search domain.

18. Indeed, Hungarian [ɒ], often transcribed as [ɔ], sounds much lower to the unaided ear—being approximately the height of the Farsi back low round vowel—than, for example, Wolof or Brazilian Portuguese [ɔ].

19. An interesting question is whether the effects of sonority hurdles can be found lower on the sonority scale—that is, with [+consonantal] elements. As discussed in section 5.1.2, Assamese has [±ATR] harmony. However, there is a systematic set of exceptions to the rightward Search-and-Copy procedure for [+ATR]: those where a nasal consonant intervenes.

(i) *Assamese nonfinal vowels cannot copy [+ATR] past a nasal consonant*
    a. sɛkɔni   'strainer'
    b. xɔmɔnia 'colleague'
    c. pʊtɔni   'dumping ground'
    d. kʰɔmir   'leavening agent'
    e. mɔni   'pearl'

This failure of the mid vowels in (i) to copy [+ATR] from the final /i/ cannot be a case of defective intervention, as nasals do not bear the feature [±ATR]. Mahanta (2007, 183) assumes that nasals are more sonorous than liquids in Assamese and follows the proposal in Nevins 2004 (and in the present chapter) that sonority hurdles are responsible for the blocking effect in harmony.

20. Metaphony processes in Spanish and Italian skip over vowels and target only the stressed syllable. I do not treat such cases of "morphemic" harmony in this book. In section 1.4, I argue that this is a principled exclusion from the pursuit of phonological locality.

21. Orthogonal to the [+ATR] copying yielding [a,ə] alternations, Kinande has an independent process whereby the [−low] applicative and reversative suffixes

harmonize in height and ATR value with the vowel to their left; this is similar to processes in languages described in section 4.4.2.

22. Goddard (1987) discusses the inconsistency in the transcription of the low front vowel that Bloomfield originally wrote *ä*, but later, for reasons of typographical preference, changed to ϵ.

Chapter 6

1. Myopia appears to be the right characterization of vowel harmony, independently of defective intervention: Wilson (2003) shows that a globally optimizing model of harmony wreaks predictive havoc.

2. See Coleman and Local 1991 for a critique of the No-Line-Crossing Constraint on formal grounds.

3. A reviewer brings up the interesting possibility that the Agree algorithm is limited to PF (the phonological branch of the grammatical computation), citing Bobaljik's (2008) proposal that verbal agreement is computed postsyntactically, within PF. While much more work is needed to verify Bobaljik's hypothesis, this possibility has the intriguing potential to localize all uses of the Agree algorithm (whether computing over segments or over phrases) to a single module.

4. Kemp, Perfors, and Tenenbaum (2007) propose a computational model for overhypothesis-learning of items with feature-values.

5. Carstens (2000) raises a number of important formal questions that arise in implementing Concord through the mechanism of Agree.

6. The closest to a case of dissimilation for ϕ-features that I have found is the phenomenon by which Hebrew numerals take the gender opposite to that of their adjacent head noun (Halle 1994). This is a concord phenomenon, and no long-distance cases exist.

7. Optimality Theory obliterates the distinction between principles and parameters, relegating the universal and inviolable properties of human language to constraints on GEN, the engine responsible for producing candidate output forms.

8. Yip (2006) raises the possibility of extending AGL paradigms to animal experiments, to determine whether some of the defining properties of human language phonology are indeed unique to humans. In my proposal, relativized and myopic locality is a mechanism shared between the modules of phonology and syntax, and a potential line of inquiry is whether the properties of relativized and myopic locality are unique to the *human* language faculty.

9. For this reason, AGL experiments with neonates (e.g., Gervain and Mehler 2008) can potentially provide some of the most exciting arguments for innateness.

References

Abels, K. 2003. The syntax of adposition stranding. PhD thesis, University of Connecticut.

Abondolo, D. 1998. Khanty. In D. Abondolo, ed., *The Uralic languages*, 358–386. London: Routledge.

Adetugbo, A. 1967. The Yoruba language in Western Nigeria: Its major dialect areas. PhD thesis, Columbia University.

Adger, D. 2003. *Core syntax: A minimalist approach.* Oxford: Oxford University Press.

Akinlabi, A. 1996. Featural affixation. *Journal of Linguistics* 32, 239–289.

Akinlabi, A. In preparation. *Yoruba: A phonological grammar.* Cambridge, MA: Harvard University, Center for African Studies.

Aksu-Koç, A., and D. I. Slobin. 1985. The acquisition of Turkish. In D. I. Slobin, ed., *The crosslinguistic study of language acquisition.* Vol. 1, *The data*, 839–878. Hillsdale, NJ: Lawrence Erlbaum Associates.

Andersen, H. 1973. Abductive and deductive change. *Language* 49, 765–793.

Anderson, G. D. 2004. The languages of Central Siberia: Introduction and overview. In E. Vajda, ed., *Languages and prehistory of Central Siberia*, 1–119. Amsterdam: John Benjamins.

Anderson, J. M. 1992. *Linguistic representation: Structural analogy and stratification.* Berlin: Mouton de Gruyter.

Anderson, L. 1980. Using asymmetrical and gradient data in the study of vowel harmony. In R. Vago, ed., *Issues in vowel harmony*, 271–340. Amsterdam: John Benjamins.

Anderson, S. R. 1976. Nasal consonants and the internal structure of segments. *Language* 52, 326–344.

Anderson, S. R. 1985. *Phonology in the twentieth century.* Chicago: University of Chicago Press.

Andrews, A. 1982. The representation of case in Modern Icelandic. In J. Bresnan, ed., *The mental representation of grammatical relations*, 427–503. Cambridge, MA: MIT Press.

Anttila, A. 2003. Finnish assibilation. In M. Kadowaki and S. Kawahara, eds., *Proceedings of NELS 33*, 13–24. Amherst: University of Massachusetts, GLSA.

Ao, B. 1991. Kikongo nasal harmony and context-sensitive underspecification. *Linguistic Inquiry* 22, 193–196.

Aoki, H. 1968. Toward a typology of vowel harmony. *International Journal of American Linguistics* 34, 142–145.

Arad, M. 2005. *Roots and patterns: Hebrew morphosyntax*. Dordrecht: Springer.

Archangeli, D. 1988. Aspects of underspecification theory. *Phonology* 5, 183–207.

Archangeli, D., and D. Pulleyblank. 1994. *Grounded Phonology*. Cambridge, MA: MIT Press.

Archangeli, D., and D. Pulleyblank. 2002. Kinande vowel harmony: Domains, grounded conditions, and one-sided alignment. *Phonology* 19, 139–188.

Ard, J. 1984. Vowel harmony in Manchu: A critical overview. *Journal of Linguistics* 20, 57–80.

Avrorin, V., and B. Boldyrev. 2001. *Grammatika orochskogo jazyka*. Novosibirsk: SO RAN.

Baković, E. 2000. Harmony, dominance, and control. PhD thesis, Rutgers University.

Baković, E. 2003. Vowel harmony and stem identity. In S. Rose, ed., *San Diego linguistic papers 1*, 1–42. San Diego: University of California, San Diego, Department of Linguistics. Available at http://repositories.cdlib.org/ucsdling/sdlp1.

Bamgboṣe, A. 1967. Vowel harmony in Yoruba. *Journal of African Languages* 6, 268–273.

Barnes, J. 2006. *Strength and weakness at the interface: Positional neutralization in phonetics and phonology*. Berlin: Mouton de Gruyter.

Battistella, E. 1982. More on Hungarian vowel harmony. *Linguistic Analysis* 9, 95–108.

Beckman, J. 1997. Positional faithfulness, positional neutralisation and Shona vowel harmony. *Phonology* 14, 1–46.

Beckman, J. 1998. Positional faithfulness. PhD thesis, University of Massachusetts, Amherst.

Beddor, P., and H. K. Yavuz. 1995. The relation between vowel-to-vowel coarticulation and vowel harmony in Turkish. In K. Elenius and P. Bran-derud, eds., *Proceedings of the 13th International Congress of Phonetic Sciences, vol. 2*, 44–51. Stockholm: KTH and Stockholm University.

Bennett, P. R. 1967. Dahl's Law and Thagicū. *African Language Studies* 8, 127–159.

Benus, S., and A. Gafos. 2007. Articulatory characteristics of Hungarian 'transparent' vowels. *Journal of Phonetics* 35, 271–300.

Bermúdez-Otero, R., and P. Honeybone. 2006. Phonology and syntax: A shifting relationship. *Lingua* 116, 543–561.

Bessell, N. 1998. Local and non-local consonant-vowel interaction in Interior Salish. *Phonology* 15, 1–40.

Bickmore, L. 1995. Refining and formalizing the Tahitian stress placement algorithm. *Oceanic Linguistics* 34, 410–442.

Bloomfield, L. 1962. *The Menomini language*. New Haven, CT: Yale University Press.

Blumenfeld, L., and I. Toivonen. 2009. A featural paradox in Votic harmony. Paper presented at the annual meeting of the Linguistic Society of America, San Francisco.

Bobaljik, J. 2008. Where's phi? Agreement as a post-syntactic operation. In D. Harbour, D. Adger, and S. Béjar, eds., *Phi theory: Phi-features across modules and interfaces*, 295–328. Oxford: Oxford University Press.

Boeckx, C., and K. Grohmann. 2007. Putting phases in perspective. *Syntax* 10, 204–222.

Bonatti, L., M. Peña, M. Nespor, and J. Mehler. 2005. Linguistic constraints on statistical computations. *Psychological Science* 16, 451–459.

Borer, H. 1984. *Parametric syntax: Case studies in Semitic and Romance languages*. Dordrecht: Foris.

Borgstrom, C. 1937. *The dialect of Barra in the Outer Hebrides*. Oslo: Norsk Tidsskrift for Sprogvidenskap.

Bromberger, S., and M. Halle. 1989. Why phonology is different. *Linguistic Inquiry* 20, 51–70.

Buring, D. 2005. *Binding theory*. Cambridge: Cambridge University Press.

Burtt, E. A. 1932. *The metaphysical foundations of modern physical science*. London: Routledge & Kegan Paul.

Butcher, A., and E. Weiher. 1976. An electropalatographic investigation of coarticulation in VCV sequences. *Journal of Phonetics* 4, 59–74.

Calabrese, A. 1988. Towards a theory of phonological alphabets. PhD thesis, MIT.

Calabrese, A. 1995. A constraint-based theory of phonological markedness and simplification procedures. *Linguistic Inquiry* 26, 373–463.

Calabrese, A. 2005. *Markedness and economy in a derivational model of phonology*. Berlin: Mouton de Gruyter.

Campbell, L. 1980. The psychological and sociological reality of Finnish vowel harmony. In R. Vago, ed., *Issues in vowel harmony*, 245–270. Amsterdam: John Benjamins.

Campbell, L. 1986. Testing phonology in the field. In J. Ohala and J. Jaeger, eds., *Experimental phonology*, 163–173. Orlando, FL: Academic Press.

Carstens, V. 2000. Concord in minimalist theory. *Linguistic Inquiry* 31, 319–355.

Casali, R. 1995. Labial opacity and roundness harmony in Nawuri. *Natural Language and Linguistic Theory* 13, 649–663.

Casali, R. 1998. *Resolving hiatus.* New York: Garland.

Cassimjee, F., and C. Kisseberth. 2001. Zulu tonology and its relation to other Nguni languages. In S. Kaji, ed., *Cross-linguistic studies of tonal phenomena,* 327–359. Tokyo: Tokyo University of Foreign Studies.

Charette, M. 1991. *Conditions on phonological government.* Cambridge: Cambridge University Press.

Cho, Y.-M. Y. 1990. Parameters of consonantal assimilation. PhD thesis, Stanford University.

Chomsky, N. 1981. *Lectures on government and binding.* Dordrecht: Foris.

Chomsky, N. 1986. *Barriers.* Cambridge, MA: MIT Press.

Chomsky, N. 1995. *The Minimalist Program.* Cambridge, MA: MIT Press.

Chomsky, N. 2000. Minimalist inquiries: The framework. In R. Martin, D. Michaels, and J. Uriagereka, eds., *Step by step: Essays on minimalist syntax in honor of Howard Lasnik,* 89–155. Cambridge, MA: MIT Press.

Chomsky, N. 2001. Derivation by phase. In M. Kenstowicz, ed., *Ken Hale: A life in language,* 1–52. Cambridge, MA: MIT Press.

Chomsky, N., and M. Halle. 1968. *The sound pattern of English.* New York: Harper and Row.

Christdas, P. 1988. The phonology and morphology of Tamil. PhD thesis, Cornell University.

Clements, G. N. 1985. The geometry of phonological features. *Phonology Yearbook* 2, 225–252.

Clements, G. N. 2003. Feature economy in sound systems. *Phonology* 20, 287–333.

Clements, G. N., and S. J. Keyser. 1983. *CV phonology: A generative theory of the syllable.* Cambridge, MA: MIT Press.

Clements, G. N., and E. Sezer. 1982. Vowel and consonant disharmony in Turkish. In H. van der Hulst and N. Smith, eds., *The structure of phonological representations, part II,* 213–255. Dordrecht: Foris.

Coats, H. 1970. Rule environment features in phonology. *Papers in Linguistics* 2, 110–140.

Cohn, A. 1990. Phonetic and phonological rules of nasalization. PhD thesis, UCLA.

Cole, J. 1987. Planar phonology and morphology. PhD thesis, MIT.

Cole, J., and L. Trigo. 1988. Parasitic harmony. In H. van der Hulst and N. Smith, eds., *Features, segmental structure, and harmony processes,* 19–38. Dordrecht: Foris.

Coleman, J., and J. Local. 1991. The "No Crossing Constraint" in autosegmental phonology. *Linguistics and Philosophy* 14, 295–338.

Collins, C. 2001. Economy conditions in syntax. In M. Baltin and C. Collins, eds., *The handbook of contemporary syntactic theory,* 45–61. Oxford: Blackwell.

Comrie, B. 1981. *The languages of the Soviet Union.* Cambridge: Cambridge University Press.

Crosswhite, K. 1998. Segmental vs. prosodic correspondence in Chamorro. *Phonology* 15, 281–316.

Csató, E., and D. Nathan. 2002. Spoken Karaim. CD-ROM. Uppsala University and Tokyo University of Foreign Studies.

Cutler, A., N. Sebastián-Gallés, O. Soler-Vilageliu, and B. van Ooijen. 2000. Constraints of vowels and consonants on lexical selection: Cross-linguistic comparisons. *Memory and Cognition* 28, 746–755.

Davy, J., and D. Nurse. 1982. Synchronic versions of Dahl's Law: The multiple applications of a phonological dissimilation rule. *Journal of African Languages and Linguistics* 4, 157–195.

de Lacy, P. 2006. *Markedness: Reduction and preservation in phonology.* Cambridge: Cambridge University Press.

Dell, F., and M. Elmedlaoui. 1985. Syllabic consonants and syllabification in Imdlawn Tashlhiyt Berber. *Journal of African Languages and Linguistics* 7, 105–130.

Dresher, B. E. 2003. Contrast and asymmetry in inventories. In A. M. Di Sciullo, ed., *Asymmetry in grammar, vol. 2*, 239–257. Amsterdam: John Benjamins.

Dresher, B. E. 2005. On the acquisition of phonological contrasts. In J. van Kampen, and S. Bauuw, eds., *Proceedings of GALA 2003, vol. 1*, 27–46. Utrecht: Utrecht University, LOT.

Farkas, D., and P. Beddor. 1987. Privative and equipollent backness in Hungarian. In A. Bosch, B. Need, and E. Schiller, eds., *Papers from the Parasession on Autosegmental and Metrical Phonology*, 91–105. Chicago: University of Chicago, Chicago Linguistic Society.

Filchenko, A. Y. 1979. A grammar of Eastern Khanty. PhD thesis, MIT.

Finley, S. 2007. Exceptions in vowel harmony are local. Ms., Johns Hopkins University.

Finley, S. 2009. Morphemic harmony as featural correspondence. *Lingua* 119, 478–501.

Fitzpatrick, J. 2002. On minimalist approaches to the locality of movement. *Linguistic Inquiry* 33, 443–463.

Fortune, G. 1981. Shona grammatical constructions. Ms., Department of African Languages, University of Rhodesia.

Fowler, C. 1981. Production and perception of coarticulation among stressed and unstressed vowels. *Journal of Speech and Hearing Research* 46, 127–139.

Frampton, J. 1991. *Relativized Minimality*, a review. *The Linguistic Review* 8, 1–46.

Frisch, S., J. Pierrehumbert, and M. Broe. 2004. Similarity avoidance and the OCP. *Natural Language and Linguistic Theory* 22, 179–228.

Gafos, A. 1996. The articulatory basis of locality in phonology. PhD thesis, Johns Hopkins University.

Gervain, J., and J. Mehler. 2008. The neonate brain's ability to detect linguistic structure. Ms., SISSA, Trieste.

Gick, B., D. Pulleyblank, F. Campbell, and N. Mutaka. 2006. Low vowels and transparency in Kinande vowel harmony. *Phonology* 23, 1–20.

Gildersleeve, B., and G. Lodge. 1895. *Gildersleeve's Latin grammar.* London: Macmillan.

Goddard, I. 1987. Leonard Bloomfield's descriptive and comparative studies of Algonquian. *Historiographia Linguistica* 14, 179–217.

Goldsmith, J. 1976. An overview of autosegmental phonology. *Linguistic Analysis* 13, 72–105.

Goldsmith, J. 1985. Vowel harmony in Khalkha Mongolian, Yaka, Finnish, and Hungarian. *Phonology* 2, 253–275.

Gómez, R., and L. Gerken. 2000. Infant artificial language learning and language acquisition. *Trends in Cognitive Sciences* 4, 178–186.

Goodman, N. 1955. *Fact, fiction, and forecast.* Cambridge, MA: Harvard University Press.

Gordon, M. 1999. The "neutral" vowels of Finnish: How neutral are they? *Linguistica Uralica* 35, 17–21.

Gouskova, M. 2004. Relational hierarchies in Optimality Theory: The case of syllable contact. *Phonology* 21, 201–250.

Greenberg, J. 1950. The patterning of root morphemes in Semitic. *Word* 5, 162–181.

Greenberg, J. 1963. Some universals of grammar with particular reference to the meaning of elements. In J. Greenberg, ed., *Universals of language*, 73–113. Cambridge, MA: MIT Press.

Hall, B. L., R. Hall, M. D. Pam, A. Myers, S. A. Antell, and G. K. Cherono. 1974. Lenition degrades information: Consonant allophony in Ibibio. *Afrika und Übersee* 57, 241–267.

Hall, T., and S. Hamann. 2006. Towards a typology of stop assibilation. *Linguistics* 44, 1195–1236.

Halle, M. 1994. The morphology of numeral phrases. In S. Avrutin, S. Franks, and L. Progovac, eds., *Annual Workshop on Formal Approaches to Slavic Linguistics: The MIT Meeting, 1993*, 178–215. Ann Arbor: Michigan Slavic Publications.

Halle, M. 2005. Palatalization/Velar softening: What it is and what it tells us about the nature of language. *Linguistic Inquiry* 36, 23–41.

Halle, M., B. Vaux, and A. Wolfe. 2000. On feature spreading and the representation of place of articulation. *Linguistic Inquiry* 31, 387–444.

Halle, M., and J.-R. Vergnaud. 1987. *An essay on stress.* Cambridge, MA: MIT Press.

Hamp, E. 1976. Palatalization and harmony in Gagauz and Karaite. In W. Heissig, J. R. Krueger, F. J. Oinas, and E. Schütz, eds., *Tractata altaica: Denis Sinor, sexagenario optime de rebus altaicis merito dedicata*, 211–213. Wiesbaden: Harrassowitz.

Hansson, G. 2001. Theoretical and typological issues in consonant harmony. PhD thesis, University of California, Berkeley.

Hansson, G. 2007a. Blocking effects in agreement by correspondence. *Linguistic Inquiry* 38, 395–409.

Hansson, G. 2007b. On the evolution of consonant harmony: The case of secondary articulation agreement. *Phonology* 24, 77–120.

Harms, R. 1987. What Helmholtz knew about neutral vowels. In B. D. Joseph and A. M. Zwicky, eds., *A festschrift for Ilse Lehiste*, 381–399. Ohio State University Working Papers in Linguistics 35. Columbus: Ohio State University, Department of Linguistics.

Harris, J., and E.-A. Urua. 2001. Lenition degrades information: Consonant allophony in Ibibio. In *Speech, hearing and language: Work in progress 13*, 72–105. London: University College London, Department of Phonetics and Linguistics.

Harris, J. W. 1983. *Syllable structure and stress in Spanish: A nonlinear analysis*. Cambridge, MA: MIT Press.

Harrison, K. D., and A. Kaun. 2001. Patterns, pervasive patterns and feature specification. In T. A. Hall, ed., *Distinctive feature theory*, 211–236. Berlin: Mouton de Gruyter.

Harrison, K. D., E. Thomforde, and M. O'Keefe. 2004. The vowel harmony calculator. Available at http://www.swarthmore.edu/SocSci/harmony/public_html/.

Hayes, B., and Z. C. Londe. 2006. Stochastic phonological knowledge: The case of Hungarian vowel harmony. *Phonology* 23, 59–104.

Hebert, R., and N. Poppe. 1963. *Kirghiz manual*. Indiana University Publications in Uralic and Altaic Series. Bloomington: Indiana University.

Hiraiwa, K. 2001. Multiple Agree and the Defective Intervention Constraint in Japanese. In O. Matushansky, ed., *Proceedings of the 1st HUMIT Student Conference in Language Research (HUMIT 2000)*, 67–80. MIT Working Papers in Linguistics 40. Cambridge, MA: MIT, MITWPL.

Hjelmslev, L. 1948. Le verbe et la phrase nominale. In *Mélanges de philologie, de littérature et d'histoire ancienne offerts à J. Marouzeau*, 235–281. Paris. Reprinted in *Essais linguistiques*, 165–191. Travaux du circle linguistique de Copenhague 12.

Hockett, C. F. 1960. The origin of speech. *Scientific American* 203, 88–96.

Hockett, C. F. 1981. The phonological history of Menominee. *Anthropological Linguistics* 23, 51–87.

Holmberg, A., and T. Hróarsdóttir. 2004. Agreement and movement in Icelandic raising constructions. *Lingua* 114, 651–673.

Howard, I. 1972. A directional theory of rule application in phonology. PhD thesis, MIT.

Hualde, J. 1989. The Strict Cycle Condition and noncyclic rules. *Linguistic Inquiry* 20, 675–680.

Hulst, H. van der, and N. Smith. 1989. Tungusic and Mongolian vowel harmony: A minimal pair. In P. Coopmans and A. Hulk, eds., *Linguistics in the Netherlands 1988*, 79–88. Dordrecht: Foris.

Hulst, H. van der, and J. van de Weijer. 1995. Vowel harmony. In J. Goldsmith, eds., *The handbook of phonological theory*, 495–534. Cambridge, MA: Blackwell.

Hyman, L. 1975. *Phonology: Theory and Analysis.* New York: Holt, Rinehart and Winston.

Hyman, L. 1998. Positional prominence and the 'prosodic trough' in Yaka. *Phonology* 15, 41–75.

Hyman, L. 1999. The historical interpretation of vowel harmony in Bantu. In J.-M. Hombert and L. M. Hyman, eds., *Bantu historical linguistics: Theorical and empirical perspectives*, 235–295. Stanford, CA: CSLI Publications.

Ihiunu, P., and M. Kenstowicz. 1994. Two notes on Igbo vowels. Ms., MIT.

Ito, J., and A. Mester. 2003. *Japanese morphophonemics: Markedness and word structure.* Cambridge, MA: MIT Press.

Jakobson, R. 1941. *Kindersprache, Aphasie und allgemeine Lautgesetze.* Uppsala: Almqvist & Wiksell.

Jensen, J. T. 1974. A constraint on variables in phonology. *Language* 50, 675–686.

Jespersen, O. 1904. *Lehrbuch der Phonetik.* Leipzig: B. G. Teubner.

Johnson, C. D. 1980. Regular disharmony in Kirghiz. In R. Vago, ed., *Issues in vowel harmony*, 89–99. Amsterdam: John Benjamins.

Jun, J. 2004. Place assimilation. In B. Hayes, R. Kirchner, and D. Steriade, eds., *Phonetically based phonology*, 58–86. Cambridge: Cambridge University Press.

Ka, O. 1994. *Wolof phonology and morphology.* Lanham, MD: University Press of America.

Kabak, B., and I. Vogel. 2009. Exceptions to stress and harmony in Turkish: Cophonologies or prespecification? In H. Simon and H. Wiese, eds., *Expecting the unexpected: Exceptions in grammar.* Berlin: Mouton de Gruyter.

Kalish, M. L., T. L. Griffiths, and S. Lewandowsky. 2007. Iterated learning: Intergenerational knowledge transmission reveals inductive biases. *Psychonomic Bulletin & Review* 14, 288–294.

Kaun, A. 1995. The typology of rounding harmony: An optimality theoretic approach. PhD thesis, UCLA.

Kawahara, S. 2004. Locality in echo epenthesis: Comparison with reduplication. In *Proceedings of NELS 34*, 295–307. Amherst: University of Massachusetts, GLSA.

Kaye, J. 1971. Nasal harmony in Desano. *Linguistic Inquiry* 2, 37–58.

Kaye, J. 1989. *Phonology: A cognitive view.* Hillsdale, NJ: Lawrence Erlbaum Associates.

Kaye, J., J. Lowenstamm, and J.-R. Vergnaud. 1985. The internal structure of phonological representations. *Phonology* 2, 305–328.

Keating, P. 1996. The phonology-phonetics interface. In U. Kleinhenz, ed., *Interfaces in phonology*, 262–278. Berlin: Akademie Verlag.

Kelepir, M. 2000. To be or not to be faithful. In A. Göksel and C. Kerslake, eds., *Studies on Turkish and Turkic languages: Proceedings of the Ninth International Conference on Turkish Linguistics*, 11–18. Wiesbaden: Harrassowitz.

Kemp, C., A. Perfors, and J. B. Tenenbaum. 2007. Learning overhypotheses with hierarchical Bayesian models. *Developmental Science* 10, 307–321.

Kenstowicz, M. 1994. *Phonology in generative grammar*. Cambridge, MA: Blackwell.

Kenstowicz, M. 1997. Quality-sensitive stress. *Rivista di Linguistica* 9, 157–187.

Kenstowicz, M. 2008. Two notes on Kinande vowel harmony. Paper presented at the annual meeting of the Linguistic Society of America, Chicago.

Kim, Y. 2005. Finnish neutral vowels: Subcontrastive harmony or V-to-V coarticulation? Paper presented at the annual meeting of the Linguistic Society of America, Oakland, CA.

Kim, Y. 2008. Topics in the phonology and morphology of San Francisco del Mar Huave. PhD thesis, University of California, Berkeley.

Kiparsky, P. 1973. Phonological representations. In O. Fujimura, ed., *Three dimensions of linguistic theory*, 1–135. Tokyo: TEC.

Kiparsky, P. 1981. Vowel harmony. Ms., MIT.

Kiparsky, P. 1993. Blocking in nonderived environments. In S. Hargus and E. Kaisse, eds., *Studies in Lexical Phonology*, 277–313. New York: Academic Press.

Kiparsky, P., and K. Pajusalu. 2003. Towards a typology of disharmony. *The Linguistic Review* 20, 217–241.

Koo, H., and J. Cole. 2006. On learnability and naturalness as constraints on phonological grammar. In A. Botinis, ed., *Proceedings of ISCA Tutorial and Research Workshop on Experimental Linguistics*, 174–177. International Speech Communication Association.

Korn, D. 1969. Types of labial vowel harmony in the Turkic languages. *Anthropological Linguistics* 11, 98–106.

Kowalski, T. 1929. *Karaimische Texte im Dialekt von Troki*. Prace Komisji Orjentalistycznej Polskiej Akademji Umiejętności nr. 11. Cracow: Nakładem Polskiej Akademji Umiejętności.

Krämer, M. 2001. Yucatec Maya vowel alternations: Harmony as syntagmatic identity. *Zeitschrift für Sprachwissenschaft* 20, 175–217.

Krämer, M. 2003. *Vowel harmony and correspondence theory*. Berlin: Mouton de Gruyter.

Kroch, A. 1989. Reflexes of grammar in patterns of language change. *Language Variation and Change* 1, 199–244.

Krueger, J. R. 1962. *Yakut manual*. Indiana University Publications in Uralic and Altaic Series 21. Bloomington: Indiana University.

Kuroda, S.-Y. 1967. *Yawelmani phonology*. Cambridge, MA: MIT Press.

Ladefoged, P. 1968. *A phonetic study of West African languages*. Cambridge: Cambridge University Press.

Langacker, R. W. 1987. *Foundations of cognitive grammar*. Stanford, CA: Stanford University Press.

Leben, W. R. 2006. Rethinking autosegmental phonology. In J. Mugane, J. Hutchison, and D. Worman, eds., *Selected proceedings of the 35th Annual Conference on African Linguistics*, 1–9. Somerville, MA: Cascadilla Press.

Leitch, M. 1996. Vowel harmonies of the Congo Basin: An Optimality Theory analysis of variation in the Bantu zone C. PhD thesis, University of British Columbia.

Leiwo, M., P. Kulju, and K. Aoyama. 2006. The acquisition of Finnish vowel harmony. *SKY Journal of Linguistics* 19, 149–161.

Levergood, B. 1984. Rule governed vowel harmony and the Strict Cycle. In C. Jones and P. Sells, eds., *Proceedings of NELS 14*, 275–293. Amherst: University of Massachusetts, GLSA.

Levi, S. V. 2004. The representation of underlying glides: A cross-linguistic study. PhD thesis, University of Washington.

Li, B. 1996. *Tungusic vowel harmony: Description and analysis*. Holland Institute of Generative Linguistics.

Lieberman, P. 2000. *Human language and our reptilian brain*. Cambridge, MA: Harvard University Press.

Lightfoot, D., and M. Westergaard. 2007. Language acquisition and language change: Inter-relationships. *Language and Linguistics Compass* 1, 396–415.

Lindblad, V. 1990. Neutralization in Uyghur. Master's thesis, University of Washington.

Linker, W. 1982. Articulatory and acoustic correlates of labial activity in vowels: A cross-linguistic study. PhD thesis, UCLA.

Lodge, K. 1995. Kalenjin phonology and morphology: A further exemplification of underspecification and non-destructive phonology. *Lingua* 96, 29–43.

Longobardi, G. 2005. A minimalist program for parametric linguistics? In H. Broekhuis, N. Corver, R. Huybregts, U. Kleinhenz, and J. Koster, eds., *Organizing grammar*, 407–414. Berlin: Mouton de Gruyter.

Łubowicz, A. 2002. Derived environment effects in Optimality Theory. *Lingua* 112, 243–280.

Magdics, K. 1969. *Studies in the acoustic characteristics of Hungarian speech sounds*. Indiana University Publications in Uralic and Altaic Series 97. Bloomington: Indiana University.

Mahanta, S. 2007. Directionality and locality in vowel harmony with special reference to Assamese. PhD thesis, Utrecht University.

Mailhot, F., and C. Reiss. 2007. Computing long-distance dependencies in vowel harmony. *Biolinguistics* 1, 28–48.

Marcus, G. 2008. *Kluge.* Boston: Houghton Mifflin.

Marler, P. 1997. Three models of song learning: Evidence from behavior. *Journal of Neurobiology* 33, 501–516.

McCarthy, J. 1984. Theoretical consequences of Montañes vowel harmony. *Linguistic Inquiry* 15, 291–318.

McCarthy, J. 1985. *Formal problems in Semitic phonology and morphology.* New York: Garland.

McCarthy, J. 1988. Feature geometry and dependency: A review. *Phonetica* 43, 84–108.

McCarthy, J. 2007. *Hidden generalizations: Phonological opacity in Optimality Theory.* London: Equinox.

McCarthy, J., and A. Taub. 1992. Review of Paradis & Prunet (eds.), *The special status of coronals. Phonology* 9, 363–370.

Milligan, M. 2000. A new look at Menominee vowel harmony. In J. D. Nichols, ed., *Papers of the 31st Annual Algonquian Conference*, 237–254. Winnipeg: University of Manitoba.

Miner, K. L. 1979. Theoretical implications of the great Menominee vowel shift. In *Kansas working papers in linguistics 4*, 7–25. Lawrence: University of Kansas, Linguistics Graduate Student Association. Available at http:/hdl.handle.net/1808/654.

Mintz, T., and R. Walker. 2006. Infants' sensitivity to vowel harmony and its role in word segmentation. Paper presented the annual meeting of the Linguistic Society of America, Albuquerque.

Mithun, M. 1998. The regression of sibilant harmony through the life of Barbareño Chumash. In J. H. Hill, P. Mistry, and L. Campbell, eds., *The life of language: Papers in linguistics in honor of William Bright*, 221–242. Berlin: Mouton de Gruyter.

Mohanan, K. P. 1991. On the bases of radical underspecification. *Natural Language and Linguistic Theory* 9, 285–325.

Moro, A. 2008. *The boundaries of Babel.* Cambridge, MA: MIT Press.

Müller, G. 2010. On deriving CED effects from the PIC. *Linguistic Inquiry* 41.1.

Müller, M. 1894. *Lectures on the science of language, series II.* Reprinted as vol. 3 and 4 of *British linguistics in the nineteenth century.* London: Routledge/Thoemmes Press. Originally published 1864.

Nash, D. 1980. Topics in Warlpiri grammar. PhD thesis, MIT.

Nespor, M., M. Peña, and J. Mehler. 2003. On the different roles of vowels and consonants in speech processing and language acquisition. *Lingue e Linguaggio* 2, 203–231.

Nevins, A. 2004. Conditions on (dis)harmony. PhD thesis, MIT.

Nevins, A. 2007. The representation of third person and its consequences for person-case effects. *Natural Language and Linguistic Theory* 25, 273–313.

Nevins, A., and I. Chitoran. 2008. Phonological representations and the variable patterning of glides. *Lingua* 118, 1979–1997.

Nevins, A., and B. Vaux. 2003. Consonant harmony in Karaim. In A. Csirmaz, Y. Lee, and M. A. Walter, eds., *Proceedings of the 1st Workshop on Altaic Formal Linguistics*, 175–194. MIT Working Papers in Linguistics 46. Cambridge, MA: MIT, MITWPL.

NíChiosáin, M., and J. Padgett. 2001. Markedness, segment realization, and locality in spreading. In L. Lombardi, ed., *Segmental phonology in Optimality Theory*, 118–156. Cambridge: Cambridge University Press.

Noske, M. 2001. [ATR] harmony in Turkana: A case of Faith Suffix >> Faith Root. *Natural Language and Linguistic Theory* 18, 771–812.

Odden, D. 1980. The irrelevancy of the Relevancy Condition: Evidence for the Feature Specification Constraint. *Linguistic Analysis* 6, 261–304.

Odden, D. 1991. Vowel geometry. *Phonology* 8, 261–289.

Odden, D. 1994. Adjacency parameters in phonology. *Language* 10, 289–330.

Odden, D. 2003. *Introducing phonology*. Cambridge: Cambridge University Press.

Ohala, J. 1981. The listener as a source of sound change. In C. S. Masek, R. A. Hendrick, and M. F. Miller, eds., *Chicago Linguistic Society 17: Papers from the Parasession on Language and Behavior*, 178–203. Chicago: University of Chicago, CLS.

Ohala, J. 1994. Towards a universal, phonetically-based theory of vowel harmony. In *Third International Conference on Spoken Language Processing (ICSLP 94)*, 491–494. Yokohama, 18–22 September. Available at http://www.isca-speech.org/isclp_1994.

Öhman, S. 1966. Coarticulation in VCV utterances: Spectrographic measurements. *Journal of the Acoustical Society of America* 39, 151–168.

O'Keefe, M. 2003. Akan vowel harmony. Bachelor's thesis, Swarthmore College.

Ola Orie, O. 2001. An alignment-based account of vowel harmony in Ifẹ Yoruba. *Journal of African Languages and Linguistics* 22, 117–143.

Osborn, H. 1966. Warao I: Phonology and morphophonemics. *International Journal of American Linguistics* 32, 108–123.

Owren, M., and G. Cardillo. 2006. The relative roles of vowels and consonants in discriminating talker identity versus word meaning. *Journal of the Acoustical Society of America*, 119, 1727–1739.

Padgett, J. 2002. Feature classes in phonology. *Language* 78, 81–110.

Palmer, F. 1970. *Prosodic analysis*. London: Oxford University Press.

Parker, S. 2002. Quantifying the sonority hierarchy. PhD thesis, University of Massachusetts, Amherst.

Pensalfini, R. 1997. Jingulu grammar, dictionary, and texts. PhD thesis, MIT.

Pensalfini, R. 2002. Vowel harmony in Jingulu. *Lingua* 112, 561–586.

Peperkamp, S., K. Skoruppa, and E. Dupoux. 2007. Implicit phonological learning in artificial language learning paradigms. Paper presented at the annual meeting of the Linguistic Society of America, Anaheim, CA.

Pesetsky, D. 1989. The Earliness Principle. Paper presented at GLOW Colloquium; Ms., MIT.

Piggott, G. 1988. A parametric approach to nasal harmony. In H. van der Hulst and N. Smith, eds., *Features, segmental structure, and harmony processes*, 131–167. Dordrecht: Foris.

Piggott, G. 1992. Variability in feature dependency: The case of nasality. *Natural Language and Linguistic Theory* 10, 33–77.

Piggott, G. 1996. Implications of consonant nasalization for a theory of harmony. *Canadian Journal of Linguistics* 41, 141–174.

Piggott, G. 2003. Theoretical implications of segment neutrality in nasal harmony. *Phonology* 20, 375–424.

Pöchtrager, M. 2006. The structure of length. PhD thesis, Universität Wien.

Polgárdi, K. 1998. Vowel harmony: An account in terms of government and optimality. PhD thesis, Leiden University.

Poliquin, G. 2006. Canadian French vowel harmony. PhD thesis, Harvard University.

Poppe, N. 1960. *Vergleichende Grammatik der altaischen Sprachen.* Wiesbaden: Harrassowitz.

Poppe, N. 1964. *Bashkir manual.* Indiana University Publications in Uralic and Altaic Series 36. Bloomington: Indiana University.

Poser, W. 1982. Phonological representation and action-at-a-distance. In H. van der Hulst and N. Smith, eds., *The structure of phonological representations, part II*, 121–158. Dordrecht: Foris.

Poser, W. 1993. Are Strict Cycle effects derivable? In S. Hargus and E. Kaisse, eds., *Studies in Lexical Phonology*, 315–321. New York: Academic Press.

Prince, A., and P. Smolensky. 1993. Constraint interaction in generative grammar. Rutgers Optimality Archive ROA-537. Available at http://roa.rutgers.edu.

Przezdziecki, M. 2005. Vowel harmony and coarticulation in three dialects of Yoruba: Phonetics determining phonology. PhD thesis, Cornell University.

Pycha, A., P. Nowak, E. Shin, and R. Shosted. 2003. Phonological rule-learning and its implications for a theory of vowel harmony. In G. Garding and M. Tsujimura, eds., *WCCFL 22*, 423–435. Somerville, MA: Cascadilla Press.

Raimy, E. 2000. *The phonology and morphology of reduplication.* Berlin: Mouton de Gruyter.

Recasens, D. 1984. An electropalatographic investigation of coarticulation in VCV sequences. *Journal of the Acoustical Society of America* 76, 1624–1635.

Reinhart, T., and E. Reuland. 1993. Reflexivity. *Linguistic Inquiry* 24, 657–720.

Reiss, C. 2003. Deriving the feature-filling/feature-changing contrast: An application to Hungarian vowel harmony. *Linguistic Inquiry* 34, 199–224.

Rice, K. 1993. A reexamination of the feature [sonorant]: The status of "sonorant obstruents." *Language* 69, 308–344.

Ringen, C. 1975. Vowel harmony: Theoretical implications. PhD thesis, Indiana University.

Ringen, C., and O. Heinämäki. 1999. Variation in Finnish vowel harmony: An OT account. *Natural Language and Linguistic Theory* 17, 303–337.

Ringen, C., and M. Kontra. 1989. Hungarian neutral vowels. *Lingua* 78, 181–191.

Ringen, C., and R. Vago. 1998. Hungarian vowel harmony in Optimality Theory. *Phonology* 15, 393–416.

Rizzi, L. 1982. Violations of the *Wh*-Island Condition and the Subjacency Condition. In *Issues in Italian syntax*, 49–76. Dordrecht: Foris.

Rizzi, L. 1990. *Relativized minimality.* Cambridge, MA: MIT Press.

Rizzi, L. 2001. Relativized minimality effects. In *The handbook of contemporary syntactic theory*, ed. by Mark Baltin and Chris Collins, 89–110. Oxford: Blackwell.

Roeper, T. 1999. Universal bilingualism. *Bilingualism: Language and Cognition* 2, 169–186.

Rose, S., and R. Walker. 2004. A typology of consonant agreement as correspondence. *Language* 80, 475–531.

Ross, J. R. 1967. Constraints on variables in syntax. PhD thesis, MIT.

Ross, J. R. (Haj). 1984. Inner islands. In C. Brugman and M. Macaulay, eds., *Proceedings of the Tenth Berkeley Linguistics Society*, 258–265. Berkeley: University of California, BLS.

Sagey, E. 1986. The representation of features and relations in nonlinear phonology. PhD thesis, MIT.

Sagey, E. 1987. Non-constituent spreading in Barra Gaelic. Ms., University of California, Irvine.

Sagey, E. 1988. On the ill-formedness of crossing association lines. *Linguistic Inquiry* 19, 109–118.

Schein, B., and D. Steriade. 1986. On geminates. *Linguistic Inquiry* 17, 691–744.

Schlindwein, D. 1987. P-bearing units: A study of Kinande vowel harmony. In J. McDonough and B. Plunkett, eds., *Proceedings of NELS 17*, 551–567. Amherst: University of Massachusetts, GLSA.

Sedivy, J. C., M. K. Tanenhaus, C. G. Chambers, and G. N. Carlson. 1999. Achieving incremental semantic interpretation through contextual representation. *Cognition* 71, 109–147.

Senghas, A. 1995. Children's contribution to the birth of Nicaraguan Sign Language. PhD thesis, MIT.

Shahin, K. 2002. *Postvelar harmony.* Amsterdam: John Benjamins.

Siptár, P., and M. Törkenczy. 2000. *The phonology of Hungarian.* Oxford: Oxford University Press.

Smith, N., and I.-M. Tsimpli. 1995. *The mind of a savant: Language, learning and modularity.* Oxford: Blackwell.

Sohn, H.-M. 1971. *a*-raising in Woleaian. In *University of Hawaii working papers in linguistics* 3, 15–36. Honolulu: University of Hawaii, Department of Linguistics.

Steriade, D. 1981. Parameters of metrical harmony rules. Ms., MIT.

Steriade, D. 1987. Redundant values. In A. Bosch, B. Need, and E. Schiller, eds., *Papers from the Parasession on Autosegmental and Metrical Phonology*, 339–362. Chicago: University of Chicago, Chicago Linguistic Society.

Steriade, D. 1995. Underspecification and markedness. In J. Goldsmith, ed., *The handbook of phonological theory*, 114–174. Cambridge, MA: Blackwell.

Stevens, K. N. 1998. *Acoustic phonetics.* Cambridge, MA: MIT Press.

Suomi, K. 1983. Palatal vowel harmony: A perceptually motivated phenomenon? *Nordic Journal of Linguistics* 6, 1–35.

Suomi, K., J. McQueen, and A. Cutler. 1997. Vowel harmony and speech segmentation in Finnish. *Journal of Memory and Language* 36, 422–444.

Surendran, D., and P. Niyogi. 2003. Measuring the usefulness (functional load) of phonological contrasts. Technical Report TR-2003-12, Department of Computer Science, University of Chicago.

Suzuki, K. 1998. A typological investigation of dissimilation. PhD thesis, University of Arizona.

Svantesson, J.-O. 1985. Vowel harmony shift in Mongolian. *Lingua* 67, 283–327.

Svantesson, J.-O., A. Tsendina, A. Karlsson, and V. Franzen. 2005. *The phonology of Mongolian.* Oxford: Oxford University Press.

Terbeek, D. 1977. A cross-language multidimensional scaling study of vowel perception. PhD thesis, UCLA.

Thorpe, W. 1958. The learning of song patterns by birds, with especial reference to the song of the chaffinch *Fringilla coelebs*. *Ibis* 100, 535–570.

Tolskaya, I. 2008. Oroch vowel harmony. Master's thesis, University of Tromsø.

Traunmüller, H. 1994. Conventional, biological and environmental factors in speech communication: A modulation theory. *Phonetica* 51, 170–183.

Travis, L. 1984. Parameters and effects of word order variation. PhD thesis, MIT.

Trigo, L. 1991. On pharynx-larynx interactions. *Phonology* 8, 113–136.

Trubetzkoy, N. S. 1931. Die phonologischen Systeme. *Travaux du Cercle Linguistique de Prague*, 4, 96–116.

Ultan, R. 1973. Some reflections on vowel harmony. In *Working papers on language universals 12*, 37–67. Stanford, CA: Stanford University.

Urbanczyk, S. 1995. *Patterns of reduplication in Lushootseed.* New York: Garland.

Vago, R. 1975. Hungarian generative phonology. PhD thesis, Harvard University.

Vago, R. 2006. Hungarian: Phonology. In K. Brown, ed., *The encyclopedia of language and linguistics*. 2nd ed. Oxford: Elsevier.

Välimaa-Blum, R. 1999. A feature-geometric description of Finnish vowel harmony covering both loans and native words. *Lingua* 108, 247–268.

Vaux, B. 1993. The origins of Altaic labial attraction. In H. Thráinsson, A. Calabrese, J. Carrier, M. Hale, and C. Watkins, eds., *Harvard working papers in linguistics 2*, 228–237. Cambridge, MA: Harvard University, Department of Linguistics.

Vaux, B. 1999. A note on pharyngeal features. In S. Kuno, and B. Vaux, eds., *Harvard working papers in linguistics 7*, 39–63. Cambridge, MA: Harvard University, Department of Linguistics.

von Soden, W. 1969. *Grundriss der akkadischen Grammatik.* Rome: Pontificum Institutum Biblicum.

Vroomen, J., J. Tuomainen, and B. deGelder. 1998. The roles of word stress and vowel harmony in speech segmentation. *Journal of Memory and Language* 38, 133–149.

Walker, R. 1999. Guaraní voiceless stops in oral vs. nasal contexts: An acoustical study. *Journal of the International Phonetic Association* 29, 63–94.

Walker, R. 2001. Round licensing, harmony, and bisyllabic triggers in Altaic. *Natural Language and Linguistic Theory* 19, 827–878.

Wechsler, S., and L. Zlatić. 2003. *The many faces of agreement.* Stanford, CA: CSLI Publications, and Chicago: University of Chicago Press.

Wilson, C. 2003. Analyzing unbounded spreading with constraints: Marks, targets, and derivations. Ms., UCLA.

Wolf, M. 2007. For an autosegmental theory of mutation. In L. Bateman, M. O'Keefe, E. Reilly, and A. Werle, eds., *Papers in Optimality Theory III*, 315–404. University of Massachusetts Occasional Papers in Linguistics 32. Amherst: University of Massachusetts. GLSA.

Yamada, N. 1983. A constraint on phonological variables. *Linguistic Analysis* 12, 29–84.

Yang, C. 2003. *Knowledge and learning in natural language.* Oxford: Oxford University Press.

Yip, M. 2006. The search for phonology in other species. *Trends in Cognitive Sciences* 10, 442–446.

Zhang, X. 1996. Vowel systems of the Manchu-Tungus languages of China. PhD thesis, University of Toronto.

Zhang, X., and B. E. Dresher. 1996. Labial harmony in written Manchu. *Saksaha: A Review of Manchu Studies* 1, 13–24.

Zoll, C. 1996. *Parsing below the segment in a constraint-based framework.* Stanford, CA: CSLI Publications.

Zoll, C. 2003. Optimal tone mapping. *Linguistic Inquiry* 34, 225–268.

Zsiga, E. 1997. Features, gestures, and Igbo vowels: An approach to the phonology-phonetics interface. *Language* 73, 227–274.

Index of Terms

Ablative
 in Classical Mongolian, 72
 in Karaim, 85
 in Shor, 101
Accusative
 in Oroch, 140
 in Turkish, 27
Agree, 11–12, 25–26, 116
Anaphora, 10–11
Aorist
 in Shor, 102
Applicative
 in Kikongo, 150
 in Kimatuumbi, 134–136
 in Kisa, 131
Artificial Grammar Learning, 205–208
Assibilation, 80–81
Assimilation, 23, 197–198
[ATR], 13, 14, 24, 39–40, 46–53, 103–105, 111–115, 126, 133–136, 136–139, 157, 173–176, 178–181, 185–189, 220n19

[back], 24, 27, 54–60, 69–71, 82, 84–88, 93, 110–111, 156, 158–162, 177–178, 181–184
Beta. *See* Distance boundedness parameter
"Blockers," 121, 125, 126
Boston subway, 3–5
Boundedness, 149

Causative
 in Khalkha Mongolian, 137–139

Class Complement Constraint, 116
Coarticulation, 8–9, 30–31, 73–76
Comitative
 in Khalkha Mongolian, 39
Concord, 198
[consonantal], 126–127
Consonant harmony, 84–88, 201–202
Contrastiveness, 70–71, 79–83
 positional, 84–88
Counter, 151, 155–156
 segment, 156–157
 syllable, 151, 161
Crossmodular Structural Parallelism, 12, 194

Dahl's Law, 163–168
Dative
 in Hungarian, 82, 158–161
Default. *See* Last-resort insertion
Defective intervention, 12, 121–125, 129–130
Deletion, 62–68
Derived-environment effects, 141, 145–146
Diminutive
 in Sibe, 93–94
Directionality (delta), 26, 39–53, 211n13
 bidirectional harmony, 40–45, 218n6
Disharmonic roots, 40–41
Dissimilation, 163–168, 197, 199–204, 214n19

Distance boundedness parameter
  (beta), 151, 154–155, 191
  0 segments, 154
  0 syllables, 151–154, 164–168
  1 segment, 156–157
  1 syllable, 157–161, 164–168
  unbounded, 161–162, 164–168
[distributed], 63–68
"Dominant/recessive" harmony, 45.
  See also Directionality
Dorsal consonants, 92–94
Duality of patterning, 193

Earliness Principle, 211n13
Epenthesis, 57–60, 91
Essive
  in Finnish, 69–71, 76–77

F. *See* Needy features
Featural affixation. *See* Morphemic
  harmony
Feature-sensitive relativization, 95, 97.
  See also Search domain
Focus
  in Oroch, 140

Gamma. *See* Distance boundedness
  parameter
Gender, 25, 43–44
Genitive
  in Karaim, 85
  in Turkish, 28

Harmonize, 26
[high], 14, 24, 123–124, 130–132, 133–
  136, 140, 142–146, 156, 215n1

Imperfective
  in Yucatec Maya, 156
Island, 169. *See also* Sonority hurdle

Kontti kieli, 38–39

[labial], 126–127
Language games. *See* Kontti kieli,
  Reduplication in Turkish

Last-resort insertion (default), 43–45,
  76–79, 94–95, 122–123, 128, 147,
  153, 174
[lateral], 199
Loanwords, 40–41, 109–111
Local apicalization, 66–68
Locality, 3, 149
[low], 24, 40–45, 90, 98–99, 156
Lyman's Law, 199

Markedness, 88–90
  Context-free, 90
  Context-sensitive, 99–102
  logical, 90–92
Microvariation, 97, 162–168, 189–190,
  191
  in Finnish, 109–111
  in Gikuyu, 163–168
  in Hungarian, 162–163, 181–184
  in Kirghiz dialects, 102–103
  in Manchu, 220n17
  in Yoruba, 103–105
Minimalist Program, 149, 192–193
Morphemic harmony, 13–14, 220n20

[nasal], 13–14, 24, 105–109, 150–154
Nasalization, 150–154
Needy features (F), 26
Nominalizing suffix, 32
Nominative
  in Icelandic, 76, 122
Nondirective gerundial
  in Yawelmani, 123–124
Nonroot, 142–146
Noun class
  in Nawuri, 126–129
Number. *See also* Plural
  in Italian, 25

PP-extraction, 169
Parametric ambiguity, 111. *See also*
  Microvariation
Parametric visibility, 80
Parasitic harmony, 123–124, 129–130
Passive
  in Kikongo, 150

Index of Terms

Past
  in Akan, 40
Perfect
  in Khalkha Mongolian, 137–139
Perfective
  in Lamba, 151–154
Person
  in Italian, 25
Phase boundaries, 154
Plural
  in Icelandic, 122
  in Karaim, 85
  in Turkish, 28
  in Uyghur, 78–79
Principles and parameters, 97
Progressive suffix
  in Turkish, 34

Reciprocal
  in Sibe, 94
Reduplication
  in Turkish, 35–38
Relativization, 191
Repetitive
  in Shona, 132–133
Reversative
  in Kisa, 131
  in Lamba, 151–154
[round], 19, 24, 27, 93, 100–103, 112–115, 123–124, 126–129, 131–133, 136–139, 140, 156, 214n19, 215n1
Rounding, 158

Search, 15, 20–22, 26, 32, 41–42, 61–62, 71, 97, 119, 121, 146–148, 151, 189–190, 191, 193, 204–205
Search domain (Tau), 26, 123. *See also* Feature-sensitive relativization
  any values, 103–105
  contrastive segments, 70–73, 78, 81–88, 97–99, 103–105, 109–111
  marked segments, 90–97, 101–102, 109–111
  set union of contrastive and marked, 111–115
[sonorant], 107

Sonority peaks/hurdles, 168–172
Source condition (R), 121, 123, 126, 130, 191. *See also* Defective intervention
Subjunctive
  in Yucatec Maya, 156
Successive Division Algorithm, 113–115

Tau. *See* Search domain

Uvularization
  in Classical Manchu, 173
  in Oroch, 112
  in Sanjiazi Manchu, 98
  in Sibe, 94–95

Vacillating stems, 82
[voice], 89, 163–168

Wh-movement, 149, 154

Index of Languages

Akan, 39–40
Akkadian, 127
Altai, 101–102
Assamese, 157, 220n19

Bantu. *See* Gikuyu, Kikongo, Kimatuumbi, Kinande, Kisa, Lamba, Londengese, Shona
Barasano, Southern, 107–109
Bashkir, 217n12

Chukchi, 154
Chumash, 63–68

Desano, 107

English, 149, 154, 169
Evenki, 112

Finnish, 38–39, 69–71, 73–77, 80–81, 109–111, 123, 176–178
Finno-Ugric. *See* Finnish, Hungarian, Khanty, Votic
French, Canadian, 134

Gaelic, Barra, 57–60
Gikuyu, 163–168
Guaraní, 107

Hindi, 122
Huave, 214n19
Hungarian, 81–82, 157–162, 181–184

Icelandic, 76, 122
Igbo, Southern, 127

Italian, 25, 43–44, 154
Indo-European. *See* Assamese, English, French, Gaelic, Hindi, Icelandic, Italian, Latin, Russian

Japanese, 199
Jingulu, 142–146

Kalenjin, 45–53
Kanembu, 13
Karaim, 83–88
Kazakh, 213n16
Khakass, Kachin, 215n1
Khanty, Eastern, 215n1
Kikongo, 150
Kikuyu. *See* Gikuyu
Kimatuumbi, 133–136
Kinande, 185
Kirghiz, 102–103
Kisa, 130–131
Korean, 14
Kwa. *See* Nawuri

Lamba, 151–154
Latin, 199
Londengese, 187–189

Maasai, 211n12
Manchu, Classical, 91, 172–176, 219n9
Manchu, Sanjiazi, 97–99
Matumbi. *See* Kimatuumbi
Maya, Yucatec, 156
Menominee, 186–187
Mixtec, 14

Mongolian, Classical, 72
Mongolian, Khalkha, 19, 21, 136–139

Nawuri, 126–129
Niger-Congo. *See* Akan, Bantu, Igbo,
  Wolof, Yoruba
Nilo-Saharan. *See* Kalenjin,
  Kanembu, Maasai, Turkana

Oroch, 111–115, 140–141

Pasiego, 14

Rotokas, 107
Russian, 122

Sakha. *See* Yakut
Semitic. *See* Akkadian
Shona, 132–133
Shor, 101–102
Sibe, 90–92, 93–96
Slavey, 107

Terena, 14
Tucanoan. *See* Barasano, Desano
Tulu, 127
Tungusic. *See* Evenki, Manchu,
  Oroch, Sibe
Tupian. *See* Guarani
Turkana, 211n12
Turkic. *See* Altai, Bashkir, Karaim,
  Kazakh, Khakass, Kirghiz, Shor,
  Uyghur, Yakut
Turkish, 2, 24, 27–38, 54–57

Uyghur, 78–79, 123

Votic, 81

Warao, 105–107
Woleaian, 40–45
Wolof, 178–181
Yakut, 92

Yawelmani, 123–124
Yoruba, 6–10, 103–105

Linguistic Inquiry Monographs
Samuel Jay Keyser, general editor

1. *Word Formation in Generative Grammar*, Mark Aronoff

2. *$\bar{X}$ Syntax: A Study of Phrase Structure*, Ray Jackendoff

3. *Recent Transformational Studies in European Languages*, S. Jay Keyser, editor

4. *Studies in Abstract Phonology*, Edmund Gussmann

5. *An Encyclopedia of AUX: A Study of Cross-Linguistic Equivalence*, Susan Steele

6. *Some Concepts and Consequences of the Theory of Government and Binding*, Noam Chomsky

7. *The Syntax of Words*, Elisabeth O. Selkirk

8. *Syllable Structure and Stress in Spanish: A Nonlinear Analysis*, James W. Harris

9. *CV Phonology: A Generative Theory of the Syllable*, George N. Clements and Samuel Jay Keyser

10. *On the Nature of Grammatical Relations*, Alec P. Marantz

11. *A Grammar of Anaphora*, Joseph Aoun

12. *Logical Form: Its Structure and Derivation*, Robert May

13. *Barriers*, Noam Chomsky

14. *On the Definition of Word*, Anna-Maria Di Sciullo and Edwin Williams

15. *Japanese Tone Structure*, Janet Pierrehumbert and Mary E. Beckman

16. *Relativized Minimality*, Luigi Rizzi

17. *Types of $\bar{A}$-Dependencies*, Guglielmo Cinque

18. *Argument Structure*, Jane Grimshaw

19. *Locality: A Theory and Some of Its Empirical Consequences*, Maria Rita Manzini

20. *Indefinites*, Molly Diesing

21. *Syntax of Scope*, Joseph Aoun and Yen-hui Audrey Li

22. *Morphology by Itself: Stems and Inflectional Classes*, Mark Aronoff

23. *Thematic Structure in Syntax*, Edwin Williams

24. *Indices and Identity*, Robert Fiengo and Robert May

25. *The Antisymmetry of Syntax*, Richard S. Kayne

26. *Unaccusativity: At the Syntax–Lexical Semantics Interface*, Beth Levin and Malka Rappaport Hovav

27. *Lexico-Logical Form: A Radically Minimalist Theory*, Michael Brody

28. *The Architecture of the Language Faculty*, Ray Jackendoff

29. *Local Economy*, Chris Collins

30. *Surface Structure and Interpretation*, Mark Steedman

31. *Elementary Operations and Optimal Derivations*, Hisatsugu Kitahara

32. *The Syntax of Nonfinite Complementation: An Economy Approach*, Željko Bošković

33. *Prosody, Focus, and Word Order*, Maria Luisa Zubizarreta

34. *The Dependencies of Objects*, Esther Torrego

35. *Economy and Semantic Interpretation*, Danny Fox

36. *What Counts: Focus and Quantification*, Elena Herburger

37. *Phrasal Movement and Its Kin*, David Pesetsky

38. *Dynamic Antisymmetry*, Andrea Moro

39. *Prolegomenon to a Theory of Argument Structure*, Ken Hale and Samuel Jay Keyser

40. *Essays on the Representational and Derivational Nature of Grammar: The Diversity of Wh-Constructions*, Joseph Aoun and Yen-hui Audrey Li

41. *Japanese Morphophonemics: Markedness and Word Structure*, Junko Ito and Armin Mester

42. *Restriction and Saturation*, Sandra Chung and William A. Ladusaw

43. *Linearization of Chains and Sideward Movement*, Jairo Nunes

44. *The Syntax of (In)dependence*, Ken Safir

45. *Interface Strategies: Optimal and Costly Computations*, Tanya Reinhart

46. *Asymmetry in Morphology*, Anna Maria Di Sciullo

47. *Relators and Linkers: The Syntax of Predication, Predicate Inversion, and Copulas*, Marcel den Dikken

48. *On the Syntactic Composition of Manner and Motion*, Maria Luisa Zubizarreta and Eunjeong Oh

49. *Introducing Arguments*, Liina Pylkkänen

50. *Where Does Binding Theory Apply?*, David Lebeaux

51. *Locality in Minimalist Syntax*, Thomas S. Stroik

52. *Distributed Reduplication*, John Frampton

53. *The Locative Syntax of Experiencers*, Idan Landau

54. *Why Agree? Why Move? Unifying Agreement-Based and Discourse-Configurational Languages*, Shigeru Miyagawa

55. *Locality in Vowel Harmony*, Andrew Nevins